REPRINTS OF ECONOMIC CLASSICS

A HISTORY OF THE ENGLISH RAILWAY

A
HISTORY
OF THE
ENGLISH RAILWAY

Its Social Relations & Revelations

1820 - 1845

BY

John Francis

[1851]

TWO VOLUMES IN ONE

REPRINTS OF ECONOMIC CLASSICS

Augustus M. Kelley · Publishers
NEW YORK 1968

7153   4238   X

First Edition 1851

(London: Longman, Brown, Green & Longmans, 1851)

REPRINTED 1968 BY

AUGUSTUS M. KELLEY · PUBLISHERS

New York New York 10010

Library of Congress Catalogue Card Number

67-20087

PRINTED IN THE UNITED STATES OF AMERICA
by SENTRY PRESS, NEW YORK, N. Y. 10019

INTRODUCTION

John Francis's *History of the English Railway* appeared in 1851. The book's publication date was well chosen, probably deliberately. The experimental stage in railway progress was over, the so-called Railway Mania past, George Hudson the "Railway King" had fallen. In short, it was the right time to take stock of some thirty years of railway history.

This book, intended for the more serious general reader, was not the first of its class, though undoubtedly it was the first comprehensive non-specialist study of the English railway system.

The opening chapters cover, with reasonable thoroughness, the development of roads and canals with their various forms of transport and motive power. From here we pass into the railway age of George Stephenson, the Peases, Thomas Gray, Nicholas Wood, William James and Henry Booth, all of whom played a part in creating the foundations of the English railway system. Having established the Stockton & Darlington and Liverpool & Manchester Railways, the way is clear for descriptions of the London & Birmingham, Grand Junction, Great Western and lesser lines, along with biographical sketches of their engineers and building contractors, Robert Stephenson, Thomas Brassey, Isambard Brunel, Joseph Locke, Samuel Peto and others.

It is difficult to name any aspect of railways which has been ignored by Francis. Their promotion, cost, prospects and misfortunes are touched upon, however lightly. The tiresome questions of gauge, Sunday travel, treatment of third class passengers, drunken navvies and many other facets receive factual treatment.

Much serious railway historical research has been done since Francis's day but his book is better left unrevised to stand upon its own legs as a contemporary record. In truth, there is very little that needs amendment; such errors as may be noticed are trivial. The absence of an index is a drawback, the table of "contents" being insufficiently detailed for easy tracing of all but major references.

Little is known about John Francis except that he was connected with the Bank of England. His other works comprise a history of the Bank in 1847, another about the Stock Exchange in 1849 and one on life assurance in 1853. That he was not the same as John Francis publisher of the *Athenaeum* is certain. The reader should not be put off by Francis's sometimes rather bombastic style and heavy nineteenth-century English. This is not an example of twentieth-century use of verbosity nicely calculated to blind the reader and camouflage the author's ignorance. Whatever his background, Francis was clearly well informed and believed in his subject. We can, despite a prejudice here and there, accept his account as honest and accurate.

C. R. CLINKER

November, 1967

A HISTORY

OF THE

ENGLISH RAILWAY;

ITS SOCIAL RELATIONS AND REVELATIONS.

1820—1845.

BY JOHN FRANCIS;

AUTHOR OF "THE HISTORY OF THE BANK OF ENGLAND; ITS TIMES AND TRADITIONS;" AND
"CHRONICLES AND CHARACTERS OF THE STOCK EXCHANGE."

VOL. I.

LONDON:
LONGMAN, BROWN, GREEN, & LONGMANS.

MDCCCLI.

INSCRIBED,

BY PERMISSION.

TO GEORGE CARR GLYN, Esq., M.P.,

CHAIRMAN OF THE LONDON AND NORTH-WESTERN RAILWAY.

THESE VOLUMES, BEING AN ATTEMPT TO INDICATE THE ORIGIN AND PRO-
GRESS OF THAT POWER IN WHICH HE HAS OCCUPIED SO PROMINENT A
POSITION, ARE TO GEORGE CARR GLYN, THE EARLY AND EFFICIENT ALLY
OF THE ENGLISH RAILWAY SYSTEM, RESPECTFULLY DEDICATED BY

HIS MOST OBEDIENT SERVANT,

JOHN FRANCIS.

A HISTORY

OF THE

ENGLISH RAILWAY.

PREFACE.

THE present volumes form an attempt to develope the origin and progress of the railway system, and, by blending with it personal sketches of many who have joined the new power—of Stephenson, indelibly associated with the mechanism of the rail; of Brunel, whose variation of the gauge has produced such serious and even sad results; of Peto, whose efforts for the railway labourer are so characteristically benevolent; of Glyn, whose name will be long remembered for his bold expression of opinion; and of Hudson, whose career and character are honestly given— to add a general interest to the subject.

The Liverpool and Manchester railway is no uninstructive record: the progress of the metropolitan lines—which are chiefly treated in detail—present no unpicturesque career: the excitement of 1836—from which period it is necessary to generalise the history —the crude attempts at legislation; the battles between the ministry and the new interest; the marked progress and power of the latter; the wrongs of the railway labourer; the frauds, perjuries, and falsehoods of 1845—appear to the writer to form no unimportant portion of commercial history.

This is not a statistical work. For those who desire the latter there is Mr. Scrivenor's elaborate and excellent " Railways of the United Kingdom ;" there are Mr. Whitehead's important pamphlets on " Railway Investment ;" there is Dr. Lardner's " Railway Economy," a book which should be in the hands of all who are interested in the subject; with many others of a similar character. The present volumes aspire only to record the rise and progress of that discovery, one phase of which was a delusion as popular as any chronicled in Dr. Mackay's interesting work.

The address of the writer is appended, as any information in correction, or in addition, will be thankfully acknowledged; particularly should it refer to the important period which ranges from 1845 to 1851.

SHOOTER'S HILL,
  KENT, 1851.

CONTENTS OF VOL. I.

CONTENTS.

HISTORY

OF THE

ENGLISH RAILWAY.

CHAPTER I.

ROADS DURING THE AGE OF CHIVALRY.—DANGERS OF TRAVELLING.—EXPENSE
OF TRAVELLING—DIFFICULTY OF CONVEYING GOODS.—THE STREETS OF
LONDON—FIRST LEGISLATIVE ENACTMENT.—FORCED LABOUR.—PRIMEVAL
STATE OF THE COUNTRY VILLAGE.—INFORMATION DIFFICULT TO TRANSMIT.
—TRAVELLING IN COMPANY.—THE PACK-HORSE.—STAGE COACHES.—OPI-
NIONS CONCERNING THEM.—JOURNEY TO CAMBRIDGE.—THE PEER IN 1750
AND 1850.—IMPROVEMENT IN THE ROADS OCCASIONED BY CIVIL WAR.—
THE IMPORTANCE OF THE PEDLER IN COMMUNICATION.—FIRST TURNPIKE
GATES.—LAND TAX.—THE HIGHWAYMAN.—THE ROADS OF LANCASHIRE.—
THE ROADS OF NEWCASTLE.—IMPROVEMENT OF THE HIGHWAY.—RAIL-
ROADS.

THERE are few subjects more interesting to the antiquarian than the science of locomotion; nor is any
topic more important to the political economist than
the roads of England. By them he traces her social
progress, and watching them as, gradually formed for
necessary intercourse, they increase with the demand
they supply, he regards them as at once a cause and

a consequence of civilization, and rejoices in the prosperity they promote.

To that imperial · people who colonized when they had conquered, England owes her first road in 415. The arts went hand in hand with arms; the Roman camp required the Roman way; and it has been remarked that the general direction of those works which excite and astonish the beholder is closely allied to that of the modern railway.

In those which have been termed the dark ages, the roads of the country, if so they may be called, were beset with danger and delay. The age of chivalry was a terrible era for the wayfarer. The great highway of Watling-street was beset, in the reign of Edward the Confessor, by violent men. Outlaws, dwelling in the woods and forests around it, came suddenly on the traveller, deprived him of his all, and, with the booty they had won, as suddenly retreated to the forest or the fastness of their solitary home. The cross of the pilgrim was no protection against their violence; the hood of the monk was no safeguard against their rapacity. Endeavours were made to remedy the evil: armed men were paid by Abbot Leofstan, of St. Alban's, to scour the forest and penetrate its depths, to punish the marauder, or to defend the wayfarer. A worse evil than death, however, sometimes awaited the passenger: protected by a ransom if rich, he was sold as a slave if poor.

The Norman baron was probably the first recipient of tolls in England; and there is little doubt that where the traveller was stored with gold, or the merchant with goods, the lowest dungeon of the castle formed at once a vault for the treasure and a grave for its possessor. It was necessary, therefore, to move in company; and from this custom arose that charming picture of English locomotive life which Chaucer drew, and which Stothard has reproduced.

Long journeys were necessarily performed on horseback. The Anglo-Saxon, indeed, occasionally used a species of carriage; and William of Malmesbury, with Matthew Paris, mention the horse-litter, which was probably used for invalids. The queen of Northumberland also is spoken of at an earlier period as travelling in her carriage; the form of the conveyance being, of course, conjectural. The difficulty of journeying alone in safety entailed great expense. In the twelfth century, Peter of Blois said the yearly proceeds of a stall in Salisbury Cathedral were less than the cost of a visit from Salisbury to London. In the thirteenth, the bishop of Hereford, with all the pomp and power attending an ecclesiastic of the period, could not proceed on his journey in Wantling without additional assistance. In the fourteenth century men were licensed to let out horses. From Southwark to Rochester the regular fare was twelve pence. From Canterbury to Dover six-pence was charged. Expeditious travelling was then, as now, only comparative. The mother of Richard II. came in one day from Canterbury to London; but this was during the insurrection of Wat Tyler, performed, too, under the influence of fear, as she " never durst tarry on the way," and the exertion was so great as to cause a severe indisposition. The herald of the king of Scotland was allowed forty days to proceed from London to the border; and twenty miles a day, if indeed the wayfarer were so fortunate as to reach his journey's end, was regarded as good and expeditious travelling.

The effect of roads so difficult to traverse was seriously and severely felt in the carriage of commodities. The conveyance of goods was so expensive that inland trade suffered in proportion. The ma-

chines which were employed to convey produce, rude
and rough in their construction, were as heavy as
they were clumsy. Even if the roads were tolerable,
it was difficult to move them; but if bad, they were
either swallowed in bogs, or fell into dykes: sometimes, indeed, they sunk into the miry road so deep,
that there was little chance of escape until the warm
weather and the hot sun made their release easy.
Markets were inaccessible for months together, and
the fruits of the earth rotted in one place, while a few
miles off the supply fell far short of the demand.
Long after coals were procured in Newcastle, London,
even then a capital of the first importance, was
contented with wood or turf, owing to the impossi-
bility of transmission. The tolls were as heavy as the
roads were bad. The thoroughfare winding through
the wooded domain of the baron, or by the rich pasture
land of the abbot, was charged with payments which
formed an additional tax on commerce and communication. It was found cheaper to export abroad than
to convey produce from the north to the south of
England. It was easier to send merchandise from the
capital to Portugal, than to convey it from Norwich
to London. Many important parts of England were

as inaccessible as the Highlands of Scotland. Coal, manure, and grain could only be carried on the backs of cattle. If waggons were ever used, eight horses were necessary to draw two tons; the expense of this, when the time taken to perform the journey is considered, was a terrible addition to the cost of the article.

" For a succession of ages," says Dr. Lardner, " the little intercourse that was maintained between the various parts of Great Britain was effected almost exclusively by rude footpaths, traversed by pedestrians, or at best by horses. Hills were surmounted, valleys crossed, and rivers forded by these rude agents of transport, in the same manner as the savage and settler of the backwoods of America or the slopes of the Rocky Mountains communicate with each other."

The roads were also exceedingly tortuous. If the hill which crossed his path were high, the passenger traversed its base; if the river were deep, he sought a shallower fording-place; if the path were too rugged, he tried a longer but smoother passage. The travelling merchants, an important ingredient in country comfort, moved in company with their fellows. From town to town, through wood and through glade, they wandered in pleasant association, seeking in each other's society mutual aid and mutual protection. Pilgrims also availed themselves of the safety and society of the trader's convoy ; nor was their pilgrimage less agreeable that the song of the merchant or the strain of the minstrel excited their mirth and cheered their way.

These were some of the modes of transport at this early period ; nor was it until 1565, according to Stowe, that the first coach—built by the Earl of Rutland—formed a new era. Horseback, however, maintained its precedence whenever speed was required. In the sixteenth century a letter was dispatched in this way by Lord Burleigh, and the envelope, yet extant, bears on it, with the direction, the receipts of the parties through whose hands it passed. It was necessarily the most expeditious mode, as fresh saddle-horses and guides were to be had at certain convenient distances. If, however, such were the difficulties of locomotion in that age, on which certain gentlemen look so lovingly and longingly, it must be added that the streets of London were worse ; nor will the following picture of them be out of place :—
" The kites, crows, and other ravenous birds were

the only scavengers of the busy streets. The traffic was comparatively so slight that the mud which collected in the uneven roads proved no inconvenience to shopkeepers ; a pack-horse might now and then pass by, a gay and chivalrous knight might call the attention of the honest burgher, but vehicles were rarely used, and the bugle of the mail never enlivened the thoroughfares of the city. Holborn, the great artery of Modern Babylon, through which pours in quick succession one loud, busy, rattling stream of life and commerce, was not paved till the commencement of the fifteenth century. Some of the minor streets were scarcely passable. Narrow lanes, with hedges broken only here and there by a straggling house, were the primitive Wood-streets, Gray's-Inn-lanes, and Ald-gate-streets, of modern times ; some would venture to traffic in them in the day, but few would risk such perilous thoroughfares at night. Some of the streets were so bad in the prosperous days of King Henry VIII., that they are described as 'very foul, and full of pits and sloughs ; very perilous as well for all the king's subjects on horseback as on foot.' Along such dangerous paths the traveller at night had to grope his way about town in total darkness, except he was near enough to be guided by the lanterns on the steeple of Bow Church, which served as the only landmark to the bewildered stranger."

It was not until the sixteenth century that the roads of England were made the subject of legislative enactment. They had hitherto been under no law, they had owned no jurisdiction. They were made at will, they were repaired at pleasure. They lay through barren moors of vast circumference, they overhung precipitous descents of the most alarming character. In the reign of Mary it was decided that the various parishes should maintain their own roads. Surveyors were chosen; and, by means of forced labour, the first step was taken in that fine system which has at once caused and increased the commerce of England. The peasant, by this act, was compelled to give six days' work in each year; where more was necessary, hired labour was payed for by a parochial rate; and to the present day, in some parts of the empire, the hind pays his tribute of work to the highway.

An improvement was effected on this plan in the reign of Charles II. It was then practically felt—it had been acknowledged theoretically long before—that there was no uniformity of way; that one road ran to the right and another to the left, in defiance of reason; that one pathway kept in good repair was useless, because that which it joined was not repaired at all; and it was determined to introduce something like a systematic principle. An act was therefore passed authorising a small toll, to pay the expense; barriers were thrown across the roads at various distances; but the people rejected the plan, opposing it as they oppose all novelty: nor was it until long after the above period that the highways could be considered at all in proportion to the importance of the country.

Such were the roads of England at a period when she had advanced far before her neighbours in adorning her capital, in pleading, trading, and in studying. Such were her roads when "the father of English poetry depicted in rich and rare language the wide varieties of English life;" when John Wycliffe first taught the people to think; when the condition of the peasant was becoming ameliorated; when between the baron and the yeoman arose that great mercantile body of which England has ever had cause to be proud, when the political institutions of the land were regarded by foes with envy, and by friends with admiration; when the prowess of Elizabeth woke the pride of her subjects; when Shakespeare gave to the world his deathless plays; when Sidney lived and died; when Raleigh carried the name of his country to new worlds; when Burleigh governed, and when Bacon taught.* The consequence was that the country village maintained its antique customs and prejudices, that, where it was far from the high road, news from the great city only reached it by accident

* It is scarcely possible to avoid reminding the reader that at this very period in another hemisphere, beneath a monarch regarded as barbaric, treated as an infidel, and doomed to die a violent death, roads were formed worthy those which the old Roman has bequeathed to us. Mr. Prescott says in his " History of Peru," speaking of its road, " It was conducted over pathless sierras buried in snow; galleries were cut for leagues through the living rock; rivers were crossed by means of bridges that swung suspended in the air; precipices were scaled by stairways hewn out of the native bed; ravines of hideous depth were filled up with solid masonry; in short, all the difficulties that beset a wild and mountainous region, and which might appal the most courageous engineer of modern times, were encountered and successfully overcome. The length of the road, of which scattered fragments only remain, is variously estimated from 1,500 to 2,000 miles, and stone pillars, in the manner of European mile-stones, were erected at stated intervals of somewhat more than a league all along the route. . . . . The other great road of the Incas lay through the level country between the Andes and the ocean. It was constructed in a different manner, as demanded by the nature of the ground, which was for the most part low, and much of it sandy. The causeway was raised on a high embankment of earth, and defended on either side by a parapet or wall of clay;

and at uncertain intervals. The massacre of the
Jews in London at the coronation of Richard I.
was not known at Stamford, Norwich, and York
for several months. The abdication of James was
not heard of in the Orkneys until three months after
his flight; and ordinary news was long ere it reached
the distant city; and longer still ere it reached
the rustic hamlet. London was a great myth to
the villager. It was the place where kings reigned
and ministers decreed justice; whence wars and
rumours of wars emanated. Queens died and
new dynasties succeeded without the fathers of the
village knowing or caring for the change. Their
luxuries were from their own vineyards and their own
orchards; their necessities were the produce of their
own farms. Their sons and daughters intermarried;
children were born to them, inheriting their prejudices along with their acres; and had it not

and trees and odoriferous shrubs were placed along the margin, regaling the
sense of the traveller with their perfume, and refreshing him by their shade,
so grateful under the burning sky of the tropics. In the midst of sandy wastes,
which occasionally intervened where the light and volatile soil was incapable of
sustaining a road, huge piles were driven into the ground to indicate the
route to the traveller."

Humboldt confirms the great American historian, and says, "The roads of
the Incas were among the most useful and stupendous works ever executed
by man."

been for the gradual improvement in our roads during the last century and a-half, the ignorance of the country would have remained unchanged, and the innocence of country life been still an article of faith. That which the turnpike-roads effected is a portion of our political economy ; that which will result from the railroads can only be known from time.

In the seventeenth century, further but not very successful efforts were made to improve travelling, and the roads remained eminently bad. The charge of conveyance amounted in many instances to a prohibition. Heavy goods cost from London to Birmingham £7 a ton ; from London to Exeter £12 was paid. Coal, even then, was rarely seen, save in the neighbourhood of the district which produced it. Pack-horses—strong, enduring animals, the breed of which is now extinct—were employed to carry the produce of the weaver's patient skill, the pottery of Staffordshire, and even the coals of Newcastle. Labouring along heavy roads, toiling beneath a burning sun, wending their way through bare, bleak moors, down steep descents, by dangerous rivers, on narrow tongues of land, between masses of mire and mud, so deep as to be dangerous if they entered

—a leading horse bearing bells to intimate the
approach of the party he heralded—the group formed a
most picturesque accompaniment to the wild, weird
scenes it enlivened. Fortunate was it if they who
heard the musical tinkle of the leader's bell could
avail themselves of the notice. The solitary horseman,
bearing perhaps intelligence which would make or mar
a revolution, was compelled to yield, and, stepping
out of his path at the hazard of not recovering it,
to wait until the procession had passed. The private
carriage—if such indeed should chance to approach—
left the track at the risk of never returning to it;
while more numerous parties either resisted the
cavalcade, or moved like the solitary passenger out of
the way, as their weakness or their strength might
dictate. With such difficulties before them, few
persons left their homes but those who were called by
some most special reason. Our great historian remarks
that "the inhabitants of London were for almost
every practical purpose further from Reading than
they are now from Edinburgh, and further from
Edinburgh than they are now from Vienna." Coaches
continued to stick fast, travellers to be benighted.
Carriers went out of the beaten track on the melan-

choly moors; and a viceroy, with all the appliances and appurtenances of wealth, was five hours going fourteen miles. Contemporary letters are full of similar illustrations. Thoresby, the antiquary, nearly lost his way in a well-known road. The attractive Pepys, with his attractive wife, were almost obliged to pass the night on Salisbury-plain. Travellers went in fear of their necks; dukes were obliged to walk in muddy roads; and the carriages of reigning princes were only saved from falling by their subjects' support.

The serious difficulties which beset travelling produced stage coaches; and great was the innovation when, in 1669, sanctioned by the doctors of the University of Oxford, the flying coach undertook to perform the journey from that place to London between the rising and the setting of the sun. "This spirited undertaking," says Mr. Macaulay, "was solemnly considered and sanctioned by the heads of the University, and appears to have excited the same sort of interest which is excited in our own time by the opening of a new railway. The success of the experiment was complete. At six in the morning the carriage began to move from before the

ancient front of All-Soul's college, and at seven in
the evening the adventurous gentlemen who had run
the first risk were safely deposited at the inn in
London." The dangers of winter, however, were
too great to compete with, and this coach was
abandoned during the dark months. In 1662 there
were only six stages in all the country; and one,
wise in his generation, John Crossdell, of the Charter-
house, thought they were six too many. Nor was Mr.
Crossdell's opinion unsanctioned by the general feeling; for in 1671, Sir Henry Herbert, a member of the
House of Commons, said, "If a man were to propose to convey us regularly to Edinburgh in coaches
in seven days, and bring us back in seven more,
should we not vote him to Bedlam? Or if another
were to assert he would sail to the East Indies in six
months, should we not punish him for practising
on our credulity?"

But the great increase of the monied interest, the
confidence which was felt in the government when the
faithless Stuarts had left the country they could not
govern, the impulse given to commerce, and the
general feeling of security, produced important results. The antiquarian traveller, who chooses to delay

his journey an hour at York, and go to the "Black Swan" hotel, may there behold the following evidence of increasing enterprise in the commencement of the century following that just treated:

York Four Days.
Stage-Coach
Begins on Friday, the 12th of April, 1706.

All that are desirous to pass from *London* to *York*, or from *York* to *London*, or any other place on that road; let them repair to the *Black Swan* in *Holbourn* in *London*, and to the *Black Swan*, in *Coney-street* in *York*.

At both which places they may be received in a *Stage-Coach* every *Monday, Wednesday,* and *Friday*, which performs the whole journey in four days (if God permits), and sets forth at five in the morning.

And returns from *York* to *Stamford* in two days, and from *Stamford*, by *Huntington*, to *London* in two days more. And the like stages on their return.

Allowing each passenger 14 lb. weight; and all above, 3*d.* a pound.

Performed by { BENJAMIN KINGMAN, HENRY HARRISON, WALTER BAYNES.

Also this gives notice, that a *Newcastle Stage-Coach* sets out from *York* every *Monday* and *Friday*, and from *Newcastle* every *Monday* and *Friday*.

This curious relic is rendered more significant by the accompaning picture from the pen of an essayist of the day, describing a journey about this period, and probably in some such vehicle, to Cambridge:—

" I resolved, since the season of the year proved dry and pleasant, to make a short journey to Cambridge. * * * By the time I got to the place of starting, the country tub-driver began to be impatient, all the company but myself being already come, and had taken up their stations in the dirty, lumbering, wooden hovel, being more in shape like a tobacco hogshead than a coach, bellying out like the stern of a Dutch fly-boat, and was built more for burthen and the horses' ease than to commode travellers. The rest of the company being most of them pretty burly, had made a shift to leave me a nook in the back part of the coach, not much wider than a chair for a jointed baby." In this "tub," drawn by "half a dozen bony hacks," the essayist proceeded, stopping at Ware, twenty miles from London, to dine, and at Barley, thirty-seven miles off, to sup and sleep; from thence, through Saffron Walden, at an "ass's gallop" he reached Cambridge, "a place so abominably dirty that Old-street, in the middle of a winter's thaw, or Bartholomew fair after a shower of rain, could not have more occasion for a scavenger than the miry streets of this famous corporation, most of them so very narrow that should two wheelbarrows meet in their largest thoroughfare they are obliged to stop half an hour before they can clear themselves of one another." This was the mode of journeying by coach to, and such was Cambridge, a century and a half ago.

In 1712, the following advertisement appeared in the *Newcastle Courant* :—

Edinbro', Berwick, Newcastle, Durham, and London stage-coach begins on Monday, the 13th of October, 1712. All that desire to pass from Edinbro' to London, or any place on that road, let them repair to Mr. John Baillie's, at the Coach and Horses, at the head of Canongate, Edinbro', every other Saturday; or to the Black Swan in Holborn, every other Monday; at both of which places they may be received in the stage-coach, which performs the whole journey in *thirteen* days, without any stoppages (if God permits), having eighty able horses to perform the whole journey : each passenger paying *four pounds ten shillings*, allowing each passenger 20 lb. of luggage; all above, 6*d*. per lb. The coach sets off at six o'clock in the morning.

These were the modes and methods which the commonalty adopted. The peer and the *parvenu* were kept at their relative distances; and the great master of modern fiction gives a graphic description of the mode in which the rich man travelled in the early part of the last century. It contrasts so strangely with the noble of the present day stepping into the first-class carriage with no more attention than is paid to a first-class passenger, mixing with the tradesman and the merchant, and joining with the architect or the attorney in familiar conversation, that the writer is tempted to show the traveller of a century and a half ago in all his greatness and grandeur :

"The privilege of nobility in those days," says Sir Walter Scott, "had something in it impressive on the imagination; the dresses, and liveries, and number of their attendants, their style of travelling, the imposing and almost warlike air of the armed men who surrounded them, placed them far above the laird who travelled with his brace of footmen; and as to rivalry from the mercantile part of the community, these would as soon have thought of imitating the state and equipage of the sovereign..... Two running footmen, dressed in white, with black jockey caps and long staffs in their hands, headed the train; and such was their agility that they found no difficulty in keeping the necessary advance which the etiquette of their station required before the carriage and horsemen. Onward they came at an easy swinging trot, arguing unwearied speed in their long-breathed calling. Behind these glowing meteors, who footed it as if the avenger of blood had been behind them, came a cloud of dust, raised by riders who preceded, attended, or followed the state carriage."

The country is indebted to the evils of war for some change in our roads. The unfortunate rising of 1715, but more especially that of 1745, rendered highways necessary for the transport of troops; and the unhappy distich so well known—

Had you seen but these roads before they were made,
You would lift up your eyes and bless General Wade,

is a further indirect evidence against them; while a direct evidence of the necessity of improvement may be inferred from the fact that when Charles Edward was only one hundred miles from Edinburgh, the meagreness and uncertainty of news concerning him was so great, that had he been in a Russian province there could not have been more ignorance of his movements.

Pedlers and pack-horses continued to the middle of the last century to form an important feature in locomotion. The former had long been the chief if not the only mode of procuring intelligence possessed by country residents; the pedler was, therefore, an ever-welcome guest. He was a collector of news by choice and by profession. He took with him the broadside, which printed in the metropolis, was eagerly perused in the village. He carried correspondence from one portion of the country to another. He wrote letters for the peasantry. The seditious intelligence of plotters was frequently entrusted to him. He purchased the spoil from the wrecker, and the first information of the wreck was often received from his public sale of the articles it contained. The " travelling merchant," as Scott makes Andrew Fair-service call his cousin the pedler, was looked and longed for by all. To the farmer he brought intelligence of the crops and the country. To the good wife he brought household necessities. To the daughter he brought the last London fashion. To the son he gave the only glimpse which he could hope to receive of the great metropolis. To the hind he told tales of terror, which have scarcely yet faded from the haunts and hearths of the peasantry. He related all the great atrocities that had excited the selfish circle of which Horace Walpole was the shrewd exponent. He detailed the executions which George Selwyn loved to witness. He repeated paragraphs from some patriotic speech which had startled London, or dilated on some piece of courtly scandal which had moved the mirth of the city. Nor was the pedler unfrequently the hero and the victim of stories similar to those which often thrilled the fireside of his auditors. Travelling rude and rugged paths, with articles often of value, and always attractive, journeying by roads where no one was near to aid—sometimes in the bed of rivers which summer had dried, and sometimes between lonely hills which winter had clad in snow—his remains were not seldom left to tell in a bloody and violent death a melancholy tale of man's rapacity.*

In 1763 turnpike-gates were first established in all parts of England, and were, for a series of years, the principal mode of supporting the expense occasioned by the repair of the thoroughfares. In vain the counties in the neighbourhood of London petitioned Parliament against the plan, alleging that they could not compete

---

* A reference to the *Autolycus* of Shakespeare will confirm the writer : "He hath ribands of all the colours i' the rainbow. He hath songs, for man, or woman, of all sizes." His ballad "to a very doleful tune, of a fish that appeared on the coast, forty thousand fathom above water;" his poetical description of his pack, show that from that early period to a very late one the pedler was a marked personage :

> " Lawn, as white as driven snow ;
> Cyprus, black as e'er was crow ;
> Gloves, as sweet as damask roses ;
> Masks for faces, and for noses ;
> Bugle-bracelet, necklace-amber,
> Perfume for a lady's chamber :
> Golden quoifs, and stomachers,
> For my lads to give their dears ;
> Pins, and poking-sticks of steel,
> What maids lack from head to heel :
> Come, buy of me ; come buy, come buy ;
> Buy, lads, or else your lasses cry."

Thus the pedler of Shakespeare's time was the pedler of a century ago.

with the remote districts in the price of produce; in vain the people tore the toll-bars to the ground; in vain the Squire Westerns of the day denounced them: the House of Commons declined to attend to the popular outcry; and experience has since decided that the improvement of our thoroughfares has been beneficial to all.

In addition to the state of the roads, they continued to be unnecessarily circuitous. In their formation public considerations had given way to private interest. The landed proprietor possessed an unlimited power over the roads of the district in which he resided: and the plantation beneath which he had sheltered himself and his children, the ornamental enclosure rendered dear by household memories, the trees planted by Sir Ralph or Sir Rupert, were sacred in his eyes. All his influence was naturally used to form the line of road in that direction which would interfere the least with, while it benefited the most, his estate. Often, therefore, through a level part of the country, where the road might have been straight, it wound for miles out of its way; while as often it ascended steep hills where it might have been level, or passed through a miry soil where it might have been on a firm foundation.

The system of forced labour, under all circumstances impolitic, even in those of despotic places, where the bow-string and the bastinado are in request, was found exceedingly inconvenient in a free country. The reaper threw down the remunerative sickle to handle the unremunerative spade; while the farmer saw his grain spoiled as the peasant worked slowly and sullenly at the work to which he was doomed. These disadvantages were obviated by a tax on land, which has effected a most beneficial change. Previous to this impost the roads of Scotland, even in the best cultivated districts, were in the worst possible state. They soon became the best in Europe.

But the plan by which turnpike-roads were managed was found exceedingly troublesome. The necessity of having a tollgate-house was also ruinously felt; and it was calculated that 40 per cent. of the receipts went in expenses. The consequence was that the business fell by degrees into the hands of capitalists, who purchased the tolls from the trustees, and undertaking their collection, saved both trouble and cost.

Highwaymen, another danger incidental to the infancy of locomotion, must not be passed over. Though nightfall saw the traveller duly housed, daylight was often no safeguard against the marauder. A crowded coach was a temptation to an Abershaw. Rash and daring, a bold and skilful horseman, it was no uncommon circumstance for the Claude Duval of the day to attack and rob, single-handed, a stage full of passengers. The arms of the riders were no alarm to him. The coachman stopped his cattle at his approach; the postilion was often in his pay. He created tremor in the minds of all as they came near his reputed haunts. The gentleman thanked heaven if he escaped a visit on Finchley-common; the lady ejaculated her delight as she passed the confines of Hounslow; the wild heath which graces Shooter's-hill was a terror to the traveller; and more fervent prayers were heard for safety on huge, desolate Salisbury-plain than were ever breathed in its fine cathedral. The highwayman was a portion of our roads then, as he is now a portion of our established literature. He is alluded to in our early essayists; he lives in Fielding and in Smollett; he is introduced into our elder dramas; he is the hero of an opera yet popular with the people; he forms a part of the polished picture presented to us by Bulwer; and, it may be added, he is met with far more agreeably in fiction than on some bare, bleak heath, where the fame of King was great, where Turpin was a terror, or where Claude Duval won the hearts of ladies and rifled the pockets of gentlemen.

Notwithstanding the establishment of turnpikes on roads in 1763, it is certain that by 1770 no great improvement had been effected. Language fails to describe the internal roads in Lancashire in that year. One gentleman charged all travellers to avoid them as they would the devil, "for a thousand to one they break their necks or their limbs by overthrows or breaking down." Ruts four feet deep, floating with mud, were common, even in summer; being primitively mended by rolling in large, loose stones, which jolted the carriage or broke the springs. It is noticeable that in eighteen miles of "execrable memory," a traveller passed three carts broken down through these and similar causes; and this was in that Lancashire which encouraged Watt, which enriched Arkwright, which gave the earliest important railroad to the world, and which is ever first and foremost in commercial enterprise. Nor were the roads near Newcastle better, but may be taken as an additional specimen of the dangers and difficulties of travelling at the very period when, and in the very neighbourhood from which, the first idea of locomotive steamengines was taken. " A more dreadful road cannot be imagined; I was obliged to hire two men at one place to support my chaise from overturning. Let me persuade all travellers to avoid this terrible country, which must either dislocate their bones with broken pavements, or bury them in muddy sand."

When, however, business between town and country augmented, and a quick transit was rendered necessary, the power of money was brought into play, and relays of horses were supplied on the roads to carry the passengers. One chief cause of reform in post-office communication arose from the fact that the post was constantly being surpassed in speed by private adventurers: and because the inhabitants of a great country town would not understand why they could travel twice as rapidly as their letters were carried.

As time proceeded, increased capital produced increased competition. The opposition of rival coach
proprietors, though often attended with deplorable
accidents, produced excellent results; and by the period
of the railroad era, it is fair to conclude the coaching
system was perfect. The cattle were changed in
a few brief seconds; the coachmen were bound by
heavy penalties to be at their destination at an
appointed hour; horses were bred especially for the
duty, and they were urged in some cases with such
inexorable rigour, that in their vain endeavours to
perform a given distance within a given time, they fell
with excitement, and died of a broken blood-vessel or
a broken heart.

The roads also had reached an almost perfect condition; the invention of Macadam rendered it a
system; and there were in 1825 few more pleasant
occupations than passing over the ground at ten
miles an hour, through a fine fertile country, over
hills, by the side of woods, skirting forests, crossing brooks, enlivening the green lane, and gladdening
the quiet village. Witnessing, as most have witnessed,
the great speed and certainty of the mail-coach, it
becomes a wonder how our friends of half a century

since could occupy so long a time in passing from one place to another; and a writer in the *Quarterly Review*, asking, "how can these hours be accounted for?" answers, "Why, if a commercial gentleman had a little business, there was plenty of time for that! If a real gentleman wanted to pay a morning visit on the road, there could be no objection to that! Half an hour was consumed in eating pork-pies in the season, and perhaps a fine specimen of church-architecture would occupy some antiquarian. Though two hours were allowed for dinner, 'Don't hurry yourselves, gentlemen; the coach is ready, but don't let me disturb you if you wish for another bottle;'" was a common saying, and thus the hours were consumed, pleasantly if not rapidly.

The preceding sketch of travelling in the good old time has brought the writer to the subject of which this volume treats. He trusts that it may not appear an unfit introduction to so analagous a topic as the rise and progress of railway locomotion; previous to which, however, its antecedent, the canal, will be briefly sketched.

CHAPTER II.

THE ORIGIN OF CANALS —FRANCIS MATHEW.—DUKE OF BRIDGEWATER'S CANAL.
—THE DIFFICULTIES IT ENCOUNTERED.—ITS SUCCESS.—JAMES BRINDLEY.—
JOHN GILBERT.—VALUE OF CANAL PROPERTY.—THE ORIGIN OF RAILWAYS.
THE WOODEN TRAMROAD.—SIMPLIFICATION OF WORK.—DESCRIPTION OF
ROGER NORTH.—WAY LEAVES.—MARQUIS OF WORCESTER.—THE RAILROADS
OF NEWCASTLE.—INCREASED DEMAND FOR COAL.—FIRST IRON RAILS.—
DESCRIPTION OF TRAMROADS IN 1765.—CLAIM OF MR. CURR FOR THE IN-
VENTION OF IRON ROADS.—THE EARLIEST LOCOMOTIVE.—DR. ANDERSON'S
RECOMMENDATION.---MR. EDGEWORTH'S PROPOSAL.—THE IMAGINARY DIFFI-
CULTY, AND VARIOUS MODES OF OVERCOMING IT.—IMPROVEMENTS IN MA-
CHINERY.—SUCCESS OF THE PRINCIPLE OF RAILROADS.—THE FIRST LOCOMO-
TIVE OF GEORGE STEPHENSON.—THE STOCKTON AND DARLINGTON RAIL-
WAY.—ITS SOCIAL AND COMMERCIAL ADVANTAGES.—LIST OF THE EARLY
RAILWAYS.

IN 1656 one Francis Mathew, deeming probably
that the repose enjoyed by England was favourable
to internal improvement, memorialized Cromwell on
the advantage of a water communication between
London and Bristol. " It is hardly fair," says a
writer in the *Quarterly Review*, " to look down from
the height of modern achievement with contempt
on a man who, at all events, did his best to call

public attention to a neglected subject. Had Mathew succeeded in fixing it upon the vigorous mind of the Protector, his feeble suggestion might have fructified, and Bridgewater and Brindley might have been anticipated by a century."

At the above period a canal was a very original idea in England; the utmost attempts of scientific men had been limited to the improvement, and not the creation, of internal navigation. So early as 1635 a Mr. Sandys formed a project to navigate the Avon, his object being the improvement of commerce. The nobility approved the scheme, and the landholders followed their example: civil war, however, broke out, and the project was abandoned. "After the Restoration," says Mr. M'Culloch, "and during the earlier part of last century, various Acts were at different times obtained for cheapening and improving river navigation. These attempts, however, were not very successful: the current of the rivers gradually changed the form of their channels; the dykes and other artificial constructions were apt to be destroyed by inundations; alluvial sand banks were formed below the weirs; in summer the channels were frequently too dry to allow of their being navigated, while at other times the current was so strong as to render it quite impossible to ascend the river, which at all times, indeed, was a laborious and expensive undertaking."

Such remained the position of this branch of loco-motion when the father of inland navigation, Francis, Duke of Bridgewater, obtained an act of Parliament to make a canal between Worsley and Manchester. It need not be said that his grace proposed to benefit himself as well as his neighbours, and that visions of a large return floated in his brain; although there is little doubt that when he had once entered with his wonted energy into the great task, the mere pecuniary results faded before the grandeur of the undertaking. The title which yet rests upon the memory of this gentleman, of "the father of inland navigation," has been disputed on the strength of an act obtained by Scroop, the first Duke of Bridgewater, in 1737, for rendering Worsley-brook navigable, and also because the Sankey navigation act was passed in 1755. The latter only is worthy of notice, and Mr. Hughes, in his life of Brindley, dis-poses of the question.

" In the year 1755, an act was obtained for making

the Sankey brook navigable from St. Helen's to
the river Mersey, but the proprietors afterwards
determined to abandon the stream and to make an
entirely new canal, using the water of the stream
merely to feed the canal. Accordingly the canal
was dug as close along the side of the stream as
practicable, and opened for navigation in 1760. In
the meantime the Duke of Bridgewater applied in
1758 for power to construct a canal, not in the bed of
any stream, not near or parallel with the course
of any stream, but entirely across the dry land."

It appears then that the first English canals are
indisputably due to the determination of the Duke
of Bridgewater, and to the mental power of that
James Brindley whose life was passed in overcoming
the difficulties which beset their creation ; who, when
asked before a committee of the House of Commons
what he considered the use of rivers ? replied in
all single-mindedness that " they were formed to feed
canals ;" and it has been said that the question
as to the propriety and probability of the duke's
undertaking that great work which bears his name,
was discussed by " three hard-headed men round
the humble hearth of the manor-house of Worsley,

or the still humbler village inn." Those men were
James Brindley, John Gilbert, and the duke.

At the early age of seventeen, his grace took
the grand tour, returned to London, and joined
its gaieties. He became an amateur jockey, and
the large, bulky man of after years was then so
slight, that bets were proposed that he would be
blown off his horse. Horace Walpole records a
ball given by him, and to one of the Gunnings,
celebrated for their beauty, the duke yielded his
heart. His judgment proved stronger than his
feelings, and when the breath of scandal fastened
on the future wife of Duke Hamilton, the Duke
of Bridgewater renounced his claim. To this,
probably, is the Bridgewater-canal owing; for the
husband of the most beautiful woman of the day
would have had other duties than that of creating
an inland navigation. That the duke consulted
Mr. Brindley as to the propriety of forming a
canal between Worsley and Manchester, argues a
thoughtful mind; and that Mr. Brindley encouraged
the idea, speaks strongly for the self-reliance of
the man who, capable of comprehending all the
difficulties which surrounded his project, felt also

capable of surmounting them. It was no ordinary
work ; and Brindley was no ordinary man. Besides
being the first canal in English history, the obstacles
which opposed it were legion. It was determined
also to preserve the level of the water without
the usual obstructions of locks ; and to do this,
it was necessary to carry it over rivers and valleys, to
pass through subterraneous tunnels, and to surmount
elevated aqueducts. Public opinion was by no means
in favour of the undertaking. The multitude had
no hesitation in declaring the duke insane, and
Mr. Brindley a penniless theorist. The duke's
aristocratic compeers thought how much better
they could spend the money ; and when the engineer
absolutely proposed to carry his great work over
the Irwell, by means of an aqueduct thirty-nine
feet above the surface of the water, there is little
doubt that his relatives considered a madhouse
the best place for a man who thus wasted his
money. That his grace was in earnest, was proved
from the fact that he limited his personal expenses
to £400 per annum, and that every penny which
by any mode or method could be collected, was
expended on his beloved project. Fortunate was

it for the duke, that associated with him as assistant
was a practical and persevering man named John
Gilbert, who, fond of mines and mechanical operations, brought to the aid of the duke an energy
and firmness as resolute as his own. He was the
duke's great aid and ally in procuring money. He
went about the country borrowing cash on all
or on any security; he was a familiar figure on
the exchange of Liverpool, where the duke's bill
for £500 could scarcely be cashed; he was a weekly
visitor among the farmers in the neighbouring districts, borrowing such small sums as they could
spare; he forestalled the rental of the duke's tenants;
and he appealed to the prestige of the ducal name, in
his earnest endeavours to support that which was
popularly known as the duke's folly. At length
the engineer brought his work to a close, and it
is impossible to do sufficient justice to the resolute
character of the Duke of Bridgewater or the genius of
Mr. Brindley. Stupendous mounds of earth, which
seemed to demand a Titanic power, were removed
from the way. Supplies of water were procured,
sufficient to exhaust mountain springs and mountain
rivulets; aqueducts were built far above the surface

of the river, rivalling those which conveyed water to
the eternal city from the mountain recesses.

The time of trial had passed and the hour of
triumph was at hand; and it is indicative of the
character of the engineer, that when the moment
arrived for admitting the water into the aqueduct,
his nerve was unequal to the crisis, and he left to
the cool, resolute Gilbert the task of superintending
the operation which would make or mar the fortunes of three great men.   That operation was
successful.   The prejudices of the ignorant multitude were uprooted; the scientific few were delighted.
They who had gone to scoff, remained to praise;
and an engineer who had sneeringly said he had
heard of castles in the air, " but never before was
shown where they were to be erected," began to
wonder as much at his own opposition as at the
simple grandeur of the work he had derided.

" When the Duke of Bridgewater," says Dr.
Aikin, " undertook this great design, the price of
carriage on the river navigation was twelve shillings
the ton from Manchester to Liverpool, while that
of land carriage was forty shillings a ton.   The duke's
charge on the canal was limited by statute to six

shillings ; and together with this vast superiority in cheapness, it had all the speed and regularity of land carriage. The articles conveyed by it were likewise much more numerous than those by the river navigation : besides manufactured goods and the raw material, coals from the duke's own pits were deposited in yards at various parts of the canal, for the supply of Cheshire; lime, manure, and build-ing materials were carried from place to place, and the markets of Manchester obtained a supply of provisions from districts too remote for the ordinary land conveyance. A branch of useful and profitable carriage, hitherto scarcely known in England, was also undertaken, which was that of passengers' boats, on the model of the Dutch, but more agreeable and capacious ; and, when set up at very reason-able rates carried numbers of persons daily to and from Manchester." Thus the markets of Manchester were supplied, country scenes and country sites were visited, the holiday of the artizan was enlivened by a trip to the rustic wood; and passengers were enabled to travel along that canal which they owed to the patient endurance and undeviating firmness of Francis, Duke of Bridgewater, and to the singular

ability of his unrivalled architect; to both of whom
personal comfort and public praise were trivial in
comparison with the achievement of a great idea.

The first canal was soon followed by others. The
duke himself was not satisfied with one attempt,
but made use of Mr. Brindley to carry out other
extensive projects. Canals were proposed by capitalists, and that frequently in places where they
were not required. They formed a novel mode
of investment; and when, in 1790, the windows
of inns were forced, and farmers met at midnight
to procure shares which would ruin them, it need
not be said that an absolute mania existed. At
the present period about 2,400 miles of canal pass
through the fields and fertile places of England,
conveying goods, assisting commerce, and creating
intercourse. Of the remarkable value of a few of
these speculations, some notion may be obtained
from the fact, that in 1846 the dividend on canal
property was as follows :—

Grand Junction Canal	6 per cent.
Oxford	26 "
Coventry	25 "
Old Birmingham	16 "
Trent and Mersey	30 "

It has been seen that commerce and communication go hand in hand; that the industrial fruits of a people are useless without a mart, and that a mart is only to be attained through the medium of a road or canal.

It has been already shown also that when the wealth of the nation consisted in its beeves and its broadcloth; when the intercourse between countries was slow and uncertain; the commodities it possessed were valueless compared to the period when civilisation made a highway for its goods, and created a demand for its produce.

The precise origin of railroads is unknown; but that the earliest approximation to the modern railway was the wooden tramroad, there can be no doubt. And simple as the first change appears from the heavy road to the smooth tram, he was probably no ordinary man who, taking the laws of nature as his guide, and her operations as his rule, seeing that the rut of the common way rendered the work of the cattle easier, applied the principle to the reduction of labour, and took the initiative in the modern system of railroads; and when, acting on this inspiration, logs of wood, placed in parallel

lines, bore the mineral product of the mine to its
place of deposit, great doubtless was the joy of him
who had reduced his work and added to his wealth.
The idea, though simple, was effective; as the
horse which, previous to this rude tramroad, could
only draw 17 cwt., was enabled after its formation,
to draw 42 cwt. without extra fatigue.   This great
change occurred, according to Mr. Wood, between
1602 and 1649; and it is certain that by 1676
the principle had been generally applied where
private property could be improved.   Roger North,
describing a visit which his brother Lord Guilford
made at the close of one of the circuits of the
latter to Newcastle, says, that among the curiosities
of the place were "way-leaves."   "When men," he
continues, "have pieces of ground between the
colliery and the river, they sell leave to lead coals
over their ground, and so dear, that the owner
of a rood of ground will expect £20 per annum
for this leave.   The manner of the carriage
is by laying rails of timber from the colliery
down to the river, exactly straight and parallel,
and bulky carts are made with four rowlets fitting
these rails, whereby the carriage is so easy, that

one horse will draw down four or five chaldron of coals, and is an immense benefit to the coal merchants." For a long period no improvement was made in these roads, which were found both useful and profitable. It was not, indeed, a period fertile in invention; the fierce intestine warfare which produced a Cromwell, which ended in the decapitation of one monarch and the exile of another, was not favourable to the development of those arts and sciences which our own age has advanced and a future time will wonder at. "They were not, it is true," says the historian of England, "quite unacquainted with that power which has produced an unprecedented revolution in human affairs. The Marquis of Worcester had recently observed the expansive power of moisture rarified by heat: after many experiments he had succeeded in constructing a rude steam-engine, which he called a fire-water-work, and which he pronounced to be an admirable and most forcible instrument of propulsion. But the marquis was suspected to be a madman, and known to be a Papist; his inventions, therefore, found no favourable reception. * * * There were no railways except a few made of timber, from the mouths of the Northumbrian coal

pits to the banks of the Tyne. There was very little
internal communication by water. A few attempts
had been made to deepen and embank the natural
streams, but with slender success. Hardly a single
navigable canal had been even projected. The English of that day were in the habit of talking with
mingled admiration and despair of the immense
trench by which Louis XIV. had made a junction
between the Atlantic and the Mediterranean."

The revolution of 1688, which has developed in
so remarkable a degree the resources of the nation,
was also, indirectly, the promoter of the railroad.
It gave an impulse to commerce, and a security
to property. A necessity for communication followed,
and slowly but surely was that necessity supplied.
The demand for the produce of the coal mine rendered
quick transit important, and although the expense
was great it is probable that by 1750 there was
scarcely an important mine which had not its
accompanying railroad : in some cases as much as
£500 a year were paid for the way leave which
Roger North described, but this was of little importance, as since the date of his visit the quantity
of coal transported from the mine had nearly doubled.

From 270,000 chaldrons it had increased to 500,000, and the competition consequent on the increased demand required every facility which imagination could devise and which capital could supply. It appears tolerably certain that up to 1738 there was no other improvement in the tramroad than in the form or the quality of the wood. The iron way, as a thing by which man or the produce of his skill could travel was not even thought of. In that year, however, the change from wood to iron seems to be indicated by the following extract from the trans-actions of the Highland Society:—"In 1738 cast iron rails were first substituted for wooden ones, but owing to the old waggons continuing to be employed, which were of too much weight for the cast iron, they did not completely succeed on the first attempt. However, about 1768 a simple contrivance was attempted, which was to make a number of smaller waggons and link them together, and, by thus diffusing the weight of one large waggon into many, the principal cause of the failure in the first instance was removed, because the weight was more divided upon the iron."

It does not appear that this invention was much

more than recorded. The usual difficulties were to be surmounted; coal owners waited probably until their wooden roads were worn out, or until others more adventurous had ruined themselves in the attempt. At any rate the following description, which evidently proves that wood was still in common use, was given of the artificial road in 1765. "When the road has been traced at six feet in breadth, and where the declivities are fixed, an excavation is made of the breadth of the said road, more or less deep according as the levelling of the road requires. There are afterwards arranged along the whole breadth of this excavation, pieces of oak wood of the thickness of four, five, six, and even eight inches square: these are placed across and at the distance of two or three feet from each other; these pieces need only be squared at their extremities, and upon these are fixed other pieces of wood well squared and sawed, of about six or seven inches breadth by five in depth, with pegs of wood; these pieces are placed on each side of the road along its whole length; they are commonly placed at four feet distance from each other, which forms the interior breadth of the road."

The usual lassitude accompanied this invention; men were contented with that which their sires had used, and the iron rail was employed by very few, notwithstanding its superior strength and imperviousness to the effects of the weather.

In 1765, then, the common railroad was of wood, but it appears clear that in 1767 the idea was entertained of practically applying iron to a similar purpose. " I, some years ago," said Mr. Robert Stephenson, " visited the great iron works at Colebrook Dale, in Shropshire, where cast iron was indisputably first applied to the construction of bridges; and, according to the information which I have been able to obtain, it was here also that railways of that material were first constructed. It appears from their books that between five and six tons of rails were cast on the 13th November, 1767, as an experiment, on the suggestion of Mr. Reynolds, one of the partners."

A claim to this novelty has been entered by Mr. Curr, who, in his " Coal Viewer and Engine Builder," says that the making and use of iron railroads were among his first inventions, and were introduced into the working of the Sheffield colliery about the year 1776.

By this period the discovery of steam had been variously applied, and reflective men were employed on that power which had been used in the mines of Cornwall, which had been pioneered by Dr. Black's beautiful discovery of the power of latent heat, and which Watt rendered applicable by those experiments that attained an unintermitted supply of steam and a continuous rotary motion. This fine invention caused Watt's thoughtful mind to recur at once to the practicability of forming an engine which should move by virtue of his novel discovery, and, in 1759, to this was his power devoted and his energy given. How far he succeeded does not appear; but it is certain that in 1769 he expressly mentioned the possibility of applying the steam-engine to domestic improvement; and that by 1787 the discovery had so far proceeded that Mr. Symington, who has such claims to the invention of the steam-boat, exhibited the model of a steam-carriage in Edinburgh, at the house of Mr. Gilbert Meason; and it must be added that in 1802 Mr. Trevithick* took out a

---

* A singular fate appeared to follow this machinist; "Trevithick, after trying one thing after another, and finding friend after friend to help him, two years after Stephenson's beginning at Killingworth, left England for the West Indies, whence he did not come back—and then penniless—until Stephenson had

patent for an invention, and brought into use in 1804 a machine of this nature on the railroad of Merthyr Tydvil, in South Wales; and the first locomotive in England, however rude or imperfect, was then and there employed for a short time.

It will presently be seen that thoughtful men were bearing in mind the power and practicability of the iron way for public use. In 1800, Dr. James Anderson recommended a general adoption of railroads, to be carried along the side of the existing turnpike-roads, specifying the way from London to Bath as the place where preliminary trials might be made. In 1802 again, Mr. Edgeworth published a similar proposal, suggesting that, besides heavy waggons

laid down the Stockton and Darlington Railway. Trevithick was taken up by Mr. Blackett, a bold, daring man, and sent a locomotive to Wylam, which, like most things in which he had a hand, was so wretchedly made that it was put to other uses. * * * Trevithick began better than Stephenson; he had friends in Cornwall and in London, and he ought not to have left Stephenson to work out the locomotive engine and the railway. Trevithick was always unhappy and always unlucky; always beginning something new, and never ending what he had in hand. The world ever went wrong with him, as he said; but in truth, he always went wrong with the world. The world had done enough for him, had he chosen to make a right use of any one thing. He found a partner for his high-pressure engine; he built a locomotive; he had orders for others; he set his ballast engine to work, and he drove his tunnel under the Thames for a thousand feet; but no one thing did well—all were afraid, and at length no one would have anything to do with him.—*Civil Engineer and Architect's Journal.* The locomotive of Trevithick was not used by Mr. Blackett on the tramway, being employed in some other duty.

at a slow pace, " stage-coaches might be made to go at six miles an hour, and post-chaises and gentlemen's travelling carriages at eight—both with one horse ; and that small stationary steam-engines, placed from distance to distance, might be made by means of circulating chains to draw the carriages with a great diminution of horse labour and expense."

The first locomotive therefore was first in use in 1804, on a Welsh railway, drawing as many carriages as would contain ten tons of bar iron, at the rate of five miles an hour. The principle was perfect, the triumph was complete; a locomotive was in absolute work in the empire; and yet for years was the fallacy established in men's minds as fixedly as an article of faith, that it could not draw heavy loads ; that the adhesion of the smooth wheels of the carriage to the smooth rails of the iron must be so slight, that though the wheels would move round, the carriage would not move with them. There was no doubt of this in the minds of scientific persons. It had been said by the pundit, it was believed by the scholar. Men published treatises, formed plans, made new discoveries, argued, wrote, pleaded, and finally took out patents to overcome a difficulty which had no existence save in their own minds. Mr. Trevithick endeavoured to provide for it by certain projections in his wheels; Mr. Blenkinsop was granted a patent. One gentleman tried to form machinery which should imitate the action of the hind legs of a horse; while another was nearly successful in producing both the fore and hind legs, when in 1811 the important difficulty was partially overcome; and Mr. Blenkinsop, of Middleton Colliery, conveyed coals by the aid of engines with toothed wheels worked into a tooth-rack. This plan was very objectionable; but as it surmounted the fancied evil, great were the rejoicings. In only two years after, the evil itself was discovered to be a figment of the brain, and the efforts to overcome it a waste of time.

To Mr. Blackett, of Wylam railway, the credit appears due of destroying the theory. Being in possession of one of Trevithick's engines, he acted like a sensible man, formed another of greater power, similar to it, and then tested its capacity. To his delight he found that nature was not at fault, but that, by virtue of one of her beautiful and unerring laws, the carriage actually moved rapidly along the road, however great the weight.

The railway on which these trials were made was by no means perfect; but the knowledge once given to the world was preserved. Experiments were made on other lines; the nature of the machinery was more perfectly comprehended; its operations were better understood; constant experience suggested successive experiments; and on the Killingworth railway, on 25th July, 1814, with an engine constructed under the superintendence of George Stephenson, was the triumphant success of the principle proved, by a carriage moving on a slight ascent, drawing after it eight loaded carriages, weighing twenty tons. Although this was a great advance, it was a somewhat cumbrous machine; the principal improvement being the introduction of two cylinders instead of one, which, acting at different portions of the wheels, produced a more regular motion, and abolished a fly-wheel hitherto used.

This was the first locomotive made by George Stephenson; and although it had been proved to demonstration that the wheels would go round,

however smooth the rails, Lord Ravensworth
was called a fool for advancing the money, and
Mr. Stephenson laughed at as a coxcomb, for
attempting that which others in their superior
wisdom declared impossible. "The first locomotive
which I made," said that gentleman with honest
pride, thirty-one years after the above date, "was
at Killingworth colliery, and with Lord Ravensworth's money. Yes! Lord Ravensworth and company were the first parties that would entrust me with
money to make a locomotive engine. That engine
was made thirty-two years ago, and we called it
'My Lord.' I said to my friends that there was
no limit to the speed of such an engine, provided
the works could be made to stand."

From this period until that of the Stockton
and Darlington railway, there is not much worthy
of note. But the forerunner of the Liverpool
and Manchester line, the first railway opened for
public traffic, the first iron road on which the
locomotive was used as the moving power for
the carriage of passengers, occupies a position by
virtue of these circumstances which it would otherwise want. Its engineer was Mr. Stephenson, its

originator was Mr. Edward Pease, another claimant,
according to *Fraser's Magazine*, to the foundation
of the new system.*

The great importance of the Liverpool and Manchester line has cast a shadow on that of the
Stockton and Darlington; the former is ever looked
to as the great starting point of the modern rail,
and practically this is true. In it the public was
appealed to, and responded; it was a public trial,
a public announcement to the people that a new
power was to be exerted for their benefit. It was
made with public money; it was opposed and supported by public men; it was to all intents and
purposes the first public line. When the latter
was projected the proposal was limited to the conveyance of coal and other mineral products: its

---

* "We hope the time may never come," says a writer in the above periodical,
"when the millions at home and abroad who enjoy the advantages of railways,
shall have forgotten that they owe them all to Mr. Edward Pease, of Darlington.
It would be idle to relate the endless opposition he received, the hostility
of antagonists, the cold support of friends, the vexatious obstacles, the absurd
objections, the doubt of some, the prejudice of others, the ignorance of all. These
matters are now being forgotten. Confident in his judgment, ready in resource,
undismayed by difficulty, with indomitable energy and perseverance, he
gradually surmounted everything. It remains a striking instance of foresight
that, without any experience, and 'with all the world before him where to
choose,' he selected what, to the ordinary observer, is an unpromising district,
and there made the first and most successful railway."

cost and capital did not exceed £250,000, although its extent was forty miles. But looked at in a higher point of view, it assumes a different appearance; it was the first line which tested the great continued power of the locomotive; it was the first railway which witnessed the public *début* of the great mind which projected it; it was the first railway which really showed how much between two towns, the personal intercourse of which was trifling, facile and cheap communication would increase that intercourse. Its act of incorporation was obtained in 1821, it was opened in 1825: its promoters had only anticipated the carriage of 10,000 tons per annum, they had not thought of passengers, and the locomotive appeared incapable of acquiring the regularity required by such traffic. They began their work, therefore, with animal power. Prior to the formation of this railroad, there had been a coach traffic of fourteen or fifteen persons weekly: the rail increased it to five or six hundred. Each carriage was drawn by one horse, bearing, in ordinary cases, six passengers inside, and from fifteen to twenty outside; "In fact," says one writer, "they do not seem to be at all particular, for in cases of urgency they are seen crowding the coach on the top, sides, or in any other part where they can get a footing; and they are frequently so numerous, that when they descend from the coach and begin to separate, it looks like the dismissal of a small congregation." The general speed with one horse was ten miles an hour. Another advantage conferred on the neighbourhood was in the unjust fact that the Stockton and Darlington railway were assessed in the amount of their net income, and paid in some parishes half the entire rates. In addition to the social advantages which accrued from increased communication—and who shall doubt the fireside union, the social pleasure, and the domestic happiness it conferred?—was the development of commerce, and the increased importance of the various places through which it passed. A new trade in lime arose; the carriage in lead was enormously reduced in cost; the price of coal fell from 18s. to 8s. 6d.; the landholders received large sums for gravel, timber, and stone, taken from their estates. An obscure fishing village was changed into a considerable seaport town. The Stockton and Darlington railway turned the shopkeeper into a merchant; erected an exchange; gave bread to hundreds; and conferred happiness on thousands.*

Before proceeding with the further progress of railways, the writer deems it expedient briefly to recapitulate those which up to the present period—that saw alike the opening of the Stockton, and the proposition for the Liverpool and Manchester—had been formed. Before this period, it will be seen, the rail had taken a purely personal and local character. It had performed no great public benefit, it had developed no great public good, and it had attracted no great public notice.

The following is a list of railways, from 1801 to 1825:—

1801. The Surrey iron railway, from Wandsworth to Croydon, with a branch to Carshalton; its length was about nine miles, and the cost of its construction £60,000. The object proposed was the facilitation of conveying agricultural produce to London, and the return of manure to the country.

---

* Various statements have been made concerning the speed anticipated by Mr. George Stephenson for the locomotive; but there is no doubt his notions were very moderate, as at the opening of this line, he positively stated to Mr. Thorneycroft that *his utmost expectations were limited to twelve or fourteen miles an hour.*

1802. The Caermarthenshire railway was con-structed for conveying limestone, coal, &c., to the basin at Llanelly, where it terminates. It is six-teen miles long, extending from a place called the Flats to the parish of Llanfihangel, Aberbythick. Its expense was £35,000.

1802. The Sirhowey tramroad was undertaken by the Monmouthshire canal company, in conjunc-tion with the proprietors of the Tredegar iron works, and extends from the canal of the former company to the Sirhowey furnace. Its length was eleven miles, and its cost £45,000.

1803. The Croydon, Merstham, and Godstone railway, is a continuation of the Surrey iron railway, and commences at Croydon, whence it runs by the Brighton road to Merstham and Ryegate: a branch connects it with Godstone Green. Its length is about fifteen miles and three-quarters, and its cost £90,000. Its object was the conveyance of coal to and from London.

1804. The Oystermouth railway commences at Swansea at the end of the canal, and runs to Oystermouth, a distance of about six miles. Its cost was about £12,000.

1808. The Kilmarnock railway connects Kilmarnock and Troon, a distance of about ten miles ; and
cost about £40,000. Its object was the conveyance
of coal, limestone, and other produce, to and from
the great works in its neighbourhood.

1809. The Bullo Hill, or Forest of Dean railway,
was formed to convey coals, timber, iron ore, and
other minerals found in the forest of Dean, for
shipment on the river Severn, to the banks of
which it proceeds near Newnham : there are
three branches from the line to the different
coal mines in the forest. Its length is seven miles
and a half, and the capital of the company
£125,000.

1809. The Severn and Wye railway connects
those two rivers. It commences at Ledbrook on the
Wye, and terminates at the lower Verge, near
Newern, in Gloucestershire. It is connected with the
Severn at Nass-point by a canal one mile long.
Its length, including branches, is about twenty-six
miles, and the capital of the company £110,000.
Its object and use is much the same as that of the
preceding railway.

1810. The Monmouth railway runs from Howler

Slade to Monmouth. The company's subscribed capital was £22,000.

1811. The Berwick and Kelso railway company was incorporated this year, but did not avail itself of its power.

1811. The Hay railway commences at the wharf of the Brecknock and Abergavenny canal, near Brecon, and ends at Parton Cross, in Herefordshire, after a course of twenty-four miles, passing through a mountainous district. Capital £50,000.

1811. The Llanfihangel railway commences near the same place, and ends at Llanfihangel Crucorney, in Monmouthshire. Its length is about six miles and a-half, and the capital subscribed was £20,000.

1812. The Grosmont railway commences at the termination of the last railway, and runs to Llangua-bridge, between Abergavenny and Hereford, about seven miles. The money raised to construct it was £13,000.

1812. The Penrhynmaur railway commences at the Penrhynmaur coal works, and is carried to Red-wharf, in Llanbedbroch, in the county of Angle-sea, with a branch for a short distance north-wards, on Red-wharf bay. It is something above seven miles long, and consists of a series of inclined planes. The capital was £10,000, paid by the Earl of Uxbridge and Mr. Holland Griffith.

1814. The Mamhilad railway runs from the bank of the Abergavenny canal to Usk-bridge, in Monmouth, rather more than five miles. Its cost was £6,000.

1815. The Gloucester and Cheltenham railway commences at the basin of the Gloucester and Berkeley canal, in the city of Gloucester, and ends at Cheltenham about nine miles.

1817. The Mansfield and Pinxton railway runs from Mansfield town to Pinxton basin, near Alfreton, in Derbyshire, where it communicates with the Cromford canal. It has a branch of about a mile and a-half in length. The whole was constructed at a cost of £32,800, and it is used chiefly for the conveyance of coal and lime.

1818. The Kington railway is a continuation of the Hay railway, running from Parton-cross to Kington, in Herefordshire, and thence to the lime works, near Burlinjob, in Radnorshire ; about fourteen miles. Its cost was £23,000.

1819. The Plymouth and Dartmoor railway runs from Sutton Pool, a short distance from Plymouth, to Bachelor's-hall, in the parish of Lydford. Its length is about thirty miles, and it cost £35,000.

1821. The Stratford and Moreton railway runs from Stratford-on-Avon to Moreton-in-Marsh, in Gloucestershire, with a branch to Shipston-upon-Stour, in Worcestershire. Its length is about eighteen miles and a-half, and was executed at an expense of £50,000.

1821. The Stockton and Darlington railway runs from the left bank of the Tees at Stockton to Witton-park colliery, about two miles and a-half from Bishop Auckland, being about twenty-five miles; which with its five branches of fifteen miles and a-quarter, makes the whole length of this line something above forty miles. Its cost was about £250,000

1824. The Redruth and Chasewater railway runs from Redruth to Point-quay, in the parish of Feock, in Cornwall. The length of the line, including branches, is about fourteen miles. It cost £22,500.

1824. The Monkland and Kirkintilloch railway runs from the latter place in Dumbartonshire, for about ten miles to Palace Craig. The cost was £25,000.

1825. The Rumney Railway runs from Abertyswg, in Monmouthshire, to the Sirhowey railway, about two miles and a-half from Newport. The expense was £47,100.

1825. The West Lothian railway runs from Ryhall, on the Edinburgh and Union Glasgow canal, in the parish of Upshall to Shott, about twenty-three miles. It was constructed at an expense of £40,700.

1825. The Cromford and High Peak railway runs from Cromford canal to the Peak Forest canal; by a series of elevations it rises to 990 feet above the starting place. Its length is thirty-four miles, and it was formed at an expense of £164,000.

1825. The Nanttle railway runs from slate-quarries near Nanttle-pool, in the county of Caernarvon, to Caernarvon itself. The capital of the company is £20,000.

1825. The Portland railway runs from the priory lands in Portland island to the Castle. The cost was £5,000

1825. The Duffryn, Llynvi, and Port Cawl railway is in Glamorganshire. The cost of its sixteen miles and three-quarters was £60,000. Its object being to open a communication between several large iron and coal mines, and quarries of limestone and freestone, and the Bristol channel.

Such, up to 1825, were the railways of this greatl and, nor is a consideration of the list unin-structive. It has been seen that from time to time the system had been improved; that enter-prising men had joined their capital together for private advantage; that wherever they foresaw a prospect of gain, so surely was the money of the commercial man, and the mind of the inventive one, employed to produce the desired result. It has been seen that the power of steam was known and applied in the eighteenth century; that the facilities of the tramroad had been patent to the world for two hundred years; that the iron way had been, probably, tried nearly a century ago; that wherever a private local line had been established, it had diminished labour, increased pro-fits, and lowered prices. Studious men had pointed out its public advantages, and private individuals had applied these suggestions to their own benefit. The locomotive had been in use the fifth part of a century, its imaginary difficulties had been over-come, and its real uses had been tested. There was scarcely a county where some form of the railway was not used. The cultivated plains of Surrey had tried, if they had not profited by, its power. The produce of that forest once reckoned the chief support of the British navy, was carried by it. The wilds of the Principality were acquainted with its uses; the cautious Scottish merchant had essayed it; it had assisted the production of coal; it was known as a tried and true power.

But with all this knowledge there was no positive benefit to the great mass of Englishmen. They still travelled by coaches, and grumbled at the stoppages; they still ate their hurried dinners at exorbitant charges; they still complained of the involuntary taxation which followed them; ignorant that at that moment the first faint dawn of one of the greatest powers the world ever knew—a power only to be classed with the invention of printing—was steadily increasing, and would ere long burst forth into perfect day. Practical men were at work, and earnest men were thinking, and inventive men were suggesting plausibly and powerfully its future operations: they spoke to and worked for the many; they were scarcely listened to even by the few.

CHAPTER III.

THE EARLIEST IDEA OF RAILROADS.—THEIR PRESUMED COST.—DR. ANDER-
SON'S ESTIMATE.—THOMAS GRAY.—IMPORTANCE OF LIVERPOOL AND MAN-
CHESTER.—IMPROVED COMMERCE.—THE MANCHESTER CAPITALIST.—HIS
SOCIAL AND COMMERCIAL IMPORTANCE.—OPPOSITION OF THE CANAL PRO-
PRIETOR.—DIFFICULTIES OF TRANSIT.—DUKE OF BRIDGEWATER'S OPINION
OF TRAMROADS.—ENDEAVOURS OF THOMAS GRAY.—FIRST SURVEY OF
WILLIAM JAMES.—RIVAL CLAIMS.

On February 11th, 1800, Mr. Thomas, of Denton,
read before the Newcastle Literary Society, a paper
on " the propriety of introducing roads on the
principle of the coal-waggon ways, for the general
carriage of goods," and an organised system of
railroads was suggested by Dr. Anderson, who, in his
" Recreations in Agriculture," in the following year
distinctly proposed that where canals could not
be established, tramroads should be laid down and
worked with horse-power. The question was so
far mooted that a committee from the Society of
Arts inquired into the subject, saw a moderate

sized horse, with a descent of one in a hundred, carry, besides the waggon, forty-three tons down, and seven tons up the incline chosen for the attempt. It was also stated that railroads might be established at a moderate expense in many difficult countries; that they would not cost near so much as canals; that they might be introduced into districts where canals could not be formed, and that wherever surveys had been made for the latter it would be wise to examine the propriety of laying down rails instead of cutting canals.

The enthusiasm of Dr. Anderson was the enthusiasm of all who devote themselves to the development of a new idea. "Diminish carriage expense but one farthing," he said with the utmost confidence, "and you widen the circle; you form, as it were, a new creation, not only of stones and earth, and trees and plants, but of men also, and, what is more, of industry, happiness, and joy." Farmers, said this gentleman, would make bye-roads of the same sort, to lead to the main road. A ton weight might then be pushed before a man to market for many miles, like a wheelbarrow.

In order to discover the practicability of introducing

iron railways into general use, Dr. Anderson entered
into some elaborate calculations respecting the expense.
In the most eligible situation, where materials are
good and labour abundant, the lowest expense of
a single railway was calculated at £1,000 a mile;
but as the inconvenience of single railways was
even then foreseen, double railways, he considered,
ought to be preferred. Those for public purposes
should be very substantially made. The metal used
should be of the strongest sort, of substance enough
to carry the proposed weight and bear any blow
to which they might be liable. Made in this way,
in favourable situations in the country, a double
railway was calculated to cost about £2,000 a mile;
but near London, where everything was dear, he was
willing to allow £3,000. Such a road would bring
a charge upon the turnpike of £150 a year, say £50
more for annual repairs, in all £200 per annum; and
as the road from Hyde-park to Hounslow cost £1,000
per mile every year, a great saving was at once shown
in the rail.

Considered with regard to consumption, it would
reduce the number of heavy road horses by seven-
eighths, it would augment the number of cattle, in-

crease consumable provisions, and lower the price of
the necessaries of life. It would decrease the cost of
carriage, it would give encouragement to agriculture,
it would produce a general prosperity, it would augment the consumption of taxable commodities, it
would increase the public revenue, and relieve taxation. He reprobated all sort of gambling speculations by monied men, and advised as highly necessary, to prevent them from even becoming private
property, that they should be made public to
all who might choose to employ them under certain regulations. They should be put, he thought,
on the same footing as public roads, under a distinct
set of commissioners, vested with authority to erect
turnpikes, to levy tolls, mortgage the produce, and
to raise money for the purchase of land and making
the roads. In the Act it should be expressly
stipulated that the produce of these tolls should
be applied solely to keeping the road in repair,
paying the interest of sums borrowed, and repaying
the principal as soon as possible. When the money
was repaid, the tolls were to be lowered until they
raised only sufficient to keep the roads in repair.
Distance would be diminished; lands originally far

beyond the influence of the town as a market, would be brought, practically, close to its gates. The value of articles would be augmented four-fold to the producer, and diminished to the public. Fossil manures, formerly confined to a narrow spot, would be attainable by all. Coals, hitherto of no value in many districts, on account of the expense of carriage, would become valuable to the owner and create employment for the labourer. Around every market he supposed a number of concentric circles drawn, within each of which certain articles would be made marketable which were not so before, and thus become the source of wealth and prosperity to many. "It is scarcely possible," he says, "to contemplate an institution from which would result a greater quantity of harmony, peace, and comfort to persons living in the country, than would naturally result from the introduction of railroads."

Such were the ideas which, twenty-five years before the first railroad era, were read with carelessness and treated with contempt. It is the habit of the world to believe in the sudden creation of that which is forced on their attention. What is new to the million, the million believe must be new to others. The name first associated with any success receives the credit, and the early rise of a grand discovery is too often lost to the annalist in its immediate greatness. The notions propounded by Dr. Anderson were sagacious and suggestive, but they took no hold of the public, partly from the ordinary indifference of the multitude, partly because the capital of the country was exhausted in loans, and partly because the time had not arrived for the thorough and earnest consideration of the railway system. Time passed, and it was long ere the idea thrown out by the Marquis of Worcester, developed by Watt, suggested by Anderson, and acted on in the Principality, was considered applicable to the wants and wishes of the country. It was, indeed, evident so early as 1820, that an increased speed between Liverpool and Manchester was necessary, as the canals which the Duke of Bridgewater had originated were the chief, indeed almost the only, resource of the manufacturer in sending the produce of his skill and of his capital to the four quarters of the globe.

The idea, however, which had thus been wisely and scientifically mooted by Dr. Anderson, found devoted followers in the persons of Thomas Gray and Walter James.

"It is now about twenty-eight years," says an anonymous writer, " since a thoughtful man "—this man was Thomas Gray—" travelling in the north of England on commercial business, stood looking at a small train of coal-waggons, impelled by steam along a tramroad, which connected the mouth of one of the collieries of that district with the wharf at which the coals were shipped. ' Why,' asked Gray, ' are not these tramroads laid down all over England, so as to supersede our common roads, and steam-engines employed to convey goods and passengers along them, to supersede horse-power?' ' Propose that to the nation,' was the reply, ' and see what you will get by it! Why, sir, you will be worried to death for your pains.' " The words were prophetic; but Gray did not take the engineer's warning. His imaginative brain saw tramroads, locomotives, and steam engines triumphant; it beheld horse-power nearly superseded. He at length broached the scheme openly, first to public men by letters and circulars, and afterwards to the public itself.

None would listen to him; and the engineer's words seemed to have been spoken in the spirit of prophecy. Yet Gray was not unwise nor unfortunate in the period he had chosen. Manchester and Liverpool, the places fixed on for his scene of action, had increased in position and power beyond any parallel. Men already looked to the latter as rivalling London. The goods of the former surpassed the graceful productions which at one time could only be procured by the aid of foreign skill, while they were produced at scarcely a tithe of the cost. The connexion between the two places was close and intimate. There had been a constantly increasing communication; they were bound together by the ties of mutual advantage. Liverpool found a purchaser in Manchester for the raw material which was imported so largely into its warehouses. Manchester depended upon Liverpool for the supplies which kept its mills in work, and its operatives contented. The improvements in machinery had, of course, contributed to this. In 1769, Arkwright originated the waterframe; in 1770 the spinning-jenny of James Hargreaves was first heard of; in 1779 Crompton's mule-jenny was invented; and in 1785 Arkwright took out

a patent for improved carding, drawing, and roving
machines. All these things necessarily increased
the importance and the trade of Manchester.

The cotton sent from Liverpool to this place
had increased fifty millions of pounds in nine years.
The docks of Liverpool had seen their shipping
augmented by 1,091 vessels in the same period.
The progress of the timber trade had been active
in proportion. From 1821 to 1824 the exports
from Liverpool had increased seven millions and
a-half. The dock duties had increased eight-fold;
the tonnage had increased from seventy-one thousand
to more than a million tons. The capital formerly
employed in loans was now employed in commerce
and manufacture, and business was flourishing. In
Manchester a similar progress was visible. In
1790 a solitary steam-engine was exhibited to the
curious spectator; in 1824 the smoke from two
hundred darkened the air: in 1814 the loom gave
its graceful produce to manual labour only; ten
years later, 30,000 machines were worked by that
power which Watt discovered, and which, first
introduced into Lancashire by the elder Peel, proved
the foundation of a fortune and a fame alike colossal.

From 1760 the trade in cotton had doubled every twenty years. In 1781 and 1785, Arkwright's patents were annulled, and a gigantic stride was the consequence. The population of Manchester and Liverpool had increased since the discovery of steam and the improvements in machinery to an unprecedented extent. Liverpool numbered, in 1824, 108,000 inhabitants more than in 1788. Manchester had increased from 1752 to 1824 by 139,000 souls. The capital of the manufacturer had more than proportionately increased. The mills of Manchester contained a working population equal to many continental cities. The capitalists of Manchester founded families, built churches, sent law-givers to the senate, mingled their blood with that of the aristocracy, and bequeathed princely fortunes to their sons. They outbid the patrician in the purchase of estates, and often employed more plebeians in one factory than the equestrian order could boast in its entirety. The painter found in them his most munificent patrons. The produce of the sculptor's skill graced their homes, and proved their taste. They were capable of appreciating, and were willing to support, the highest aspirations of science. They were intelligent representatives of an interest which had spread with the growth of machinery throughout England. At first a clique, gathered in particular localities for a particular purpose, despised by the great landed aristocracy as the founders of their own fortunes, they expanded to a class alike antagonistic and dangerous to that power which once refused to recognise them. The cotton lord of Manchester was then as much a feature in the history of commerce as he is now a feature - in the history of the senate. There were more opulent fortunes in the dark streets of that unrepresented town than in the fairest continental cities. There were men, too, with minds as enlarged as their fortunes, capable of grasping any subject, of advancing any capital, of embracing any practical plan.

Although the wealth, the wisdom, and the importance of Manchester and Liverpool had thus increased, there was no increase in the carriage power between the two places. The canal companies—the Irwell and Mersey navigation, the duke's canal, and the Leeds and Liverpool—enjoyed a virtual monopoly; and, with that singular want of foresight which so often accompanies unrivalled success, they had abused their power and controlled their customers.* The agents of these companies were despotic in their treatment of the great houses which supported them ; they formed agreements to charge the same rates, and adopt the same plans. The charges, though high, were submitted to, but the time lost was unbearable to the active spirits thus controlled. The canal proprietors were dilatory to the public, until they became dangerous to themselves. Although the facilities of transit were manifestly deficient; although the barges employed to carry goods often got aground, and were sometimes wrecked by storms; although for ten days during summer the canals were closed; although in very severe winters they were frozen up for weeks: yet they established a rotation by which they sent as much or as little as suited them, and shipped it how or when they pleased. They held levees, attended by crowds, who, admitted one by one, almost implored them to forward their

---

* Mr. Sandars, the father of the Liverpool and Manchester line, proved that the canal carriers had raised the freight of corn from 6s. 8d. to 12s. 6d. per ton, and that of cotton from 6s. 8d. to 15s., and that the freight in 1822 was three times what it was in 1795.

goods. One firm was thus limited by the supreme
wisdom of the canal managers to sixty or seventy
bags a day. The effects were really disastrous:
mills stood still for want of material; machines
were stopped for lack of food. Of 5,000 feet of
pine timber required in Manchester by one house,
2,000 remained unshipped from November, 1824,
to March, 1825. Every large concern was compelled to keep an extra clerk in consequence of
the scarcity of conveyance. In addition to the difficulty of conveying at all, another feature was the
extreme slowness of communication. The average
time of one company was four days, of another
thirty-six hours, and it is on record that it sometimes occupied a longer period from Liverpool
to Manchester, than from Liverpool to New York,
while the commodity, although conveyed across
the Atlantic in twenty-one days, was often kept
six weeks in the docks and warehouses of Liverpool
before it could be conveyed to Manchester. " I
took so much for you yesterday, and I can only
take so much to-day," was the reply when an
urgent demand was made. One company would
not take timber at all; another would only take

a particular sort; a third extended its prohibitions to wheat. A peculiar kind of cotton was objected to by all because it was of great bulk. They limited the quantity; they appointed the time; until the difficulties of transit became a public talk, and the abuse of power a public trouble. The Exchange of Liverpool resounded with merchants' complaints; the counting-houses of Manchester re-echoed the murmurs of manufacturers. The moral and material evil which occurred, when, owing to the absence of supplies, thousands of operatives were thrown out of a day's wages in some large mill, must by its political importance and its personal injury, account for the strong increasing dislike to the agents of the canal proprietors. Even in 1792 the conveyance for timber had been found insufficient, and in 1822 the quantity imported was double. The difficulty of moving it created a positive nuisance, which only the police of Manchester could treat. The public thoroughfares were encumbered with it; the quays were loaded with it; the crowded streets of that great commercial town were often impassable, owing to the carts and carriages which conveyed it, but which could find no legal resting place for their burden. It was sometimes deposited so long on the shore that the owners were fined; while corn, of all articles the most important, was bonded and injured by being kept warehoused in one place, because it could not be sent to the other. These pictures are not exaggerated, they are not even highly coloured; Mr. Huskisson, our early free trade minister, confirmed these assertions, and was cognisant of the mischief when he said in the House of Commons that, "Cotton was detained a fortnight at Liverpool, while the Manchester manufacturers were obliged to suspend their labours, and goods manufactured at Manchester for foreign markets could not be transmitted in time, on account of the tardy conveyance."

Various attempts were made to supersede the necessity of the canal, and men submitted to send their most valuable goods on the open road, exposed to pillage and plunder, rather than submit to the delay. Remonstrances being met by rudeness, it became perceptible to all that something must be done, and that the facilities of transit between Liverpool and Manchester must be improved, if those great places were to retain their relative importance. It was obvious to every thinking man that the gentlemen of Manchester—whose very names were synonymous with intelligent adventure—must feel indignant at the trouble they experienced and the treatment they received; and there seems a decided fatuity in the indifference of the canal owners towards such powerful opponents. The great duke who originated the canals would have behaved otherwise. That he knew the danger which environed his beloved property is evident. "They will last my time," he said; "but I see mischief in these —— tramroads." It was a sentence spoken with that spirit of forethought which had produced canals, and which would at a later period, had he lived, have made the duke one of the most strenuous supporters of the railway.

Such was the peculiar position of Manchester and Liverpool when Thomas Gray went to the principal inhabitants and urged them to take the new mode of locomotion into their consideration· The book which bears his name, published at this period, is remarkable for its foresight; but the energy with which he pressed and pushed the doctrines he taught was more so. The title of his work was as follows:—" Observations on a general iron railway, or land steam-conveyance, to supersede the necessity of horses in all public vehicles; showing its vast superiority in every respect over all the present pitiful methods of conveyance by turnpike-roads, canals, and coasting traders. Containing every species of information relative to railroads and locomotive engines. By Thomas Gray.

> No speed with this can fleetest horse compare,
> No weight like this canal or vessel bear;
> As this will commerce every way promote,
> To this let sons of commerce grant their vote."

A similar confidence is expressed in the volume. There was no wavering and there was no hesitation. "No obstacles," said the preface, confidently, " can long impede what is found essential to the general welfare." The plan would supersede the necessity of horse-power in all public waggons, stage-coaches, and post-chaises. By the establishment of a general iron railway in a direct line, the distance between the capital and the manufacturing districts and principal cities might be reduced one quarter, and in many cases one-third, instead of the ridiculously winding course the stage and mail-coaches then daily ran. The permanent prosperity which would arise to commerce from this rapid communication would soon be felt in every corner of the United Kingdom. The mails from London to Manchester and Liverpool might be conveyed within the space of twelve hours, and those to Glasgow and Edinburgh within twenty-four. The farmer would likewise greatly participate in this national improvement. The land now required to produce food for his horses might be cultivated to produce something far more profitable. The various products of the farm, as well as live stock of every description, might be conveyed to any market, in one half the time, at half the expense now incurred.

" If a public meeting were convened by the wealthy merchants and capitalists of the metropolis, the example would soon be followed in the manufacturing districts and principal cities, and the many millions now annually squandered in purchasing and feeding unnecessary horses, might be divided by the holders of shares in a general iron railway company, and in the numerous branch companies which would be established throughout the United Kingdom."

The trouble which this enthusiast took is worthy

of remembrance. In 1820 and 1821 he memorialised Lord Sidmouth. In 1822 he sent five separate petitions to as many ministers of state. In 1823 he again addressed them; in 1824 he petitioned the lord mayor and corporation of the city of London, from whom, however, as from the others, he met with little or no practical attention.

For some time the name of Gray was associated in the minds of those who thought on the subject with the idea of a clever, curious man, who having no capital of his own, was willing to employ the capital of others for his own benefit. It is probable that the enthusiast was not remarkable for caution ; that he possessed a mono-mania on his favourite subject is indisputable. "About twenty years ago," says Mr. Howitt in one of his delightful books, " Mr. Thomas Gray, then, like myself, residing in Nottingham, used to be noted for what was considered a whimsical crotchet, namely, that a general system of iron railways might and ought to be laid down, on which trains of carriages drawn by locomotive steam-engines should run, and thus supersede the use of coaches, and also, in a great measure, canal-boats and stage-waggons for goods. This scheme, it was said, had for years completely taken possession of and absorbed Mr. Gray's whole mind; that it was the one great and incessant subject of his thoughts and conversation; that begin when you would, on whatever subject—the weather, the news, the political movements of the day—it would not be many minutes before, with Thomas Gray, you would be enveloped with steam, listening to a harangue on a general iron railway. Of course Thomas Gray was looked on as little better than a madman, a crotchetty fellow, a dreamer, a builder of castles in the air, one of the race of discoverers of the elixir of life, the philosopher's stone, the perpetual motion. With one consent he was voted an intolerable bore. Thomas Gray and myself came in contact, and true enough he soon broke out on this railway topic: visions of railways running all over the kingdom, conveying thousands of people and hundreds of thousands of tons of goods at a good round trot; coaches and coachmen annihilated; canals covered with duckweed; enormous fortunes made by good speculations, being talked of as sober realities that were to be."

But other claimants have arisen to the pioneer-

ship of the rail at this particular juncture : and
the friends of William James, of Snowford Manor,
assert that he was the only successful agitator
of the subject—the first person who gave the
impulse by which the movement was commenced.
But, notwithstanding this, and although the last
reserve of his fortune was declared to have been
expended on the project of the railway system,
although he himself said he pursued the cause
" with a missionary's zeal, though not with a missionary's salary," it is the writer's conviction that
he followed rather than led, availing himself of a
public feeling instead of instilling a public taste.*
That he adopted the idea of a Liverpool and Manchester railway from or about the same time with
Gray, that he was the first who absolutely surveyed the ground between these two important towns,
that he suffered pecuniarily, that he drew attention
to the scheme, and endured mortifications similar
to those of his exemplar, cannot be doubted.   In
1822 the above survey between these two places
was made under the auspices of Mr. Sandars,

* This gentleman also proposed the London, Rochester, and Shoreham railway in 1825. It was to be worked by locomotives, and was assisted by his pen
in the shape of a pamphlet.

who was greatly disposed to assist the system
which promised so much. This, though executed by Mr. James, was for various reasons abandoned : but these facts are due to the memory
of the Lord of Snowford Manor, and the services
of Mr. James will be appreciated when it is said
that in a testimonial, intended to benefit the children of this gentleman—signed, too, by the principal engineers of the day, including the names of
Stephenson, Rennie, and Brunel—it is stated that
his pecuniary sacrifices entitled his family "not
only to public sympathy, but also to compensation,
it being an acknowledged fact that to their father's
labours the public were indebted for the establishment of the railway system."

The claims of Mr. Gray and Mr. James have
been well and variously urged : their partisans have
persisted in looking only on one side of the shield ;
and while the friends of Mr. Gray have repudiated
the claims of Mr. James, the supporters of Mr.
James have thrown doubts upon the originality of
Mr. Gray. The following is one claim entered :—

" Mr. W. James of London, was the actual originator of the railway system, by his proposing a

line from Strafford to Birmingham, and subsequently by his more grand project, the Manchester and Liverpool line. William James in his letter to the Prince Regent in 1815, shows that he entertained the idea of rapid locomotion by steam and other agents. William James was really the leader and the only successful agitator of the subject, the first person who gave the impulse by which the movement was commenced. No one could have succeeded in that undertaking but such an one as William James, who all his life had been accustomed to struggle with, and execute difficult projects, who possessed a wide connection with the nobility and great landed proprietors, with whom he was accustomed to mix. To William James belongs the merit of being its earliest agitator in all parts of the kingdom, in making the survey of the first line, in organising the first company, and lodging the first reports and plans of the Manchester and Liverpool railway; and he had done much in experiments and surveys in various places, but without patronage, at his own expense."

There is little doubt in the writer's mind that Gray was, to all practical intents and purposes,

the pioneer of the railway. Although he was neither
the inventor nor the improver, he was the adapter;
although, as it has been seen, the principle of the
locomotive was in operation at various collieries,
and although the idea which possessed Gray's mind,
as it originated from his visit to these places, had
also occupied the thoughts of many others—among
them Sir Richard Phillips—yet the application of
the principle to public transit, the patience with
which the facts were investigated, and the wisdom
with which they were brought to bear upon the
new theory, rests with Thomas Gray.*

---

* The following claim, made by our German friends, must be left to the
judgment of the reader :—

"It appears that the original inventor of the railroad system was the late
principal engineer, Mr. Friederichs, son of a miner in that part of the Herrynian
district which belongs to Hanover. His talent for mechanics was soon perceived
by an influential gentleman, who solicited the Hanoverian government to furnish
him with the means for increasing his practical knowledge in mechanics, and
generally cultivating his mind by a tour though Europe. The request was
granted, and young Friederichs set out on a tour of several years. Two of them
he spent in the salt mines of Gallicia; and it was there that the thought occurred
to him of constructing a new machine for the easier conveyance of heavy loads.
Certain circumstances compelled Friederichs to consider his plan of a new conveyance; and he finally invented iron rails (exactly as they still are in use), a
locomotive engine, and a cart to run from the pit to the silver smelting-house.
The cart is a four-wheeled one, and on its frame is placed a wooden chest, which
may be filled up with minerals to the weight of from 60 to 80 cwt. The
guide sits before the chest, just as the coachman sits on the driving-box;
by pressure he is enabled to direct the cart, and also to arrest it at any time,

But honour is due to all. He who in his chamber
or study watches through the midnight hour in
the inspiration of a great idea, and he who, witnessing
the steam ascend, first thinks of its application
to scientific purposes, must alike be named with
praise. Nor is that great mechanical genius which
gave a vigorous life to the locomotive; or that
earnest unsubdued spirit which combated with the
prejudiced and convinced the capitalist; or that
determined man who, in his desire for the public
benefit, made surveys and urged schemes, less worthy
of honour. It is much to conceive a new idea;
it is much to diffuse that idea throughout the land;
it is much to apply a new theory to an established
power; and it is, indeed, much to devote a life to

however fast it may run. The arrangement is so certain and safe, that to the
present day no accident has occurred. The locomotive engine is all of iron.
When, in 1811, the King and Queen of Westphalia visited the Herrynian district,
the director of mines caused a carriage of the invention of Mr. Friederichs
to be fitted up for an excursion; the king, attended by ten gentlemen of his
court, mounted the first vehicle, and the queen, attended by the ladies of her
suite, stepped into the second carriage, which closely followed the first. They
started at the same time, and the distance which usually occupied forty-five minutes
took only five. This invention was transferred to England, where Mr. Thomas
Gray, of Exeter, advocated it zealously. The simple fact that Mr. Friederichs
having invented the railroad system, and communicated his invention to an English gentleman, was all along known among the inhabitants of the Her ynian
district and the adjacent country. Wooden rails were never used in the above
district.

the propagation of a public principle. All these things were done by men who will long be remembered. The brass on the wayside is not so lasting as their reputation. The names of Anderson, of James, of Gray, will not be readily forgotten: that of George Stephenson is honoured in the present; and at some far-off period, when the " traveller from New Zealand shall, in the midst of a vast solitude, take his stand on a broken arch of London-bridge to sketch the ruins of St. Paul's;"* when the gigantic works, dark tunnels, stupendous bridges, and massive excavations of a dead and decayed nation shall excite the wonder and move the admiration of a new race, it is not impossible that George Stephenson may be to them, as Cadmus was to the elder world, a myth and mystery; his origin lost in the uncertain past, while his memory is an object of reverend respect, if not of religious worship.

* Macaulay's Critical and Historical Essays.

CHAPTER IV.

It has been said that the first survey for the first
railroad was made in 1822, by Mr. James, who,
adopting about the same period a similar idea to
that of Gray, considered that locomotive engines
might be successfully employed on a railway applicable to commercial purposes. It is not to be
supposed that such a town as Manchester would
long submit to the arbitrary controul of the canal
companies ; and the insufficiency of the existing
modes of conveyance for the increased commerce
between Liverpool and Manchester, together with
the absolute monopoly enjoyed by the three canal

interests, induced several gentlemen to lend their
countenance and aid to any scheme which promised
to rid them of so unsufferable a tyranny. Foremost
among them was Mr. Sandars, of Liverpool, who,
when Mr. James was introduced to him, exhibiting
his drawings and explaining the working of the
locomotive, treated him with all the attention he
deserved. That it was not cold, or lukewarm,
may be judged from the fact that, when James
offered to make a preliminary survey of the country
for £10 a mile, Mr. Sandars at once agreed to
pay the £300 necessary to complete the entire distance. The agreement was entered into, the survey
was made ; and well may the friends of Mr. Sandars
claim for him the title of " father and founder of
the Liverpool and Manchester railway."

The scheme was, however, temporarily abandoned ;
partly on account of the engineering difficulties,
and partly because the opposition of the landholders was excited by the canal proprietors, who
delaying until too late a reduction of their charges,
the only opposition that could be effectual, found,
when they could not avoid it, that they had made
a great mistake.

At length the fate of the canal was sealed. The annoyance to which the commerce of Liverpool had been subjected, the difficulties which the manufacturers encountered, the pecuniary loss, and the mental irritation, together, probably, with a great increase of unemployed capital, combined to bring about the first phase of that extraordinary change in locomotion which is not even now fully developed. A declaration was signed by one hundred and fifty of the leading merchants that a new line of conveyance was absolutely necessary. A meeting was convened at Liverpool to consider the preliminaries and the practicability of the plan. A railway was determined on, and a subscription entered into to defray expenses. A committee was then formed; but as they were anxious, if possible, not to quarrel with the canal proprietors, provided only they could obtain proper business facilities, a formal application was made to the agent to reduce the charges and increase the accommodation. The application proved vain; an unqualified refusal was given, and the committee retired. Disappointed, but not dismayed, they returned to the charge. The agent was then informed, that if no extra assistance were given by the canal, the capitalists of Manchester and Liverpool were prepared to form a railway between the two towns. The assertion was probably disbelieved, or the power doubted. A railway was a kind of fable. It had been talked of until it became a tradition. When, therefore, an offer of shares in the new undertaking was made to the canal agent, his answer, owing, probably to the above feeling, manifested as much ignorance of a railroad as it did insolence towards the proposers. " All or none," was his contemptuous reply. " They scouted," says a writer of the time, " the very notion of the smallest reduction ; they wallowed in their dividends with a confidence that must always be impolitic and presumptuous ; when not perfectly secure, they engendered the elements of that opposition they at first ridiculed, but now respect ; and they frittered away their concession in a manner that excited the mirth of their opponents and the pity of their friends." " The fact is notorious," wrote another, " that the manner in which irresponsible power had for some time been exercised, accelerated a crisis which might have been delayed." Great fear and confusion of mind fell upon canal proprietors; nor was the coach owner particularly happy with the prospect which opened before him.

The 29th October, 1824, was the date attached to the first prospectus of the Liverpool and Manchester railway company; and that prospectus, in the calmness of its utterance and the almost dignity of its tone, formed a marked contrast to many which have succeeded it. The opposition of the landowner was alluded to and deprecated. " The road," said the document, " does not approach within about a mile and a half of the residence of the Earl of Sefton, and traverses the Earl of Derby's property over barren mosses, passing about two miles from the hall." The first names in the district were attached to it, and " the importance to a commercial state of a safe and cheap mode of transit for merchandise," was made a prominent consideration. " It is competition that is wanted, and the proof of this assertion may be deduced from the fact that shares in the old Quay navigation, of which the original cost was £70, have been sold as high as £1,250." " The canal establishments are inadequate to the great object to be accomplished—the regular and punctual convey-

ance of goods at all seasons and periods. In the
summer time there is frequently a deficiency of
water, obliging boats to go only half loaded. In
winter they are sometimes locked up for weeks
together." The total quantity of merchandise
passing between Liverpool and Manchester was
estimated at 1,200 tons a day, of which the
average time of passage was thirty-six hours, and
the average charge 15s. a ton. The astonishing fact already given to the reader, that goods
were frequently brought across the Atlantic from
New York to Liverpool in twenty-one days, while
cotton had been longer on its passage from Liverpool to Manchester, was solemnly recorded. And,
pursued the paper, " By the projected railroad, the
transit of merchandise between Liverpool and Manchester will be effected in four or five hours, and
the charge will be reduced one-third. Here then
will be accomplished an immense pecuniary saving
to the public, over and above what is perhaps more
important—economy of time. Nor must we estimate this saving merely by its nominal amount,
whether in money or in time: it will afford a
stimulus to the productive industry of the country;

it will give a new impulse to the powers of accumulation, the value and importance of which can
be fully understood only by those who are aware
how seriously commerce may be impeded by petty
restrictions, and how commercial enterprise is encouraged and promoted by an adherence to fair
competition and free trade."

The principle, therefore, on which the country
was invited to co-operate in the great experiment,
was the public good. It was a principle at which
the canal proprietors scoffed, and which the coach
proprietors ridiculed.

The estimated expense of the entire line was
given at £400,000 ; and the passenger traffic—that
traffic which has formed so marked a feature in
railroads—was cautiously alluded to. " Moreover,"
continued the prospectus on this point, " as a cheap
and expeditious means of conveyance for travellers,
the railway holds out the fair prospect of a public
accommodation which cannot be immediately ascertained."

This prospectus created great interest. The excitement which was prevalent throughout England at
the period, the freedom with which money was

invested in foreign mines and foreign loans, in domestic milk companies, and domestic umbrella societies, was an additional assistance to those who were promoting the project, and the shares were taken without difficulty. The line previously examined by Mr. James was abandoned, and Mr. George Stephenson was employed to make a new survey. An application was immediately made to the House of Commons to grant a bill, and a most determined opposition ensued : every clause of that great argument was opposed ; every fallacy which had been refuted was again repeated ; facts were most obstinately mis-stated, and falsehoods confidently asserted as facts. The bill was argued against by one gentleman, " because there were already three canals between Liverpool and Manchester. They were rival companies, interested in opposing each other, and the competition produced a reduction of rates. It would interfere with private property. He knew one individual whose land was bounded by a canal on one side, and by the high road on another, and now they were going to run the railway through the centre of his estate." This logical reason why the proposed railway bill

should not become the law of the land was probably conclusive only to canal proprietors and to
the honourable member himself. Mr. Huskisson
said, and the remark is worthy notice, coming
from this eminent man, "that the promoters of
the scheme had a higher object than the mere
accumulation of wealth through this channel. They
would render a great commercial benefit to this
country. The subscribers were the merchants,
bankers, traders, and manufacturers of Liverpool
and Manchester. They had agreed that no person
should hold more than ten shares each. He had
seen the parties interested, and they had declared
they were willing to limit the amount of dividends
to ten per cent., and that they would be perfectly
satisfied with five per cent."

When the canal companies saw that the railway
was likely to become what has since been termed
a great fact, a wonderful change took place. Their
fear conquered their pride, and they attempted to pro-
pitiate the merchant. They, who once had laughed
at such an application, now lowered their charges.
They, who once had haughtily declared it to be
impossible, now increased their accommodation.

One canal company offered to reduce its length three miles out of forty-two, at an expense of many thousands of pounds. They saw now, as the father of canals had seen half a century before, "mischief in those —— tramroads." But despite of this, though they deprecated where they once had defied, they found their efforts vain, and their offers of accommodation too late.

The railway was determined on; and every interest, direct or indirect, which the canal proprietary, as influential, perhaps, as any company that ever existed, could exert, was brought to bear on their formidable and fatal opponents. Next to the canal owner, the most important opposition was naturally expected from the landholder, and by both interests every art was used to produce an effectual hindrance. Every report which could promote a prejudice, every rumour which could affect a principle, was spread. The country gentleman was told that the smoke would kill the birds as they passed over the locomotive. The public were informed that the weight of the engine would prevent its moving; and the manufacturer was told that the sparks from its chimney would burn his

goods. The passenger was frightened by the assertion that life and limb would be endangered. Elderly
gentlemen were tortured with the notion that they
would be run over. Ladies were alarmed at the
thought that their horses would take fright. Foxes
and pheasants were to cease in the neighbourhood
of a railway. The race of horses was to be extinguished. Farmers were possessed with the idea
that oats and hay would no more be marketable
produce; cattle would start and throw their riders,
cows even, it was said, would cease to yield their
milk in the neighbourhood of one of these infernal
machines.

The provincial and metropolitan press were busied
with argumentative articles. The *Birmingham Gazette*
of 6th December, 1824, invited opposition in an
advertisement bearing sixty-three signatures; which,
when subjected to a severe examination, proved
to be in the proportion of eighteen landowners and
canal proprietors, to forty-five of their tenants.
The Leeds, and Liverpool, the Birmingham, and
other corporations, called on every navigation company in the kingdom to oppose railways wherever
contemplated. The *Quarterly*—and it is most

important to examine the views of these exponents of public opinion—wrote in 1825, "The gross exaggeration of the powers of the locomotive steam-engine, or, to speak more plainly, the steam-carriage, may delude for a time, but must end in the mortification of those concerned. * * * It is certainly some consolation to those who are to be whirled at the rate of eighteen or twenty miles an hour, by means of the high-pressure engine, to be told that they are in no danger of being sea-sick while they are on shore, that they are not to be scalded to death nor drowned by the bursting of the boiler, and that they need not mind being shot by the scattered fragments, or dashed in pieces by the flying off, or the breaking, of a wheel. But with all these assurances we should as soon expect the people of Woolwich to suffer themselves to be fired off by one of Congreve's ricochet rockets, as trust themselves to the mercy of such a machine going at such a rate. * * * We will back old father Thames against the Woolwich railway for any sum."

Such were the opinions of the disbelievers; nor were some who were favourable much more propitious in their views: anxious not to excite too great a hope, they tended to produce depression. Thus, " it is far from my wish," said Mr. Nicholas Wood, " to promulgate to the world that the ridiculous expectations, or rather professions, of the enthusiast speculator will be realised, and that we shall see engines travelling at the rate of twelve, sixteen, eighteen, or twenty miles an hour. Nothing could do more harm towards their general adoption and improvement than the promulgation of such nonsense."

These opinions were thoroughly justified by the existing state of mechanical science in comparison with the difficulties to be overcome. The reviewer was not alone in his opinion. He was supported by scientific men, who denounced railroads as wild and visionary; but it has become a habit with most writers to quote the opinions of the press generally, and the above paragraph in particular, as evidence of a remarkable want of foresight. It must be remembered, however, that the period was one of intense excitement; that bad, base men were projecting companies under any and every pretence; that schemes were proposed and capital called for under circumstances which made every thinking person watchful. It was at this period that railways were schemed for every county in England; and that some one, far in advance of that day, projected an iron way from Dover to Calais. The wants and wishes of every class were addressed with specious and special care. The public was tempted to throw its money after delusive schemes, and it became a peremptory duty of the press to caution that public against projects, which, appearing to address themselves to reason, were only fit subjects for ridicule. The proposal of an iron road, of carriages moving by steam, of thirty miles an hour, of excavated rocks, of deep cuttings, of high embankments, of long tunnels, of tremulous bogs bearing gigantic weights, of effects produced in two hours which sometimes occupied two weeks, appeared both false and frivolous. For the reviewer to have argued differently, would have required the gift of prophecy or the practical power of a Stephenson. At any rate the opinions expressed were honest; and, therefore, honourable to all save those who, making them the subject of a disingenuous ridicule, evidence their wit at the expense of their

wisdom.   The ideas of Mr. Wood and the *Quarterly*
reviewer were then the ideas of nearly the whole
world.   They remained the general opinion for a
long period.   It will be seen that, ten years after
this, the indignation of the many descended upon
railroads ; that when even they had become an
established fact, and when they had changed the
face of the land, educated, intelligent men were
not wanting to declare we must return to our old
established habits.   It is a recorded fact that, twenty
years later, the learning of Southey, and the imaginative power of Wordsworth, only taught the
former to speak disparagingly of, and the latter to
vent his indignation in a sonnet on the iron way.   It
is necessary to remember these things as this history
proceeds, that the wrath of the reader may be modified by his reason.

When the bill went into committee, the opposition
was strong and severe.   Satire and argument were
alike brought to bear upon the subject.   The wit-
nesses were subjected to a severe cross examination ;
Mr. Stephenson was attacked with an undeserved
severity ; the claims of the land-owner were placed in
a prominent position ; the locomotive was laughed

at, the speed was denied, and the Exchange of Liverpool denounced for having aided and abetted so preposterous a plan. "It was the most absurd scheme that ever entered the head of man to conceive." "Public profit," said another, "is always the plea for private benefit." Another "would sooner give £10,000 than have the steam-engines come puffing near him." A third declared it afforded no practical advantage over a canal. "If this railroad is to be made," said a fourth, with a bathos rarely equalled, "we must quit the place where we have lived so long and happily ; we must leave it—we must go away."

Vegetation, it was prophesied, would cease wherever the locomotive passed. The value of land would be lowered by it ; the market gardener would be ruined by it. The canal could carry goods cheaper. Steam would vanish before storm and frost ; property would be deteriorated near a station. It was called the greatest draught upon human credulity ever heard of. It was erroneous, impracticable, and unjust. It was a great and scandalous attack on private property, upon public grounds. The most contradictory reports were current. Prejudice rode paramount; and while one class was informed that the locomotive would travel so fast that life and limb would be endangered, another was told that it would be too heavy to travel at all.

A great point with the disaffected was Chatmoss. Over this wavering, trembling place the locomotive was to travel. There was nothing, said the opposition, but long, sedgy grass to prevent it from sinking to the shades of eternal night. No engineer in his senses would try to make a railroad through Chatmoss; and if this bill were got, another would be required to emerge from it. It was an immense mass of pulp, which swelled in wet and sunk in dry weather.

But the most vehement abuse was bestowed upon Mr. Stephenson; the most virulent opposition reserved for him: and the following, extracted from a mass of gross assertion, is a curious specimen of the liberality of feeling which attends the promoter of a new scheme. He was said to be utterly devoid of common sense. He was taunted with attempting an impossible ditch by an impossible railway; with making schemes without seeing the difficulties; with being industrious only to deceive; with being anxious to get everything but the truth. "I say," said one, "he never had a plan; I do not believe he is capable of making one. His is a mind perpetually fluctuating between opposite difficulties; he neither knows whether he is to make bridges over roads or rivers: or of one size or another; or to make embankments, or cuttings, or inclined planes, or in what way the thing is to carried into effect."

"Mr. Stephenson speaks of an arch which is to cost £375. How high is it to be? He does not know. At what rate per yard? He cannot tell. Whenever a difficulty is pressed, as in the case of the tunnels, he gets out of it at one end; and when you try to catch him there, he gets out at the other." He had embankments where he should have had cuttings; he had cuttings where he should have had embankments. So great a specimen of rashness and ignorance was never before exhibited. There was a shuffling manner of going into the whole of his estimates. There was nothing to which he would not bend himself, nothing to which he would stick.

Such were a few of the personal expressions of

wrath towards Mr. Stephenson ; and the locomotive
came in for its share.   Expeditious it could not
be, whenever " Providence in Lancashire sent mizzling
weather."   The wind, if higher than usual, would
prevent it from running ; the rain would stop it ;
the snow would upset it.   It was quite idle and
absurd to say the present scheme could be carried
into execution under any circumstances or in any
way.   The subscribers would lose all their money ;
the scheme was bottomed on deception and fallacy.
They would not go so fast as the canal or so
safe as the coach.   The engine would burst, and the
wheels would fly off.

The most dangerous and important opposition,
however, was that which proved errors in the
sections and surveys of Mr. Stephenson ; and though
that gentleman candidly allowed that they were so,
it was a most important feature in an examination
on which the fate of the bill depended.   The difficulties thrown in his way must be accepted as
the defence.   Although by their resistance they
drove him to take his survey secretly, they did
not hesitate to charge him with the consequences
of their own opposition.   He had " trodden down the

corn of widows," he had " destroyed the strawberry-
beds of gardeners," he had " committed trespasses,"
he had " violated private rights." He was threatened
by peers, he was attempted " to be ducked" by
commoners. With such difficulties in his path, the
wonder is not that his survey was incorrect, but that
he was able to take one at all.

Mr. Stephenson said, in after times, that he was
scarcely in the witness-box before he wished himself
well out. The picture of such a mind exposed to
vulgar taunts, to sneers, to satire, is painful, yet
instructive. The professional pathos of counsel, the
jargon of men crammed for a purpose, the free and
fluent speech of those who were paid to

Make the worse appear the better cause,

must have filled the mind of Mr. Stephenson with pity
allied to contempt. Nor is it to be wondered at, that
the " untaught, inarticulate genius," as he has been
finely called, stood confounded before the class which
opposed him. But be it remembered that, if he
hesitated, it was from depth and not from shallowness
of thought; it was because he feared to astonish
rather than feared to inform his hearers. Let it

be remembered, too, that he had to accommodate his language to his listeners; that his directors implored him not to express fully his opinion; that even when, in obedience to their wishes, he only recommended a speed of eight miles an hour with twenty tons, and four miles with forty tons, the committee deemed him mad, and the counsel ridiculed him; that he was sneered at as a visionary and pitied as a lunatic. The bill failed. A discussion of thirty-seven days in the committee of the House of Commons was closed by the two first clauses being negatived.

It is both curious and interesting to look back on the state of public opinion and the lassitude of public feeling. The world of England would not believe in railways, and a small proprietary was forcing it on them. And so it ever is; the few fight the battle, the many claim the benefit. From his obscure home the student emits the first ray of light, and he is called a dreamer. In his workshop, or at his loom, the mechanical genius broods over the thought, applies it mentally, spends his last shilling on it, and dies ere he has been able to offer it to the world. It comes into the possession of one contemptuously pronounced a projector, who sees its value and seizes on the idea: he passes his time in waiting on the capitalist, in exhibiting its uses, in showing its profits. The monied man assists; a company is formed; efforts to penetrate the apathy of the public are made. The opposition of the interested is neutralised. The world is told that a great and beneficial change is at hand; but, indifferent to that which it cannot comprehend, it shouts the hackneyed cry of innovation. The shrewd, sagacious merchant employs the pamphlet and the press; he has given his capital, and there is no pause. Onward, silently and surely, the good cause speeds, unheard-of or uncared-for by the many, but still day by day increasing, until the discovery is perfected, the invention is complete, and the public rejoice in the good which they lately abused. It is thus with all our great inventions; thus with all that graces the person or gratifies the taste; thus with all which gives a comfort to the poorest or a luxury to the richest home: and the inventor, the adapter, the capitalist, are all links in one great chain of human good. To all and each belong the several meeds so justly their due, while to the public alone belongs an apathetic indifference. The writer has previously written on the same subject, but he feels so acutely for the dark hours of those whose doom it is to create in silence and in sadness, and to project amid ridicule and contempt, that he trusts he may be pardoned this digression in a volume devoted to the progress of the greatest idea of the century.

CHAPTER V.

NEW PROSPECTUS ISSUED. — PROPITIATION OF A CANAL COMPANY. — NEW
SURVEY.—OBJECTIONS IN PARLIAMENT.—THE BILL PASSED.—ANALYSIS OF
THE RAILWAY DIRECTORATE.—NAMES OF FIRST AND SECOND COMMITTEE.
—LOCOMOTIVE CHOSEN. – PRIZE OFFERED FOR THE BEST LOCOMOTIVE.—
GAINED BY THE ROCKET.—CHATMOSS.— HENRY BOOTH.

THE first attempt in parliament had failed, but
the directors had lost no jot of heart or hope. They
assembled their friends, discussed their difficulties
calmly, and the more closely the question was canvassed the more evident it became that railways
must form the locomotive power of England. The
difficulties thrown in their way were temporary,
but the principle was true. Their first efforts were
therefore turned to the errors discovered in the
sections and levels. These were corrected; attempts
were also made to soften and subdue the landowners. A new prospectus was issued. The estate
of Lord Sefton, who had opposed the bill, was

entirely avoided, while a few detached fields of the estate of Lord Derby—" far removed from the Knowlsby domain "—were the only portions dese-crated. " The committee have to state," pursued this interesting document, " that they have spared no pains to accommodate the exact route to the wishes of proprietors whose estates they cross, by removing the road to a distance from the mansions of proprietors, and from those portions of estates more particularly appropriated to game preserves." But the important part of the document was the following : " The opposition of the most powerful of the existing establishments has been removed, by the Marquis of Stafford having for himself, and those of his family who are beneficially interested in the profits of the Duke of Bridgewater's canal, become a subscriber to the extent of one thousand shares."

Thus was the great canal proprietor propitiated, and thus was the way paved for success. But the storm, though subdued, was not entirely silenced. The streets through which the new line was to pass arose in a mass against it. The old Quay company objected because a bridge was to be formed

over the Irwell; the Leeds and Liverpool canal
resisted because it was to pass under their stream.
So the streets which objected were avoided, while
the objection of the companies was subdued by the
line neither crossing the canal nor tunnelling the
river.

When the railway directors determined once more
to try their fate in parliament, it was thought
better, as Mr. George Stephenson was comparatively
unknown, to employ as engineer to the company
some name better known to the world. George
and John Rennie were, therefore, invited to the
post; and being appointed to make a fresh survey,
the committee, on the recommendation of these gentlemen, determined to adopt a new route, passing to
the south of that surveyed by Mr. Stephenson.
The energy of the proprietors was employed to
carry this plan into operation. The necessary documents were prepared with due diligence; great
exertion was made by the engineers; and so successful were the operators, that in three months
the standing orders were complied with. The errors
which had been almost unavoidably committed were
candidly acknowledged. Every sacrifice, save that

of honour, was made, to further the great scheme ;
the very locomotive was temporarily abandoned rather
than peril the passing of an Act on which so much
depended ; and the inconvenience which in the first
survey had been made a subject of complaint, of
crossing public thoroughfares, was removed or obviated. That the directors were in earnest was
proved ; that there was no factious feeling on their
part, is now acknowledged , while all must admire
the moderation with which they appealed to public
opinion in their new prospectus.

" It becomes a question of serious import whether
this country, which is indebted for so much of her
wealth, and power, and greatness to the bold and
judicious application of mechanical science, shall
now pause in the career of improvement, while it
is notorious other nations will adopt the means of
aggrandisement which we reject ; whether England
shall relinquish the high 'vantage ground she at
present possesses, not more with a reference to
the direct operations of commerce and manufactures than generally in the successful application
of the most important principles of science and
art."

When the bill was once more introduced into parliament, an interesting discussion occurred, and the objections brought against the innovation were given with all the force of senatorial dignity. Mr. Stanley undertook to prove that the railway would take ten hours in its journey, and that the trains could only be worked by horses. Sir Isaac Coffin denounced it as a most flagrant imposition. He would not consent to see widows' premises invaded; "and how," he added, with great and dignified feeling, "how would any person like to have a railroad under his parlour window?"

It was in vain that Mr. Huskisson announced his main object to be the destruction of the overgrown monopoly enjoyed by the canals; and it was in vain he informed the members that, whereas the canals divided a hundred per cent., the railway would be contented with ten. He was met with arguments which even Mr. Huskisson was unable to answer satisfactorily to the recipient.

"What was to be done," said his opponent, "with all those who have advanced money in making and repairing turnpike-roads? What with those who may still wish to travel in their own or hired carriages, after the fashion of their forefathers ? What was to become of coach-makers, and harness-makers, coach-masters, coachmen, inn-keepers, horse-breeders and horse-dealers. The beauty and comfort of country gentlemen's estates would be destroyed by it. Was the House aware of the smoke and the noise, the hiss and the whirl which locomotive engines, passing at the rate of ten or twelve miles an hour, would occasion ? Neither the cattle ploughing in the fields or grazing in the meadows could behold them without dismay. Lease-holders and tenants, agriculturists, graziers, and dairy-men would all be in arms. * * * Iron would be raised in price one hundred per cent., or, more probably, it would be exhausted altogether. It would be the greatest nuisance, the most complete disturbance of quiet and comfort in all parts of the kingdom, that the ingenuity of man could invent."

Notwithstanding such verbal and vituperative objections, the bill was this time successful, and the directors believing, after mature deliberation, that Mr. Stephenson, from his extensive practical knowledge, was most desirable as an engineer, appointed him to that important situation, although the survey which had been passed by parliament had been formed by Mr. Rennie.*

The bold and business-like conduct of the company had met with its reward; and, to use the words of Mr. Whishaw in his great statistical volume on railways, " They truly should be numbered among England's benefactors, whose names are recorded in the prospectus first issued by this company. So great was their zeal in this formidable undertaking, that notwithstanding the violent and costly opposition which they met with in their first application to parliament, they proceeded with renewed vigour during the recess to prepare themselves with more perfect plans and sections for a second application in the following year, so fully were they convinced, that though they might incur a vast outlay before they could even obtain an act of parliament, their efforts would be crowned with success, and the results prove nationally advantageous."

The directorate of this railway was composed of

---

* Mr. Booth states that Messrs. Rennie, if they undertook the superintendence of the works, could only make six visits yearly, of seven or ten days each visit. They claimed also the privilege of naming the resident engineer. These propositions were declined, and thus originated what some have termed a grievance towards Mr. Rennie.

men who could scarcely be paralleled in importance by any place in the world, save that which produced them. The names which were on its list were the names of merchants and of manufacturers responsible for millions. But great as their pecuniary power, their moral and intellectual importance equalled it. The firm of Gladstone—a name now regarded by England as that of one of her trusty statesmen—gave an assurance that the motto of that great local house was "*en avant*." Another name, that of Cropper, represented the wealthy interest which was founded by Fox, and has since been adorned by a Fry. The mercantile character of this gentleman was only equalled by his private character; and the man who, having placed his family in the position which was their due, could devote his entire energy, intellect, and fortune to the benefit of others, demands our praise, and deserves the honour bestowed upon his memory by those who know him.

The following are the names appended to the first and second prospectus:—

COMMITTEE

OF

LIVERPOOL AND MANCHESTER RAILWAY.

Charles Lawrence—Chairman.

Lester Ellis,
Robert Gladstone,
John Moss,
Joseph Sandars.
} Deputy Chairmen.

Robert Benson	Isaac Hodgson
H. H. Birley	Joseph Hornby
Joseph Birley	John Kennedy
Henry Booth	Wellwood Maxwell
Thomas Shaw Brandreth	William Potter
James Cropper	William Rathbone
John Ewart	William Rotheram
Peter Ewart	John Ryle
William Garnett	Thomas Sharpe
Richard Harrison	John Wilson
Thomas Headlam	
Adam Hodgson	George Stephenson—Engineer.

SECOND PROSPECTUS.

Charles Lawrence—Chairman.

Robert Gladstone,
John Moss,
Joseph Sandars.
} Deputy Chairmen.

Robert Benson, Liverpool	R. Harrison, Liverpool
H. H. Birley, Manchester	Thomas Headlam, do.
Joseph Birley, do.	Adam Hodgson, do.
Benjamin Booth, do.	Isaac Hodgson, do.
Henry Booth, Liverpool	Joseph Hornby, do.
T. S. Brandreth, do.	John Kennedy, Manchester
John Ewart, do.	Aaron Lees, do.
Peter Ewart, Manchester	W. Maxwell, Liverpool
R. H. Gregg, do.	William Potter, do.

William Rathbone, Liverpool	Thomas Sharpe, Manchester
William Rotheram, do.	John Wilson, Liverpool
John Ryle, Manchester	George and John Rennie—Engineers.

Among the many dangers and difficulties which beset the directors, was the nature of the power to be used. The opposition which the railway had received on personal grounds was extended to the locomotive. Its unpopularity with the ignorant can scarcely be described ; the horrors of the infernal regions were figured by it. Death and dismay were familiarly connected with it, and it argues great boldness and perseverance in its friends, that, anxious to avail themselves of every invention which science had placed at their disposal, competent persons were employed to report from personal inspection on the powers and practice of the engines they saw, and the tramroads they visited. In October 1828, therefore, three of the directors, aided by Mr. Booth, went to Darlington and the neighbourhood of Newcastle. On their return, although they brought with them a fund of information, it was of so mixed and contradictory a character that the question still remained unsettled. One step was gained; as the deputation was convinced that for so immense a portion of traffic, anticipated by the Liverpool and Manchester line, "horses were out of the question."

Another movement was then made: Mr. James Walker, a London, and Mr. Rastrick, a northern engineer, were employed to report on the merits of the locomotive and the fixed engine; and the opinions of these gentlemen are worth recording, because they prove that the locomotive, even with the profession, was unfavourably regarded. "As a general answer," says Mr. Walker, "I should say that the stationary is the safer, chiefly from the locomotives being high-pressure engines and accompanying the goods or passengers on the way." Mr. Rastrick considered that "locomotives weighing more than eight tons could not be conveniently used to get a speed of more than ten miles an hour;" but he said, "I am decidedly of opinion that fifteen miles per hour on a railroad may be travelled in perfect safety, both to goods and passengers."* An answer, considered theoretically con-

---

* It need not be said that recommendations and suggestions poured in on the gentlemen who formed the direction. If the engineers generally were against the locomotive, Mr. Sandars and his friends supported it, and Mr. Stephenson was earnest for it. Mr. Booth, in his "Account of the Liverpool and Manchester Railroad," a pamphlet now difficult to be procured, says,

clusive, from Mr. Robert Stephenson and Mr. Locke, was followed by the determination to try the locomotive.   " The nature of the power to be used," said the report which ensued, " for the conveyance of goods and passengers becomes now a question of great moment ; after due consideration, the engineer has been authorised to prepare a locomotive engine, which, from the nature of its construction, and from the experiments already made, he is of opinion will be effective for the purposes of the company without proving an annoyance to the public."

A most judicious resolve was the result ; a public announcement being made that a premium of £500

with a humour not always found among the class to which he belongs, "multifarious were the schemes proposed to the directors for facilitating locomotion. Communications were received from all classes, each recommending an improved power, or an improved carriage ; from professors of philosophy down to the humblest mechanic, all were zealous in their proffers of assistance.   England, America, and Continental Europe were alike tributary.   Every element, and almost every substance were brought into requisition and made subservient to the great work.   The friction of carriages was to be reduced so low that a silk thread would draw them, and the power to be applied was so vast as to rend a cable asunder.   Hydrogen gas and high-pressure steam; columns of water and columns of mercury ; a hundred atmospheres, and a perfect vacuum ; machines working in a circle without fire or steam, generating power at one end of the process and giving it out at the other ; carriages that conveyed every one its own railway; wheels within wheels to multiply speed without diminishing power, with every complication of balancing and countervailing forces to the *ne plus ultra* of perpetual motion."

would be given to the owner of the locomotive which, on a certain day, should perform certain conditions in the most satisfactory manner.* This challenge to the engineers of the country produced its effect. Independently of its proving the power of the locomotive, it was calculated to remove prejudices from the minds of those who might witness the trial, and thus create a certain moral effect on its behalf throughout the country.

The sixth of October, 1829, was chosen for the day of trial, and great was the interest. The adjacent country poured forth its thousands. Every class of social life sent a representative. The farmer who had anathematised it, came to wonder ; the operative who could understand it, came to praise.

* The conditions given forth on 25th April, 1829, were,

1. The engine should consume its own smoke.

2. An engine of six tons should draw twenty tons, at ten miles an hour, with a pressure of not more than fifty pounds.

3. For two safety valves, one beyond the reach of the engine man.

4. The engine to have springs and six wheels, and not to be more than fifteen feet high to the top of the chimney.

5. The engine, with water, not to weigh more than six tons, and if less, would be preferred, on its drawing a proportionate weight, and an engine weighing only four and a-half tons might be put on only four wheels.

6. For a mercurial gage, showing the steam pressure above forty-five pounds to the inch, and to blow out at a pressure of sixty pounds.

7. The engine to be sent to Liverpool not later than 1st October.

8. The price of the engine to be not more than £550.

Wherever a glimpse could be caught of the new machine, the space was filled with expectant eyes. Engineers from all quarters of the kingdom looked significantly on. The man of science interested in the dawn of a great change, awaited eagerly the result. The representative of letters was there to record the advent of a power as fruitful as his own. The Earl of Derby came to rejoice in its failure ; the directors were there to enjoy its success. Many a youthful student of mechanics left his books, and many an intelligent artisan forfeited his wages to catch the first glimpse of that power which was to renew the youth of England.

The engine termed the "Novelty," built by Messrs. Braithwaite, was the favourite. Light, elegant, and compact, the boiler, which in the "Rocket" of Mr. Stephenson bore a somewhat ungainly aspect, was in the "Novelty" almost hidden from the sight. With curious, wondering eye, the public gazed on the cumbrous machines ; and great was the pleasure of assembled thousands when they saw its huge bulk moving at a speed which wearied the eye and excited the brain but to follow it. For several days the initiatory movements continued, and the excitement lasted. Shops, warehouses, and counting-houses were thinned, that their owners might enjoy the public triumph. Liverpool forgot its commerce and Manchester its trade. Weighing four tons three hundred-weight, dragging also three times its own weight, the "Rocket" performed the conditions prescribed on the second day; and when, detached from all encumbrance, the bye-standers saw the engine dart along the road with a rapidity analagous to that with which the swallow cleaves the sky, the air was filled with sounds of praise and wonder.

In the definite trial, to which the others were only introductory, the "Sans Pareil" of Mr. Hackworth, the "Novelty" of Mr. Braithwaite, and the "Rocket" of Mr. Stephenson, tested their capabilities; the result was that the machinery of the "Sans Pareil" failed, the boiler of the "Novelty" burst, while the "Rocket," after fulfilling all the conditions imposed, performed various amateur journeys with amateur passengers, yielding the honour of that noble victory to him whose name is indelibly associated with the triumph of the rail.

The engineers were said to be surprised at their

own success; the public which once doubted now believed ; and it is probable that Lord Derby saw the folly of denying the power he could not stay.

The greatest speed attained by the "Novelty" was rather less than twenty-three miles an hour, while that of the "Rocket" was rather above twenty-nine miles in the same time. If the success of the locomotive were great, the effect on the shares was equally so. The price rose £10 per cent., and the £500 paid Mr. Stephenson sunk into insignificance compared with £65,000 increased value on the capital stock.

It was little thought by those who wondered at the rapid movements of the "Rocket," that on it as driver sat one whose name, nearly a quarter of a century later, would be identified with the great triumph of the year 1851. Son of a medical practitioner, destined for the same profession, marrying for love at an early age, and immediately finding that "fathers have flinty hearts," Charles Fox, the future builder of the Crystal Palace, determined if he could not gain his living by his head to earn it with his hand; and greatly to his honour is the fact that he guided the engine which Stephenson built, and aided to win the prize which Stephenson received.

Although this line was only thirty miles in length, some notion of its engineering character may be formed from the fact that, independently of culverts and footways, there were sixty-three bridges, thirty of which passed under the turnpike road, twenty-eight over it, four over streams, and one over the river Irwell; while, in its formation, the various excavations yielded upwards of three million cubic yards of stone, clay, and soil.

The reader will have seen that the attempt to make a road over Chatmoss excited great derision. Extending four miles on the line of road; composed of a dreary impassable waste; celebrated by Michael Drayton as having its origin at the deluge; chronicled by Camden as " a swampy tract of great extent ;" the abode of the plover by day, and lighted only by the fire-fly at night; it seemed to the uninitiated as easy to tunnel Tartarus as to send an engine over Chatmoss. And it is characteristic of the engineer who proposed it, that though unable to develope his plan to a public audience, he was yet able to carry it out for the public benefit. The words of Mr. Stephenson will best relate the difficulties with which he contended, and the skill with which he executed his task, "Chatmoss," he says, in a letter dated 1st November, 1828, "extends four miles on the line of road; on each side of the moss the land lies low; on the western side an embankment is formed of moss nearly a mile in length, and varying from ten to twenty feet in height, which stands extremely well; the slopes of this embankment are a little more upright than the angle of forty-five, which, from our experience, stands better than if more inclined. It is now covered with a material, from two to three feet thick, consisting of sand and gravel. The permanent road is laid upon this covering, and remains very firm; the quantity of excavations made in the moss to form the embankments adjoining, amount to 520,000 cubic yards. That portion of the moss, about three-quarters of a mile from the western edge, called the "flow-moss," from its extreme softness, is also covered with sand and gravel; underneath I have laid hurdles thickly interwoven with twisted heath, which form a platform for the covering. Two years ago a person was not able to walk over this portion of the moss, except in the dryest weather ; at present we have horses travelling with loads of from six to twelve tons."

Over this moss, which had, in an attempt to cultivate it, destroyed the fortunes of the polished historian of Leo and Lorenzo, the carriages of the railway now pass hourly. And seldom does the passenger bestow his tribute on the power which triumphed over so great a difficulty—which, in opposition to the sneer of the sceptic and the anxious silence of friends, in spite of the doubt of some and the despair of others—carried out a plan, where to fail would have been ruinous, and to succeed was to be depreciated. It must be some pride to the proprietary, that at this juncture they supported Mr. Stephenson ; and some satisfaction to the men of the two great Lancashire towns, that they gave their capital to the genius of their engineer when most men would have retired in dismay.

The name of its particular promoter must not be omitted in recording the services of those who forwarded the project and assisted the prospects of the line. Interested in railways generally, the author of an improvement in the early locomotive, the writer of an important pamphlet on the subject to which he devoted his life,* the name of Henry Booth is not only associated with this line, it is associated with the entire system.   He, among others, has been termed the founder of modern locomotion; and the writer has seen sufficient confidently to assert that to this gentleman not only the Liverpool and Manchester, but the entire world of railways, is greatly indebted.   More than a quarter of a century has now elapsed since Mr. Booth first agitated for this line, and he has lived to see his agitation successful; to witness the discomfiture of those who opposed him; to rejoice in the success of those who assisted him; and to behold that system for which he so zealously fought, an integral portion of English commerce, of English capital, and of English comfort.

---

* It is scarcely asserting too much to say that Mr. Stephenson was indebted to Mr. Booth for his success at Rainhill, as from a suggestion of this gentleman the "Rocket" was made by Mr. Stephenson to present a greater surface to the fire than its competitors.

CHAPTER VI.

RAILWAY EXCITEMENT OF 1825.—ITS FEATURES AND PROMOTERS.—THE KENTISH RAILWAY.—LIST OF PROPOSED RAILWAYS.—OPENING OF THE LI-VERPOOL AND MANCHESTER.—ITS FIRST LOCOMOTIVE.—COMPARISON OF TRAFFIC WITH THE ESTIMATES.—PERSONAL SKETCH OF GEORGE STEPHENSON.

WHILE the Manchester and Liverpool was thus in its incipient progress, various lines which were afterwards carried out, were attempted unsuccessfully. Many a survey of many a future line was then made under the auspices of far-sighted men, capable of foretelling the future power of the rail, which on calm calculation it was found either inexpedient to adopt, or for which the calls could not be raised. It was thus with the London and Birmingham, thus with the Northern, thus with the Great Western, thus with nearly every trunk line we now possess. A capital of £21,942,500 was demanded for railways in 1824-5, on which

£219,425 was actually paid; what became of the money it would be difficult now to say; though there cannot be a doubt that to the great mania of 1825 England is indebted for her railway system. Amid the many schemes which Mr. Canning described as " springing up after the dawn of the morning, and passing away before the dews of the evening descended," the railway has been forgotten in the delusions which surrounded them. But there was a very general feeling in favour of the companies which have since been so popular. A great number of lines were prepared to go before the House; several ventured, but were thrown out; a large amount of capital was raised upon them; and nearly all the principal routes which are now occupied by railways were, during that memorable year, proposed and pressed on the public attention. It was the misfortune of some, that persons known in the city to possess darkened reputations, were connected with them, and there was, therefore, no chance for these. The writer is prepared to assert, on an authority which cannot be gainsaid, that many of the merchants and bankers of London were not backward in the matter. But they commenced cautiously; before they gave their money, they gave their time; and for a considerable period, men whose names would have been an assurance of the honour of any company, entered into close calculations of chances, collected information of traffic, estimated expenses and receipts, and did all which wise men should do before they join societies, the failure of which, if trifling to them, is ruinous to others. The result was that, unable to foresee the fact that railways create trade; seeing, too, that there was not sufficient traffic existing to sanction them, they abandoned the proposition, and returned the deposits. It must also be remembered, that in that fierce and fatal crisis which followed, when bankers suspended their payments hourly, when merchants followed their example, when bullion was scarce and coin a novelty, when the bank begged a customer to postpone presenting his notes, when its governor scarcely saw his home for a week, when terror and confusion reigned paramount, and England was within twenty-four hours of barter, there was no chance of collecting deposits, no hope of carrying on projects, no time to think of railroads or of locomotives. A sketch, therefore, of one of these railroads, will represent the progress of many.

In 1824 the Kentish railway was proposed, not as one of the bubbles so finely described by Mr. Canning, but as an actual endeavour to apply the force of steam to the iron way. The names in its introduction bore the stamp of respectability; the manner of its treatment was sound. The prospectus appealed to no violent feeling; it stirred no strong passion. It was worthy the directors whose names were on its surface. " The application of steam to locomotive and stationary machines, for the conveyance of passengers and goods, will give a new and extraordinary impulse to the industry of this country. Reducing the cost of transporting and exchanging commodities, has an effect upon agriculture and manufactures, precisely analagous to that which would be produced by improving the quality of the soil, or increasing the skill and energy of the workmen. * * * The cheap and rapid communication about to be established will give an incalculable impulse to the prosperity of Kent, and confer the most important advantages on all its inhabitants; every article which they do not produce, they will be able to sell more advantageously. Their home trade with London, their foreign trade with France, especially in fruit, fish, and game, and all perishable articles, will be simultaneous."

This company was abandoned, not because the shares were unapplied for, not because the scrip came out at a discount, nor because railways were deemed impracticable, but because some of the gentlemen in the direction, applied themselves personally and patiently to investigate the project, and because these gentlemen, many of whom bore names greatly honoured in the city, imagined that the immediate prospects of such a line were insufficient to warrant their involving a numerous proprietary; that the idea, though just, was then in advance of the period, although with time it would afford a fine field for enterprise. The line alluded to would have occupied nearly the same ground as the present North-Kent, which, with all the unnecessary expense it has incurred, is understood to pay well; and the proposition of this line in 1824 was as honourable to the foresight as its abandonment was honourable to the principle of its directors. Another cause is also said to have operated. Mr. Peter Moore was one of the directors, and Mr. Moore—who was connected with half the companies of 1825, declaring them all to be as safe as the Bank—was of opinion that his services as director should be liberally remunerated. The late Sir Charles Price, and others of the directorate, did not agree with the gentleman, and this tended to abolish the company.*

The following list will confirm the writer's assertion that the first railroad era was 1825.

Liverpool and Mancherter Railway	London, Portsmouth, and Southampton Railway
London, Rochester, and Shoreham, do.	
Birmingham and Liverpool, do.	Manchester and Leeds, do.
Biistol and Bath, do.	Manchester and Bolton, do.
London and Birmingham, do.	Limerick and Waterford, do.
London and Bristol, do.	Newcastle and Carlisle, do.
London and Northern, do.	Garnkirk and Glasgow, do.

* In the early history of the railway world, the Croydon, Merstham, and Godstone company was a curious exponent of railway failure. The names on the direction were bankers, baronets, and members of Parliament. The prospectus, like all other prospectuses, spoke confidently of profit. The estimate of income was professed to have been most scrupulously examined. The committee were as confident as committees generally are, asserting that, at the very outset of the trade it would pay an ample interest on the capital, and that the returns would soon produce double the amount estimated. The shares were taken, £100 were paid up on each, and the reader may judge of their value when he is told that many years after (in 1836) the £100 share was valued at 30s., and that in the same year, forty shares which had cost originally £4,000, were absolutely sold for £60. Had this company, which was incorporated in 1801, proved successful, it is propable that England would have advanced much further than she has done in steam locomotion.

Edinburgh and Glasgow Railway
London and Brighton, do.
Grand Junction, do.
Taunton, do.
Norfolk, Suffolk, and Essex, do.
Leeds, Selby, and Hull, do.
London and South Wales, do.
Birmingham and Bristol, do.
Kentish, do.
Grand Western, do.
East London, do.
Canterbury and Whitstable, do.
Severn and Wye, do.
Stroud and Severn, do.
Hibernian, do.
Colchester and Halstead, do.
Ipswich, Diss, and Eye, do.
Exeter and Exmouth, do.
Cromford and High Peak, do.
Duffryn, Lynvi, and Porth Cawl, do.
London and Edinburgh, do.
London and Newcastle, do.
Maidstone and Tunbridge, do.

Manchester and Oldham Railway
Bolton and Leigh, do.
Rhymney, do.
Berwick and Kelso, do.
East Lothian, do.
Edinburgh and Dalkeith, do.
West Lothian, do.
Glasgow and Rosebank, do.
Kelso, Melrose, and Dalkeith, do.
Dundee and Strathmore, do.
Monkland and Kirkintilloch, do.
Galligate, do.
Tees and Weardale, do.
Kennet, Avon, and Old Sarum, do.
Dublin and Kingston, do.
Dublin and Belfast, do.
Brighton and Shoreham, do.
Wormsley, do.
Flintshire, do.
Portland, do.
Festiniog, do.
Huddersfield and Wakefield, do.
Redworth, do.

The 15th of September, 1830, will be memorable in the history of railways; on that day the Liverpool and Manchester was officially opened. By sunrise the people flocked to the parts where the best view could be obtained. Mr. Huskisson, who from the first had interested himself in this fine mechanical undertaking, and had declared that he deemed it his bounden duty to do so, was there. There, too, appeared the Duke of Wellington, destined in after times so greatly to influence their fortune. Members of the senate were there: heads of old aristocratic houses also came to test the power they had not assisted. The engines with waving flags and bright colours, added to the scene, and curiosity was at its height when the carriages started; one portion on the down, and the other on the up line. Nothing could exceed the success of the undertaking, and all was pleasant until the arrival at Parkside, where the engines were stopped for a fresh supply of water. The company had been requested not to leave their carriages, and the caution was repeated in the printed directions. The advice was unfortunately misunderstood or disregarded. Most of the gentlemen in the "Northumbria," in which the directors and the more distinguished of the guests were placed, left the carriages when the train stopped, and unsuspicious of the extraordinary power which they were witnessing, gathered in groups on the line, mixing sociably together, in utter ignorance of the danger which menaced them. The alarm suddenly arose that the "Rocket" engine was rapidly approaching, and the various groups dispersed to places of safety. Some sheltered themselves beneath the embankment;

others forced their way into the carriages ; confusion was paramount amid all. Mr. Huskisson only hesitated in his course ; and instead of seeking shelter where others had done, hurried to the "Northumbria," grasped the door of the train, and attempted to enter. The door swung back, the statesman fell to the ground, the engine swept on with fearful velocity, and the representative of Liverpool was practically a dead man. "God bless you all! Now let me die at once!" were his words when he had kissed, and bade farewell to his wife; and his prayer was not long delayed. His remains were placed in the cemetery of the town for which he was member, and a marble pillar to his memory may be seen near the spot which witnessed the doom of our first free-trade minister.

Such was the tragedy which darkened the opening of this railway ; and the tribute paid at its accomplishment by Lord Brougham is so eloquent a contradiction to some of his later vituperations of the iron road, that the writer is tempted to present it below.* On the 4th December, 1830, the first

* When I saw the difficulties of space and time as it were overcome; when I beheld a kind of miracle exhibited before my astonished eyes; when I surveyed

locomotive engine bearing merchandise passed along
the line from Liverpool to Manchester, and the
contents form an interesting specimen of the traffic
between the two towns. The train consisted of
eighteen waggons, containing one hundred and thirty-
five bags and bales of American cotton, two hundred
barrels of flour, sixty-three sacks of oatmeal, and
thirty-four sacks of malt, weighing altogether fifty-
one tons, eleven hundred weight, one quarter. To
this must be added the weight of the waggons and
oil cloths, *viz.*, twenty-three tons, eight hundred-
weight, three quarters; the tender, water, and fuel

mosses pierced through, on which it was before hardly possible for man or beast
to plant the sole of the foot, now covered with a road, and bearing heavy waggons, laden not only with innumerable passengers but with merchandise of the
largest bulk, and heaviest weight; when I saw valleys made practicable by
the bridges of ample height and length which spanned them; saw the steam
railway traversing the surface of the water at a distance of sixty or seventy
feet perpendicular height; saw the rocks excavated and the gigantic power
of man penetrating through miles of the solid mass, and gaining a great, a
lasting, an almost perennial conquest over the power of nature by his skill and
industry; when I contemplated all this, was it possible for me to avoid the
reflection which crowded into my mind—not in praise of man's great success,
not in admiration of the genius and perseverance he had displayed, or even
of the courage he had shown in setting himself against the obstacles that
matter opposed to his course—no! but the melancholy reflection that all
these prodigious efforts of the human race, so fruitful of praise, but so much
more fruitful of lasting blessings to mankind, have forced a tear from my eye,
by that unhappy casualty which deprived me of a friend and you of a representative.

four tons; and of fifteen persons upon the train, one ton; making a total weight of eighty tons, exclusive of the engine, which, "under the disadvantage of an adverse wind, was carried in two hours and fifty-four minutes."

The report from the directors which followed the opening of the rail was one continued swell of triumph. Within fourteen days the passengers amounted to eight hundred a day, and immediately after to one thousand two hundred. The journey, instead of occupying two hours, was done in one hour and a half; "and thus in a few months was produced a new and effective system of intercommunication, highly important to the interests of a mercantile community, and so extraordinary and complete as to form an era in national improvements, and an epoch in mechanical science." "The company have not been required to wait for gradual and partial transition." Out of 130,000 passengers only two trifling accidents had occurred. The increase of the merchandise traffic had been gradual and satisfactory. In four months it had quadrupled; from 1,432 tons, it had increased to 5,104 tons. The winter which followed was one of marked severity: but it was triumphantly said, "on no one day were the goods trains prevented from passing, or the coach trains diminished." A bill was again introduced to raise £865,000 by the creation of new shares, and it was added "the directors have great satisfaction in being enabled to recommend to the proprietors a dividend at the rate of £8 per cent. per annum." The calculations of the originators as to the receipts on various items, were singularly erroneous in some cases, and singularly successful in others. The gross receipts of merchandise were estimated at £50,000; and so close was the calculation that they were within £2,960 18s. 5d.: being that sum above the estimate. The coal carriage was expected to realise £20,000; it only produced £910 16s. 9d. On the other hand the passenger traffic was greatly underrated: instead of £10,000 from this source, £101,829 12s. 5d. was received. The bridge over the Irwell was not included in the first statement, nor was any allowance made for building waggons, carriages, or warehouses; for accidents, or for the wear and tear of material. No sum was estimated for the purchase of houses and land, under which the tunnel passed. Only

£39,574 were allowed for contingencies, one of which
consumed the entire amount. The original estimate
was £400,000, the cost was £800,000 : carriages
and warehouses increased this sum to £1,000,000.
The net income of the line was expected to be
£62,500, it proved to be upwards of £83,000;
£510,000 was considered sufficient to complete the
works entirely; the cost arose ultimately to nearly
£1,200,000. The expenses were calculated at thirty-
three per cent. ; they amounted to sixty-two per
cent.

The revenue derived from passengers was double
that from merchandise. The distance by the newly
formed line was thirty-one miles, performed in one
hour and a half. The fare at the opening was 7s.,
but was soon reduced to 4s. Only one passenger
out of the first 700,000 was killed, and this death
was entirely owing to the rashness of the sufferer.
£4,000 were contributed to the parish rates. Not
only cotton, but sugar, with many other articles of
consumption for the poor, were carried at a cheaper
amount. Goods placed in the railway at Manchester
in the afternoon were shipped from Liverpool for
America in the evening. The £100 shares soon

rose to £200, although many causes conspired to
keep down the profits. Constant improvements
were made in the locomotives, constant alterations
were suggested, defects were remedied, old engines
were abandoned for new ones of a superior construction, magnitude and form were both changed,
nor was anything omitted which could possibly support the character of the line, increase the comfort of the passengers, or maintain their safety.
Nothing, however, could prevent evil or idle reports.
It was confidently stated—and the remark of Mr.
Huskisson in the house had justified the notion—-
that the company could not divide more than ten
per cent., the fact being that when the profits
amounted to more the public were to divide with
the proprietors. Accidents were wilfully exaggerated : if a passenger injured himself because he
would leap from a train in full motion, it was
changed by report into an upsetting of the carriages ; and when money was wanted to establish
a carrying department, and an attempt was made
to raise 5,000 quarter shares, the reports of the
disaffected and disappointed lowered the premium
on the shares a hundred and twenty per cent.   With

the following sketch of their increased passenger traffic the writer concludes his history of the first line.   In 1832 the number was upwards of 356,000; in 1833 it was augmented by 30,000 ; in 1834 an additional 50,000 was the result; and in 1835 the number that travelled amounted to more than 473,000, being an increase in four years of 117,000.

The form of George Stephenson, its engineer, rises so naturally to the imagination, in connexion with this line, that a sketch of his career must not be omitted here, even at the risk of anticipating portions of railway history.

Born in a small cottage in Newcastle, and dying owner of the fine estate of Tapton ; commencing life on a coal-heap, and ending it in a mansion ; mending the peasants' clocks to pay for his son's schooling, and living to see that son a senator; dining in his youth in the mine of Killingworth, and amusing his age in a horticultural contest with a duke; taught arithmetic at four-pence a week, and planning the most difficult railways in the kingdom; consulted by the premier, receiving honour from kings, a kind son, a faithful friend, and a loving father, the name of George Stephenson is one to which all men delight in doing homage. His life was a lesson to the world. Dragged, not brought up, as Charles Lamb expresses it, he early learned to gain his bread. He worked when other children played. "He led the horse at the plough," it was graphically said, "when too young to stride across the furrow;" he picked the dross from the coal heap; and so alive was the child to the importance of the two-pence a-day he gained, that he hid himself when the overseer passed, lest he should be deemed too young for his occupation. Scarcely had he passed boyhood when he found employment on one of those tramways which he lived to make so general. At Killingworth, earning his shilling a day and thankful for it, was his apprenticeship served to mechanics; and when, skill and strength increasing, he gained double that sum, and joyously told a comrade he was a man for life, it argues the narrow boundary of his early notions.

He married early, and his only son, the future member for Whitby, was the fruit of this marriage. He had no other child, and on this was the love of his strong mind concentrated. Feeling the absence of education personally, he determined that want at least should not be transmitted to his son; and he who worked when others slept to pay for a son's schooling, was the man to love and respect. Deeply lamenting his own want of lore, he endeavoured to remedy it. He was never idle. He cut out the pitmen's clothes, he taught the pitmen's wives, he made shoes and gave them to his poorer kinsmen: and when it is remembered that a daily labourer's wages are earned by the sweat of his brow, and that George Stephenson was early and late at work, it will be seen that he was one to make his way in the world. Here, accordingly, he acquired a name which enabled him to quit the close work of the stoker for something more akin to that power which has done so much for England.

In the early life of Stephenson the working man had little to hope. There were war prices and war profits for the farmer, but in these the hewer of wood and drawer of water had no share. Provisions were fearfully high—wheat was at one hundred and sixteen shillings a quarter; labour was depressed; the labouring man was unrepresented; the poors' rates rose to four millions, with a population of nine millions; the legislature was only employed in taxing; the social questions of 1850 were disregarded in 1800; the worker had not even hope, and Stephenson, like many of the class to which he belonged, thought seriously of seeking the New World, of carving out a new fortune, of sitting under his own porch, of becoming a landed proprietor, of working for himself and not for a master. These were the dreams which filled his imaginative brain. But like others he felt that emigration was a fatal step; like others, too, he clung to the soil on which he first trod; and as he passed from his daily labour to his evening rest, it is said he wept when he approached his home at the thought that he soon might leave it.

It was about this time that his fine mechanical power was first developed. He effected some improvement in a condensing machine. He became known in the neighbourhood; he made two or three engines do the work of a hundred horses; he won the faith of those who trusted him; and he felt, perhaps, that his power was more likely to be recognised in England, where capital was plentiful, than in America, where money was scarce.

By 1813 it is impossible to doubt that Mr. Stephenson had made a local fame. There are a thousand objects to which a scientific man can turn his attention: small things often evince as much ingenuity as great, and traditional stories are extant which show that even then he could accomplish much which was impossible to others. And when it is remembered that by the above year he had attained the important post of engine overlooker at Killingworth, and in this position was so highly appreciated that he was advanced capital to form a locomotive for the colliery he served, it is an evidence of the estimation in which he was held.

The friends of Mr. Stephenson have claimed for him the discovery of a safety lamp the honour of which is now exclusively given to Davy; but this is not the place to enter into the discussion which arose. The fame of Stephenson cannot be greater than it is; the invention of a thousand such would not heighten it. The man who could conceive a locomotive could surely conceive a lamp; and the claim itself is only of importance because it proves the position he had assumed. It was much to Stephenson to enter the lists with a Davy; it was something even to be beaten by the future president of the Royal Society: but to have a large

and influential section of scientific men supporting
him, to be able to postpone a meeting called to do
homage to his opponent, to have a motion openly
made whether Davy or Stephenson were really
entitled to the honour, speaks trumpet-tongued in
favour of the young mechanical genius. A paper
war, which occurred on the subject, was as unsatisfactory as such warfares ever are, and the only
pleasant result was when Mr. Stephenson, invited
to a public dinner in 1818, received as a tribute a
silver tankard and a thousand guineas.

At forty years of age, then a mature, well-informed
man, George Stephenson began his first important
work, being at this period called on by Mr. Pease
to assist in constructing the Railway called the
Stockton and Darlington ; and it is honourable
to both that, in return for the care he bestowed
on their interests, the proprietors lent him money
to commence some locomotive works. To this
manufactory, now known as that of Robert Stephenson and Co., may his fine fortunes be traced; and
the same year which saw him his own master saw
him also engineer to the Liverpool and Manchester
railway. From this period his name is blended

with the tramroad; it is part and parcel of the
locomotive: by 1824 he had made sixteen of them;
and when Mr. Brunel conceived the notion of the
broad gauge, Stephenson showed a littleness of
feeling which is recorded with pain. He was to
some extent jealous. The locomotive was the offspring of his own brain—the creature of his own
cunning, wrought by his own right hand, the
produce of his own skill; and when Mr. Brunel
threatened to interfere with it, when he changed
the gauge and altered its character, Mr. Stephenson waxed wroth. It was touching the apple of
his eye, and he resented it proportionately. No
one can justify his intense dislike to the broad
gauge, or his hatred of the atmospheric. He called
the latter, and he thought the former, "the greatest
humbug in the world." But a kindlier feeling
would have bade him remember that this expressive term had been often applied to himself and to
the produce of his own thought; and that it would
be better to help than to thwart one who, if not
his equal, had no other superior. The cause may
be found in the fact that Stephenson and his pupils
having been paramount in three-fourths of the rail-

ways of England, hungered after the remainder;
and when Mr. Brunel incautiously vaunted a hundred miles an hour, it excited a feeling which Mr.
Stephenson never lost. With the faith of a great
mind in those powers which had never deceived
him, regarding other persons' schemes with supine-
ness, if not with suspicion, his temper mastered his
judgment. Lord of the locomotive, it was his
cherished idol, and woe to those who did not bend
in its worship. Objections have been urged against
his lack of courtesy; but due allowance must be
made for persons in the position of Mr. Stephenson
and of his son, if found wanting in that kindness
which should be the mark and heritage of genius.
Their minds absorbed, their train of thought broken
by some unfortunate intruder, worried by speculators who only propose what has been proposed
a hundred times before, applied to by writers, intruded upon by theorists, and the target for projectors, their time and their attention are often
unnecessarily lost.

These evils the subject of this sketch must have
felt; and if he told the friend of one who
aimed at achieving that which Mr. Stephenson

thought impossible, "not to leave him by himself, but to get some one to take care of him;" or if he lost his temper at the notion of a locomotive on a common road, be it remembered that to a poor man he gave advice, refused remuneration, and sent a generous letter to the press in support of his invention. Like other people, he must be taken as we find him. If, with strong powers, he lacked great patience; if he sometimes overstepped the bounds of propriety, and violated the decorum due to the society with which he associated; if he were coarse enough to tell an ancient enemy that he was "the best fellow in the world to tell a lie and stick to it," it must be borne in memory that there are injuries which some minds can never forgive, and that the person to whom he said this had been a fierce and dangerous opponent when Mr. Stephenson's strength was not sufficient to produce magnanimity.

His name became synonymous with success. He shared with Mr. Hudson the growing glories of the rail. His assistance sent shares to a premium. The jobbers of the Stock Exchange thought little of a line without it. In public he was worshipped;

in private he was beloved. Shrewd in his conversation, but simple in his habits, this single-minded man might have been met seeking nuts and nests, and enjoying the wild melody of birds. His vines and his melons were dear to him, and he tried, by the aid of science, to grow his pines as large as pumpkins. Careful of the moral and physical improvement of those he employed; ever impressing on the young the advantages of literature and science; liberal in assisting, not with his purse, but with employment; always pleased to offer advice and encouragement; he never forgot that he had once been a "swart slave of the mine," or that he earned his bread then by the sweat of his brow, as he afterwards earned it by that of his brain.

From 1840, when he left the locomotive business to his son, his life was a perpetual ovation. Premiers and princes honoured him. The Belgian monarch knighted him. The railway king did homage to him. The painter gave life to his shrewd, sarcastic brow. The sculptor carved him in enduring marble. Scientific men acknowledged his power. Commercial men were proud of him. He was on social terms with the most princely spirit in England, telling his grace, in homely, intimate language, that when he went to Paradise he would not be better off than at Chatsworth; and it was in an injudicious rivalry with the owner of the latter that he lost his life; for the spirit of superiority was strong in this gifted man, and that which others could do at all, he rightly thought he could do better. He fell in the fullness of health and strength. Struck down by fever, he lingered but a few days, and died on 12th August, 1848, at the age of sixty-eight.

It is difficult to describe the feeling of those to whom he had endeared himself: his death was regarded as a national loss. Innumerable honours followed him to his grave: the mourning border on the newspaper; the public tribute on the platform; the private sympathy by the fireside; were alike given him. The marble statue; the life-like engraving; the eulogium at the railway meeting; the polished periods of Mr. Glyn; the unstudied oration of Mr. Hudson, were all his. It was felt that a bright light had gone out; that a great spirit had passed to its rest; that it would be long before the dark colliery and the humble cottage would yield his fellow. It was felt that though his pupils might carry out his plans and inherit all of his knowledge which could be transmitted, yet between them and him "there was a great gulf fixed." It was bitterly felt, too, that the inheritance of genius could not be bequeathed, and that a genius of the purest water had departed in George Stephenson, fondly and affectionately termed the founder and the father of the railway system.

The journals of the day, and the press generally, delighted to eulogise him; nor will a few extracts be improperly employed to conclude the record of the man they praised.

" We apprehend," says the *Westminster Review,* "that George Stephenson is perfectly aware of the value and uses of money; but no mere pecuniary interest could have led him to persevere in his onward course from boyhood; when he toiled as a slave to the great steam-engine of the mine, up to the period when he had forced his way through all the difficulties, natural and artificial, of the Manchester and Liverpool, and ridden his ponderous fire-steed with arrowy swiftness over that very Chatmoss whereon a natural horse could not find foothold.

No calculation of per centages and dividends wrought this work. It was the high, heroic soul, the strong English spirit, the magnificent will, the indomitable energy, breaking forth, to win a world from chaos."

"His mechanical genius," said another, "was of that order that it may without exaggeration be asserted that, if Watt had not previously invented the steam-engine, he was capable of achieving it. Others before him had prepared the way, others since have contributed valuable improvements in detail; but to George Stephenson unquestionably belongs the proud title of the author of the railway system. He gathered the many threads of ingenuity and enterprise, and weaved them into the wide-spreading network which promises in its manifold extension to envelope the whole world in bonds of commerce, civilisation, and peace."

"Tracing the progress of railways," said a minute of the London and North-Western directors, "they found Mr. Stephenson foremost in urging forward the great railway movement; earning and maintaining his title to be considered, before any other man, the author of that universal system of locomotion which has effected such mighty results through-

out the civilised world." And in allusion to a statue
which had been ordered, it was gracefully added, " they
did not anticipate that on the completion of this work
of art the great original would be no more ; that they
should be constrained to accept the marble effigy of the
engineer in lieu of the living presence of the man."

" In private life," said the *Athenæum*, " he earned
the regard of all who appreciate worth and liberality.
* * * His affections were warm, his manners pleasant and vivacious, bearing that stamp of originality
indicative of the man."

" On the death of a great man," said a beautiful
article in the *Civil Engineer*, to which the writer is
much indebted, " it is a good time to think of what he
has done. We are struck by the loss ; the thought
comes gloomily that he who so lately stood among
us, whose smile still beams upon us, whose sayings
are fresh in our ears, and whose looks have not faded
from our sight, has ended his days here, and sought
another world. * * * He has given the engineers
of England an European name ; he has opened for
them a new field of employment at home, a wider
field of honour and wealth abroad, and they owe
him heartfelt thanks."

The directors of the Midland railway declared " he had left a memory that princes might be proud of, and that the most distinguished man living would be glad to exchange his fame for that which would surround the name of George Stephenson."

Mr. Hudson said, " His departure was a national calamity. He was a benefactor of his species. He had benefited the poor as well as the rich."

This was a part only of the praise which followed him to his last resting-place. In a book like the present, it is delightful to dwell on such a man and such a memory; to think that he who did so much for commerce did as much for humanity; and to remember that the greatest of all projectors, the projector of the locomotive, died in the fulness of years, and escaped the fate which has darkened the lot of so many.

CHAPTER VII.

FROM 1825 to 1830 the railway, with the entire
commercial interest, was depressed. The languor
which followed the great panic remained; money
was by no means plentiful : men watched with
curiosity, mingled with contempt, the movements
of the Manchester and Liverpool line, nor was it
until the locomotive proved its power at Rainhill
that much more than curiosity was excited. In
1829 an act was passed for the Newcastle and Car-

lisle railway, the distance between the two places being sixty-one miles; and so many were its difficulties that it was not opened throughout for ten years. Following this act came a desire to form trunk railways from the metropolis. One of these, the London and Birmingham, now known as the London and North-Western, though first thought of and surveyed during that great excitement in 1825, of which its elder brother, the Liverpool and Manchester, was born, was abandoned when the panic followed that excitement, not because it was impracticable, but because it was considered that, with the existing traffic, there was not a sufficient prospect of profit. In 1830 the project was again placed before the public view, and all eyes fixed on the great experiment which they of Liverpool and Manchester had tried; the time was propitious. Unfortunately rival lines were proposed. One of these was under the auspices of Sir John Rennie, the other under those of Mr. Giles. The former was to pass the collegiate town of Oxford, the latter by that place renowned for the exploits of the fair Godiva. The merits of these plans were discussed with due plausibility: each projector endeavoured to demonstrate that there was no scheme like his own. Each engineer sought to prove that there was no route so proper as that which he proposed. If one line were difficult and expensive, it had the merit of promising a proportionate traffic. If the other went through less populous districts, it would create traffic and increase population. Directors and engineers, solicitors and secretaries, entered warmly into the warfare, and every prospect appeared of a social strife similar to that which disgraced the city at a later period. Fortunately all concerned saw the propriety of amalgamating. Proposals were made to join the two companies ; and, fearful in that early stage of the railway interest lest they should damage themselves without injuring their opponents, an union was effected. The next question that arose was the line to be adopted. Mr. George Stephenson was called on to adjudicate on the merits of the rival routes ; the directors agreed to select the line which the majority should approve ; and as Mr. Stephenson decided in favour of that by Coventry, the gentlemen of Lancashire, who in this as in most other railways were personally and pecuniarily interested, supported their favourite's opinion, and decided by their support that the line through Coventry should be that chosen by the united company.

Mr. Stephenson and his son were appointed engineers, and by September the companies were formally united. Thus early did the directors of this fine property evince their wisdom. During the period devoted to negociations, great but unobtrusive efforts had been made to model public opinion, and to produce a general feeling in favour of the line. It was known that opposition must ensue; that there would be the outcry of the selfish, and the demand of the unjust; that the weak would assert a power which would be better softened than irritated; and that the strong would open a contest which must be met on expedient and not on fair grounds. In addition to this, the public were far from enlightened on the subject of railroads. They heard of the success of the old line, but did not apply its chances to the new; urging all the ancient objections, and stirring all the old opposition, regardless that the former had been answered a hundred fold, and that the latter was only formidable in proportion to its landed strength. To obviate this difficulty the press was unsparingly employed, the public mind was prepared for another adoption of the new power, and a committee appointed to establish a communication with the engineers.

Every possible exertion was made to forward the undertaking; the necessary documents were ready by November 1830; but so great had been the haste, and so unsatisfactory was the result to the engineers, that it was deemed judicious to postpone the application for a bill until the following year. In November, 1831, therefore, plans and sections, marking the line almost as it now exists, were lodged with the proper authorities.

The first crude idea had been to form a single line of rail, the expense of which was calculated at £6,000 a mile. The capital was to be a million and a quarter, and the shares rose to £10 premium. A more matured thought suggested the necessity of a double line. This was determined on; but so little faith had commercial men in there being sufficient traffic to pay for the increased capital, that the shares soon descended to a discount. It would be idle now to argue upon the advantages of any line of railway, but it is necessary to prove the relative power, position, and traffic of the two places, to show that though the directors of the London and Birmingham railway were, with wit more sarcastic than sound, called a " patriotic party of speculators coming forward for their country's benefit," they had good reason for the faith which was in them. The connection of Birmingham with London was most important : the population of the former was extending with its business. Between 1751 and 1831 it had increased from 50,000 to 110,000. Its trade had more than proportionately improved. Its fine productions were celebrated all over the world. Its mechanical power was almost marvellous. The most trifling trinket and the most ponderous machine issued from its factories. In half a century one hundred and sixty-nine steam-engines had been erected. With all this the mode of carriage had not greatly enlarged. The shortest journey by canal—then the only mode of sending bulky articles—occupied three days. More than a thousand tons came weekly, and business was hourly lost for want of a more rapid communication. The beautiful city of Liege was beating us out of the markets in which we had long been paramount.

Increase of speed was necessary to compete with the foreign merchant; and the Birmingham manufacturer was gradually yielding the Italian, Spanish, and Portuguese business to the continental trader, who, procuring the raw material on the spot, could only be rivalled through the assistance of a railroad. Orders were daily refused because they could not be undertaken by specified dates. The canal transit was most objectionable—the goods being detained by the way, sometimes lost altogether, and at others rejected because they were not received by the appointed time. The goods for the Baltic were stopped by frost for the whole winter : entire trades had left the country and become only traditional, because the coach proprietors could not take articles of much weight. These were a few of the absolute evils which the railway proposed to rectify : nor were the directors backward in assertions connected with the future, which that future has more than ratified.

The time of travelling—such were the temptations held forth—would be reduced six hours, and the cost decreased in proportion. The wholesale dealer would be able to turn his capital oftener. The

cheapness of all articles would be increased by facilities of communication. Freight, which averaged
from Birmingham to London, and from London back,
80s. a ton, would be greatly reduced. Money then
scarcely returned in eighteen months would be
returned in nine.

Coal mines,* valueless without a railway, could be
worked to advantage with it. Provisions could be
brought at cheap rates to and from the various towns
through which the locomotive passed; and many a
secluded village would find its property improved by
the rail. But above all, it was asserted that there
was a great struggle between this country and the
continent in supplying manufactured articles, and that
it was a question not of personal but of political
advantage.

This reason, independently of the important fact,
that the surplus capital of the country would be well
and wisely employed in constructing roads which the
population of the country would use, produced its
effect on the commercial world. In January, 1832,
the London and Birmingham railway issued its

---

* An inestimable blessing which the country owes to the rail is the reduction
in the price of coal: the cost of which is one-third less, owing to the former
monopoly of the coal-owners being broken.

first circular, and the following were the calculations :—

ESTIMATED EXPENSE.

Excavation, embankments and tunnels . .	£1,098,000
Masonry, including bridges, and walling in depôts	334,672
Rails, &c.	316,368
Ballasting and fencing	205,920
	£1,954,960
Ten per cent. for contingencies, including engineering, surveying, parliamentary conveyancing, and other law charges .	195,496
Land and compensation . . .	250,000
Total estimate	£2,400,456

ESTIMATED REVENUE.

Passengers	£331,272
Goods	339,830
	671,102

The gradual progress of opinion since the proposal for the Liverpool and Manchester railway was somewhat curious. Mr. Hardman Earle, who had been an avowed and strenuous opponent of that line, came himself forward to state that he had been mistaken, that no inconvenience was experienced from the train passing through his grounds; that the smoke was not offensive, that the noise was not troublesome, and that the passage of the carriage was a pastime rather than a nuisance. Many of the farmers gave evidence that it would be a great benefit to them. Lords Derby and Sefton, who had also contested the first line, consented to the London and Birmingham. The Earl of Chesterfield, who had been one of the malcontents, followed the good example. Many who had opposed the railway because they thought it would annoy them, gave way when they discovered their error, and yielded their allegiance to the new power. Some agriculturists, who had vehemently declared it would ruin their property, discovered that property was increased in value, and withdrew from the contest; and some landowners, who had combatted it because it was to ruin the country, found that houses grew in the place of corn, and that ground rents more than compensated for grain.

This was the conduct of a few. But the ranks of the discontented are easily swelled; and when the new line was in progress, the old cries were not wanting to prove how evil it would be and how absurd the scheme. These opponents, blinded by ignorance and obstinacy, could not see that the produce of their land could be carried to remote districts;

that places which were deprived of pure dietary would pay liberally to procure it, or that millions spent in the employment of the poor would relieve them in their poors' rates. While some, therefore, had changed their opinion, and avowed that change, others formed themselves into an opposition which might almost be called organised; and the echoes of those " sweet voices " which had condemned the Liverpool and Manchester to destruction, were heard throughout the empire against the London and Birmingham.

It was said with great boldness and bitterness of spirit, that the new railway would be "a drug on the country;" that its "bridges and culverts would be antiquarian ruins;" that "it would not take tolls sufficient to keep it in repair;" that "the directors were making ducks and drakes of their money;" that "every hill and valley between the two towns would behold falling arches and ruined viaducts." It was said once more that game would cease to be, and that agricultural communication would be lost; that not a field existed but what would be split and divided; springs would be dried up, meadows become sterile, agricultural operations would be suspended. Like an earthquake it would create chasms, it would upheave mountains; and it was pathetically added, the railway promoter was like an evil providence, unrighteously attempting that which nature was too kind to effect. Hundreds of innkeepers, and thousands of horses—that antique, ancient cry—would be thrown out of employment; while hundreds of thousands would be ruined for the benefit of the few. Labour for the poor would be lessened, the rates for the poor be increased. Canals would be destroyed; those who lived on them would be beggars; houses would be crushed by embankments, corn thrown out of cultivation, land made barren, landholders beggared. "Long before the London and Birmingham is ready," wrote one sapient expositor, "such are the improvements now making in canals, that not only may the charge be expected to be many times less than the railway, but the time will be considerably saved." "Our estates," said a second, with apt alliteration, "will not only be deteriorated, but destroyed. It is not a question of pounds, but a question of principle." The prospects of one peer were said to be blighted; the Countess of Bridgewater and Lord Brownlow declared that the advantage to the public would not equal the injury to their estates; not only would it be a nuisance to the county, it would positively be a nuisance to my Lord Southampton. It was coolly asserted that no acceleration of speed was desirable, although in the same breath it was added that canals were increasing their rapidity of transit; and, with a boldness worthy the old English gentleman, their objections were said to be not on personal, but on public grounds: while the general ignorance may be estimated from the fact that, though the Liverpool and Manchester railway had been running some time, one of the parliamentary committee innocently exclaimed, " Why, you don't imagine they will leave in the dark?" The survey was violently opposed. Dark lanthorns were employed to do that which could not be done by the light of day. The grounds of one reverend gentleman were surveyed while occupied in his Sabbath duties. Artifice was used to counteract force, and had it not been for the ingenuity of the engineers, the line would never have been finished. Extortionate demands were made; advantages were taken of every trifling want. £3,000 was given for a piece of land, with £10,000 for consequential damages, although its value was increased twenty per cent. One man who had demanded four bridges, found out when the agreement was signed, that half the money they would cost the company would be more serviceable to him than the bridges, and proposed a compromise which the directors accepted.

Probably few private bills ever sustained so much combined opposition. Those whose purses were interested, refused to be convinced; those whose prejudices were attacked, would not listen to the voice of reason.

Meeting after meeting was held to counteract this. Reports and circulars were issued to neutralise the efforts of its opponents. It bore the appearance of a great national undertaking.

It must not be forgotten that signal difficulties, irrespective, perhaps, of the object for which the capital was demanded, beset the directors of the company. Twenty years ago, when this railway was in progress, the commercial houses of London were principally of that class which could claim ancestral honours. Their fathers had fought for commercial rights, and been graced with commercial dignities. They had been honoured with titles,

they had founded great charities, they had ever
been ready to aid an impoverished state with their
capital, they had often been called on to assist a
falling ministry with their counsel. By 1830, the
position of these houses was beginning to change.
The fearful crisis of 1825 had ruined some, and
weakened more. Many who had stood the crash
had been severely shaken, and unwilling at a
future time to run a similar hazard, they had withdrawn their capital from their narrowed business,
and remained in dignified isolation. In addition
to this, a new race of traders had arisen to push
them from their stools. Such men made up for
a small capital by great activity. Hitherto the old
houses had been paramount in their business, and
peremptory in their mode of conducting it. They
had fixed their own terms in the old times, and
they refused to change them in the new. They
could scarcely be said to have sought their profits,
so easily had those profits fallen to them. They
rarely ventured on anything novel, and the utmost
stretch of speculation was when some young adventurous member of the firm startled his seniors by
sending a courier to Vienna to take advantage of

the exchanges, or an *estafette* to St. Petersburg to forestall the tallow-market.

The " new men " saw at once the position of these houses, and the prospect which opened to their own ambition. They introduced that mode of dealing for time which had its origin in the Stock Exchange, and which the writer has elsewhere had occasion to moot. They bought and sold for delivery, paying or receiving the difference. They lowered the rates of commission, they relaxed the dignified terms maintained by their competitors. They were the type of that earnest, progressive spirit which for good or for ill has increased for the last twenty years. They were emphatically the men of the time ; they carried that competitive spirit into the higher branches of commerce which had long been in existence in the lower orders of trade.

The consequence was so far as the railway is concerned, that while the old commercial houses rejoiced in placing their sons in the directorates of insurance companies, engrossed the shares in the New River company, or gave their imperial sanction to the gas corporations, they were too determined to support their order at once to recognise the new and mighty power which silently, but surely, was abolishing all that they regarded as sacred. They feared at once to involve their character and their capital, and for a short time they held aloof.

If the old houses wanted the will, the new houses wanted the power. Every shilling of their funds was employed in what they were pleased to call legitimate speculation. Independently of this, they were not desirable men. They had no traditional names which spoke at once for the respectability of the company. They possessed no character to charm the multitude ; and they could not dispose of the shares. They could not influence the senate ; they were, therefore, worthless to the railway promoter.

The London merchants had doubted the practicability of the iron way ; they had derided the notion of the locomotive ; they had scarcely even adventured in the shares. Contenting themselves with watching its progress, they were ready to rejoice in their prudence, or to benefit by its success. When, therefore, they were persuaded it would pay, they raised their voices in its favour as heartily as they would have denounced it had it failed.

Under these circumstances the following list,

representing much of the then solidity and capital of the London houses, is somewhat remarkable. The names are familiar to all commercial readers : —

George Pearkes Barclay	James Pearson
Edmond Calvert	William Phipson
William T. Copeland	John Lewis Prevost
Edward Cropper	Theodore W. Rathbone
James Foster	Henry Rowles
William Francis	Isaac Solly
Robert Garnett	Timothy Smith
George Carr Glyn	John Sturge
Pascoe Saint Leger Grenfell	Thomas Tooke
Daniel Ledsam	John Turner
Joseph Frederick Ledsam	Joseph Walker
John George Shaw Lefevre	Henry Warre.

From this it may be seen that in this list of the early directors of the London and Birmingham railway company, the merchant and the manufacturing interest had each its symbol. The names of George Carr Glyn, and Pascoe Saint Leger Grenfell, represented the banking interest of London ; that of Copeland gave a pledge that the class in which he stood prominent appreciated the power. The merchants of London sent members, in the persons of Barclay, Prevost, Tooke, and the name of the latter, since known as the exponent of a new principle in political economy, gave an additional sanction and

surety to the conduct of the company. The character of the gentlemen on that list of directors
afforded evidence that if the provinces had taken
the initiative in railways in 1825, the metropolis
would not be backward in joining them with cash
and credit in 1832. And yet it was composed of
mixed materials. The country and the London
banker was side by side with the provincial share-
broker. The directors of some of our most ancient
London corporations went hand in hand with the
Birmingham manufacturer. The chairman of one
of our oldest insurance companies did not disdain
the companionship of the Cheapside factor ; and
to the honour of Robert Garnett, merchant, of Manchester, be it recorded that he was one of the largest
contributors to this fine undertaking.

The course of proceedings in parliament was
interesting. On the 20th February in the above
year, the bill was read a first time in the commons.
On the 28th it passed a second reading by a majority
of seventy-nine. A rigorous examination of the evidence followed, and the bill was carried in the lower
estate. No division occurred in the House of Lords
on the first and second reading ; and after the com-

mittee, of which Lord Wharncliffe was chairman, had sat for six days hearing conflicting evidence and reconciling conflicting statements, an adjournment was agreed to with the idea that some amicable arrangement might be effected between the company and its opponents. The negociation, however, failed; in other words, the directors could or would not bribe high enough : the opposition was stoutly maintained; and on the 10th July, 1832, the bill was lost.

A most indignant spirit was stirred throughout that important commercial interest which had joined the movement. It was felt that the house of peers had been moved by more aristocratic influences than those of trade. It was thought that a company which partook so completely of a monetary character, which proposed at its own risk to form a highway and to increase communication, should have been dealt with on catholic and not on sectarian grounds. It was felt that a bill which affected the acres of every farmer, and the comforts of every artisan, should have been treated on the broad basis of justice, and not on the narrow considerations of expediency. The wisdom of our highest

representative body should have taught such a
lesson to those who would have crushed the company, as its own dignity demanded; and above all
it should have remembered, with such a spirit of
change in the people as marked the period, it would
be wise to encourage that, in a beneficial movement,
which might otherwise be turned to a destructive
one. If ever the eyes of the people of England were
on the House of Peers it was when, having failed
in stopping the progress of reform, it lowered its
character by rejecting the bill of the London and
Birmingham railway company. The power which
produced this unhappy result was fully known and
appreciated. "There is no doubt," said Lord Wharncliffe, with honest indignation, "that to landowners
the failure of this bill must be attributed." "Had
the aristocracy assisted them?" asked Mr. Glyn,
on a future occasion. "No! they had done all
they could to keep the company back. Had
the landed interest aided them? No! for they
had tried to smother the company by the high
price they demanded for their property." "The
London and Birmingham," said another, "was
thrown out of the House of Lords through the

influence of a single peer, because it would approach a mansion he did not occupy. The noble proprietor and his friends did not attend to hear the evidence, they came only to the division, and threw out the bill." The *Westminster Review* took a severe and stronger tone : " Why," said the writer earnestly, " why has not the land resounded with the indignation which the rejection of the Birmingham railway bill by the lords ought to have excited ! * * * There is a blindness which will not see, and how can it be expected that they should be able to calculate whose schooling has gone little beyond counting the feet of an hexameter verse." Three days only elapsed before a meeting of peers and members of parliament, favourably disposed to the undertaking, was held at the Thatched House Tavern. Various resolutions were carried affirmative of the benefits of the line; and the country was plainly told that the plan was deferred but not abandoned, while the opponents saw that their efforts were temporarily not permanently successful.

Six months after the bill was thrown out, another circular was issued. That circular speaks as plainly as language can speak, the mean spirit of its opponents. In it the directors stated that they had no hesitation in proceeding with the bill, "provided they could remove that opposition of dissentient landowners and proprietors," which was the sole cause of their failure. They there distinctly avowed that they had adopted this plan with some, that the negociations with other "most influential parties" had only very recently been concluded; that "these measures had been successful to a greater extent than they had ventured to anticipate; and that the most active and formidable had been conciliated."

These things are written with pain, for they display a low tone of moral feeling in that class which by virtue of inheritance of birth and of blood should possess a high and chivalrous sense of honour. The writer is far from wishing to blame those who honestly opposed the rail. The conscientious feeling which prompts a man even in an unwise action, if mistaken, is at least respectable. There is much to palliate the honest opposition of the landowner. Scenes and spots which are replete with associations of great men and great deeds, cannot be pecuniarily paid for. Sites which bear memories more selfish, yet not less real, have no market value. Homes in which boyhood, manhood, and age have been passed, carry recollections which are almost hallowed. Such places cannot be bought and sold: nor are the various prejudices which cling to the country to be overlooked. If the nobleman disliked the destruction of his fine old English park, the yeoman deplored the desecration of his homestead. The one bore its splendid remembrances, the other its affectionate recollections. If the peer hallowed the former for the sake of its royal visits, the farmer cherished the latter for the sake of those who had tilled the land before him. There are fancy spots in this our beautiful England which it would pain the most indifferent to destroy; what then must be the feelings of those who have lived and only wish to die there?

It is the trafficker in sympathies, it is the dealer in haunts and homes, at whom the finger of scorn should be pointed. It is the trader in touching recollections only to be soothed by gold that should be denounced. It is the peer who made the historic memories of his mansion a plea for replenishing an impoverished estate; it is the farmer who made the sacred associations of home an excuse for re-

ceiving treble its value; it is the country gentleman who made his opposition the lever by which
he procured the money from the proprietor's pockets,
who should be shamed: and a double portion of
ignominy must rest upon these, when it is remembered that the money thus immorally obtained is
a constant tax on the pleasures of the artizan, on
the work of the manufacturer, and on the wages
of the railway official.

Such was unhappily the case with those whom
the directors of the London and Birmingham propitiated. They who professed to oppose the bill
not on private but on public grounds; they with
whom it was not a question of pounds, but a question
of principle; they who had stood in the van of a
popular opposition, and they who predicted with a
feeling not equalled by their fear that the country
would be ruined, and the farmer exiled, if the London
and Birmingham line were carried out, changed their
opinion at the instance of its directors, and formed
an alliance with the speculators they had denounced.

" Nearly all those who were the most active
and the most formidable," said the report, " have
been conciliated, and the directors have the pleasure

to announce that their measures"—in other words their money—" have been successful;" and a most instructive commentary on the value of this conciliation is in the fact that the land which was over estimated at £250,000, cost three times the amount.

By these means the bill was passed; but though the directors, in the circular which followed, said it had met with little opposition, and at an expense of not more than half the amount incurred in the previous application to parliament, they did not also hesitate to assert the power which had been in operation, leaving their shareholders to mourn over their expenses.*

* " It is well known," says Sir Francis Head, "that one of the results of Mr. Robert Stephenson's elaborate investigation was that the London and Birmingham railway ought to pass through the healthy and handsome town of Northampton. The inhabitants, however, urged and excited by men of influence and education, opposed the blessing with such barbarous fury, that they succeeded in distorting the line *viâ* the Kilsby tunnel, to a point five miles off." The Kilsby tunnel is a specimen of engineering which tells with double force after the above relation. Let to a contractor for £99,000, a quicksand soon stopped his progress, and though the company relieved him from his engagement, the vexation killed him. Mr. Stephenson then undertook the task, and confronted the difficulty with a most inventive spirit. Though the water rose and covered the works, though the pumping apparatus appeared insufficient, though the directors were inclined to abandon the task, the engineer, by aid of their capital and his skill, with 1250 men, 200 horses, and 13 steam-engines, raised 1800 gallons of water per minute night and day, for eight months, from the quicksand alone, and infused into the workmen so much of his own energy, that when either of their com-

Another difficulty with which the company had
to contend was a great dislike to tunnels. The
public could not or would not understand that
it was as safe to travel in a dark tunnel as on
a dark night. It was said, too, that the chill of
a two miles subterranean passage would deter any
person of delicate health from ever entering them.
Sir Antony Carlisle asserted that "tunnels would
expose healthy people to cold, catarrhs, and consumption." "The deafening peal of thunder,"
said another medical man, more poetically than pro-
fessionally, "the sudden immersion in gloom, and the
clash of reverberated sounds in a confined space, com-
bine to produce a momentary shudder, or idea of
destruction, a thrill of annihilation." The "resound-
ing echo," the "rattling wheels," the "panting,
puffing engine," the "clanking chains," the "dismal
glare of lamps," the "darkness made visible," were

rades were killed by their side, they merely threw the body out of sight, and
forgot his death in their own exertions.

Three hundred thousand pounds was the cost of this great work. Thirty-six
millions of bricks were used in its formation; 177,452 cubic yards of soil were
taken from the tunnel in eight months; 286,480,000 gallons of water were
pumped from it; and for all this the shareholders of the company are indebted to
the "men of influence and education," who excited the people of "the healthy
and handsome town of Northampton."

themes on which much more was prophecied than time has supported, and were arrayed in all the horrors which vivid imagination and alarmed pockets could suggest.

On the other hand it was replied that tunnels were better than the open air, being more uniform. That safety would be more insured in a tunnel than out of it, because more care would be taken. With much grace of diction it was said they ought rather to be called "lighted galleries;" while Dr. Paris and Dr. Walsh, Messrs. Lawrence and Lucas, together with Mr. Phillips, lecturer on chemistry, reported, after their visit made purposely under unfavourable circumstances, that "the air for many feet above their heads remained clear, and apparently unaffected by steam or effluvia of any kind, neither was there any damp or cold perceptible." They found—what no scientific or unscientific man has since discovered—that the atmosphere of the tunnel was "dry, of an agreeable temperature, and free from smell." That the danger incurred in passing through a properly constructed tunnel, would be no greater than that incurred upon an open railway or on a turnpike road, that apprehensions of such tunnels proving detrimental to health or inconvenient to the feelings, were futile and groundless, adding, that the sensation was "like passing in a coach by night through a narrow street; that the sound was not greater than in the open air, and that the noise did not prevent easy conversation."

The public has long since decided that a tunnel is a necessary nuisance, and that when persons can avoid one, they avail themselves invariably of the opportunity.   Besides the ordinary

> Troubles which environ
> The men who meddle with cold iron,

many incidental difficulties were experienced by the directors of this line.   From the great and general increase in prices, seven contracts were thrown on the company's hands.   They were obliged to forfeit some shares on which recreant proprietors refused to pay the calls.   They quoted the seasons as against them.   They partially changed their route, they wisely chose a terminus in town, and were compelled to apply to parliament for new powers.   They found additional capital would be necessary, and in February, 1837, they announced that instead of £2,400,000, the expense would probably reach four and a-half mil-

lions. At length these various difficulties were surmounted; and on 17th September, 1838, the railway
was opened the entire distance.

It has been said that George and Robert Stephenson were appointed engineers. A sketch of the
former has been given; and in considering the latter,
as well as other members of a profession to which
the railway owes so much of its success; in glancing
at all which they have promised, and all which they
have done, astonishment cannot fail to be excited
at the fine staff which has grown with the demand
for engineers. In sketching, therefore, the career
of Robert Stephenson, the gifted son of a most
gifted father, the difference between inspiration and
ingenuity forces itself on the notice and compels
attention. It is as old as the hills that genius is
no birthright, yet we see Robert Stephenson bearing
honours akin to those of his father; the younger
Brunel acquiring a name equal to that he inherited;
and Locke, the favourite pupil of George Stephenson, performing tasks worthy the master of whom
he learned. Other names also claim similar honour,
and it is certain that no sooner had the country
demanded a power to mark the course of railways,

and to form the gigantic works connected with them, than capable men arose. But they were created, not creators; and an exception must be taken when for these gentlemen the honours due to genius are demanded. It is certain that all history has no such record; and though there have been intellectual eras and Augustan ages in every kingdom, there has been no power passed from father to son, or from master to pupil. The scholars of a Michael Angelo could not rival the works of their teacher. Raphael, Rubens, or Correggio, left no immediate inheritors of their fame. The skill of a Chantrey and the inspiration of a Newton die with them. The genius of a Watt is not transmissible. A Bacon or a Brindley cannot bequeath their power. The poetic impulse of a Byron, and the genius of our own Sir Walter, have passed away. Napoleon lived not in his son. His great antagonist forms no exception, and these examples tend to prove that, whatever form genius may assume, it is rarely, if ever, transmitted. It seems, therefore, scarcely probable that the inspiration of George Stephenson should have passed to his son, or that the creative power of Mark Brunel should have been inherited by the engineer of the Great Western. That Isambard Brunel and Robert Stephenson have achieved great works, in opposition to great obstacles, is undeniable ; but the difference between their productions and those of their fathers, is almost the difference between mind and matter. When George Stephenson, unknown and untaught, wrestled with hazardous difficulties to introduce a great discovery, it was creative impulse : when Robert Stephenson, an engineer by the force of association, after much thought conceived the tubular bridge, it was a high order of design. When the elder Brunel devised the tunnel beneath the Thames, it was genius : when his son devised the broad gauge, it was a lower order of the inventive faculty. If the children of George Stephenson and Mark Brunel inherit the inspiration of their parents, and if the pupil of the former rival the works of his original, it follows that the scholar of a Robert Stephenson may equal the inventions of his master ; or that genius in one long line of engineers may descend from an Isambard Brunel. This is in opposition to all we know, and it is more natural to believe that the names which adorn our age, obeying the laws of political economy, have supplied the demand which their master created, continuing the work which their master commenced. This view is confirmed by the remembrance that when the simple-minded Brindley was the good genius of the Duke of Bridgewater, and canals became a fashion, men then arose with the demand, and engineers were not then wanting to form works for which capitalists could pay.

These remarks do not appear an unfitting introduction to the somewhat eventful career of Robert Stephenson ; and little does the ordinary tourist think, as he passes his summer vacation in examining the manufactories of Liege, the chair of Charlemagne, or the tomb of the three kings, that to this gentleman, no less than to his father, he is indebted for the facility of passing in twelve hours from Ostend to Cologne ; or that to their ability and foresight he owes that fine scheme of continental travel, which is familiar to most ; and when with due dignity Mr. Stephenson rises in the House of Commons, as little do his brother legislators think that his great father mended the pitmen's watches and cleaned the neighbours' clocks in after hours, to pay for the schooling his son received.* It is only in England that these strong lights and shades appear; and it is rare even in England that so much dignity of character is displayed, as when, fond and proud of his successor, George Stephenson related facts to which Robert Stephenson points with pride.

Born at Wilmington in 1803, sent to school in 1813, leaving it in 1819, to be apprenticed as coal-viewer to Mr. Nicholas Wood, with whom he served three years underground, Robert Stephenson was enabled by his father's growing fortunes to attend in 1821 the university of Edinburgh, at which there was no more diligent inquirer, and where, with every hour employed in suitable studies, it is said he acquired in one session as much as others learned in three; nor is it unworthy of remark that Mr. Stephenson believes his knowledge of chemistry to surpass his attainments in engineering.

In 1822 he joined his father's manufactory at Newcastle, where so close was his application and

---

* I was, however, a poor man, and how do you think I did? I betook myself to mending my neighbours' watches and clocks at night, after my day's work was done, and thus I got the means of bringing up my son.—*Speech at Newcastle.*

so intense his study, that although to external appearances his athletic frame seems capable of anything,
his health failed beneath the labour.

The year 1824 was the era of gold mines, and
in charge of an expedition from one of those companies which ruined so many, Mr. Robert Stephenson
went to South America. With a fresh air and a
new country, he soon recovered his health, performed
his duties, employed his leisure time in studying
various sciences; and in 1828, on his way home,
met with that Mr. Trevithick, whose career has
already been given, and from whom he received
information concerning the steam-engines in Cornwall,
which on his return he applied to the locomotive,
and was one cause of their success. When in 1824
Robert Stephenson left England to explore the
mines of Columbia, there were not many of these
engines in existence; when he returned in 1828 the
Liverpool and Manchester railroad was nearly finished,
his father had become a great man, and his father's pupil was on the high road to fame and
fortune. For the next few years, encouraged by
the success of the "Rocket," he devoted himself with renewed earnestness to the locomotive.

He simplified its works, he increased its capacity, he varied its proportions, he experimentalised, until year after year witnessed an increased improvement and an increased power. He made the factory of which he had become a partner known in every civilised city of the old world ; he supplied to the New World engines with which they could scarcely hope to compete ; and he has manufactured nearly a thousand of those machines so familiar to the traveller.

The chief part of Mr. Stephenson's life has been passed in connexion with railways. He surveyed the line for the London and Birmingham ; he undertook the entire controul of its works, until it was open to the public ; and its success is patent to all the world.

From its commencement his name obtained a power which augmented with time. He was sought after by directors, he was longed for by scrip-holders ; his assistance was regarded as an omen of good. It sent shares to a premium, and made rival lines hide their diminished heads. He is the hero of many a parliamentary battle ; the conqueror in a hundred parliamentary fights. He stood foremost in the fray when the guage question was mooted.

He executed all the iron lines from London to Berwick; he united Yarmouth with Holyhead; he has been prominent in the formation of one thousand eight hundred miles of railway; and a mere list of all he has accomplished would fill a chapter. The largest stone viaduct in the world—that of the Tweed —with its million cubic feet of masonry and its two million and a-half of bricks, was contrived by him. The Chester and Holyhead railway, with its forty-four hundred yards of tunnel and its forty-five-arch viaduct, was the work of his brain; and though that which has truly been termed the crowning triumph of engineering—the Britannia tubular bridge—will be detailed at a future period, it may be added for the present to his list of achievements.

There is something striking in the career of this gentleman, who at the early age of forty-eight has made so fine a reputation and performed works "which Egypt and the ancients might have been proud of, but could never have executed." It seems difficult to reconcile him as one and the same person in the various phases of his life. It is scarcely possible to think of him "working for three years under ground," as Mr. Nicholas Wood's apprentice, and then as a senator of the greatest legislative assembly in the world. It is painful to remember him as emphatically one of the people, and then to regard him opposing free trade and abetting a traditional conservatism. It is curious to think of him as taken away from college for pecuniary reasons, and then to see him rejecting honours proffered by his sovereign; it is equally remarkable to recollect him at the early age of twenty-two examining a South American mine, and a quarter of a century later receiving degrees from colleges, rewarded with orders and crosses by kings, planning railways for a republic through the Alps or forming lines for the successor of the noble Egyptian pacha. This, however, has been the career of one whose name will long be remembered in the annals of engineering.

The progress of railway statistics and railway calculations so far as regards expenses and traffic is exceedingly interesting. The various corporations and companies have been blamed for suggesting receipts which they could not possibly expect, and for promising dividends which they could not possibly pay. The error into which they fell is common to all new undertakings; but if they understated their expenses, it is noticeable that they also underrated their receipts. Railways have produced results which the wildest prospectus never dared to exhibit. They have found sources of profit which the most vivid imagination never conceived. They have carried millions instead of thousands, and that at a rate so low as to compel traffic where none previously existed. They have created towns, erected manufactories, built churches, educated children, peopled villages, filled heaths with houses, given the poor man the luxuries of the rich, placed the wealthy on a level with the poor, enforced a punctuality which was before wanting, have taken the townsman from the smoke of the city, have given the yeoman a glimpse of the town paved with the gold of imagination, have shed a light and life over many a country village, and by the power of that great discovery for which Franklin was derided, which Wheatstone has developed, and which Cooke has applied, have made the uttermost parts of the land converse with the speed of light.

The boldest prospectus never spoke such language;

the most arrant enthusiast never imagined such things. But the first half of the nineteenth century has witnessed them, and the development of the second will in all probability surpass the first, provided peace be maintained in the land.

No one will wonder then, that though the passenger traffic of the London and Birmingham was only estimated at £331,272, it amounted to more than £500,000 the first year; that the goods traffic calculated at £339,830, scarcely reached £90,000; or that within twelve years from the opening it did not attain the large sum expected. These things are curious, but more so when it is remembered that the expenses were estimated by Mr. Stephenson at two and a-half millions, and it was his conviction if so large a sum should be exceeded, it would not pay the proprietary: while Mr. Rastrick, on the other hand, deemed it much too heavy. The expenses reached five and a-half millions, but the investment paid ten per cent.

The assertion that land and compensation on the line to which Mr. Robert Stephenson was engineer, which was estimated at £250,000 amounted to £750,000, appears to call for some additional remark; and the question which is now proposed, is, how far the right is with the railroads to demand, and the passengers to pay an increased fare, in consequence of bargains which, unjust in principle, ought never to have been allowed? It is now a historic fact that every line in England has cost more than it ought. That in some, where, too, the directors were business men, large sums were improperly paid for land, for compensation, for consequential damages, for fancy prospects, and other unjust demands, under various names. These sums being immorally obtained, is it right that the public should pay the interest on them? Is it just that the working man should forego his trifling luxury to meet them? Is it fair that the artisan should be deprived of his occasional trip, or that the frequenter of the rail should pay an additional tax?

Other influences were at work to increase the capital stock. Law expenses swelled some bills, parliamentary opposition increased others, competing lines augmented the charges of a few, arrant jobbery was not wanting with many. It has been computed that sufficient money has been spent in unnecessary legal costs to form a direct line from one end of the country to another; and some notion can be formed of the difference of law charges from the following. Assuming that the engineering and direction would vary considerably, still the difference is greatly attributable to the legal expenses :

LAW, ENGINEERING, AND DIRECTION.

London and South Western . . .	£ 900	per mile.
London and Birmingham . . .	£1,500	do.
London and Brighton	£1,800	do.
Great Western	£2,500	do.

Another specimen of opposition, be it remembered, too, causing increased fares, is to be found in the

PARLIAMENTARY EXPENSES.

London and South Western . . .	£ 650	per mile.
London and Birmingham . . .	£ 650	do.
Great Western	£1,000	do.
London and Brighton	£3,000	do.

The following statement completes a brief but painful sketch of how much the country has had to pay for the opposition which it is the endeavour of one part of this volume to display :

LAND AND COMPENSATION.

London and South Western . . .	£4,000	per mile.
London and Birmingham . . .	£6,300	do.
Great Western	£6,300	do.
Brighton	£8,000	do.

The entire expense per mile amounts in the case of

the London and Birmingham to £8,450, or about
£4,500 more per mile than it should have cost.
Thus £504,000 on the one hundred and twelve
miles was spent through avarice and rapacity : ten
per cent. interest on which was paid for years in
the shape of dividend out of the pockets of many
who could ill afford it.   The question is worthy
consideration.

The record of this line must not be concluded
without mention of one whose services at its formation and whose aid during its progress were of
essential value.   Filling the office of secretary, the
assistance of Richard Creed was of the first importance to the company ; and when, in acknowledgment
of this fact, the directors paid the personal tribute
of placing him in their body, it was equally honourable to them as to him ; while the mode in which
it was done speaks loudly for the moral and the
mental character of the men who did it.   " On
his honesty and integrity," said Mr. Glyn on one
occasion, emphatically, " I pin my faith, and you
may pin yours also !"   " Co-operating as we have
done with my valued friend for years and years,
a co-operation of which I feel we ought as a body

to be proud, and from which I individually have received the greatest amount of assistance which one gentleman can receive from another, I have the satisfaction of knowing that co-operation is to be continued."*

Such were the remarks of one as competent to form an opinion as he is capable of paying a tribute; nor must it be forgotten that, when Mr. Creed by virtue of his position was placed over many subordinate officers, he produced the greatest benefit to the employer, with the least annoyance to the employed; that it was felt a privilege to associate with, and a pleasure to serve under him. He was always accessible, and ever considerate ; and it is doubtful, when, in after times, the period of his elevation arrived, whether his loss was lamented or his rise was rejoiced in the most. His kind and genial spirit has produced an effect which will not soon be effaced, and, within the time, with any other secretary, it is uncertain whether the prosperity of the London and Birmingham railway would have been so signally developed.

---

* The testimonial to this gentleman, in 1844, was worthy the munificence of the givers. It is not often that a cheque for two thousand one hundred guineas accompanies an expression of opinion, or that the rich man's praise fructifies into a service of plate.

The Grand Junction railway deserves notice in
connexion with the line just detailed. Petitioned
for under a different name in 1824, and opposed
by the usual interests, it failed in procuring its acts.
In 1826 a similar result followed a second application; and when, in 1832, under its present title,
a petition was once more presented, the opposition
not being renewed, the bill was passed without difficulty. Public attention was but little excited; the
works proceeded with vigour; the distance was under
a hundred miles; and when the whole was opened
for public traffic in 1837, it was probably one of
the most important provincial railways ever formed.
Its effects, viewed at a distance even, appear great,
and at that early period were peculiarly striking.
It passed through most important districts; it affected
manufacturing and commercial interests alike; it
afforded extra facilities for forwarding correspondence, and it gave a great and general stimulus to
the business of those towns it united. By its aid
the letter-bags sent from London at eight o'clock
in the evening were delivered before noon the next
day at Manchester, and the dinner tables of the
inhabitants of Birmingham were supplied with fish

purchased the same morning at Liverpool. Thus what was once a costly luxury became a common habit, and the operative was enabled to purchase that which previously was scarcely attainable by his master.

On this line was the first contract taken by one of those men whose fortunes and misfortunes form a feature in railways; and Thomas Brassey probably little thought when he made the agreement for a small portion of the Grand Junction line, that it was the opening of a career which, commencing with ten miles only, would lead to the construction of more than a thousand.

There is something striking in the enormous undertakings of railway contractors; and a glance at those of Mr. Brassey seem enough to overwhelm one man. A thousand miles of railway is no small distance; many thousands of labourers is no trifling responsibility; nine millions of pounds on his own account, and nine millions more in conjunction with two others, is no small sum; yet in fifteen years has Mr. Brassey undertaken and succeeded in these things; and at the early age of forty-five is able to look back on a useful, laborious, and—if measured by deeds—a long life, spent in works which have contributed to the happiness of thousands.

A prominent exception to this gentleman's general success, was in the fall of a viaduct built by him on the Rouen and Havre line, composed of twenty-seven arches, very nearly completed, and costing £30,000. An accident like this would have quenched the zeal of most persons. But it proved a memorable illustration of the character of Mr. Brassey, and was a marked test of the man. Although there could be no moral claim, as, during its construction, he had repeatedly protested against the material, and although the lawyers expressly repudiated all legal responsibility, the fine and almost chivalric spirit of the " descendant of the Brasseys of Bulkeley " burst forth when he said, " *He had contracted to make and maintain the road, and no law should prevent Thomas Brassey from being as good as his word.*"

The engagement was made good ; the viaduct was rebuilt ; and the word which the contractor maintained inviolate is not inaptly typified by the stability of the work he re-formed. The energy of this gentleman will be appreciated when it is

known, that though sixteen million bricks were required to re-build the viaduct, and though fourteen millions of these were made on the spot,
the stupendous erection was finished in seven
months.

CHAPTER VIII.

In 1832 government determined to assist their
ways and means by the taxation of railway travelling.
The amount charged was a halfpenny a mile for
four passengers, or half a farthing for one. It is
always a question how far a government should
tax communication, and the question is more important when that communication is on a novel
principle, struggling into existence, and untried on
a grand scale. A wise executive will only impose
those charges which are required by the state's necessities, as all imposts which restrict commercial inter-

course are sure to fall eventually on the government which imposes them.

In the present instance the Liverpool and Manchester railway boldly asserted that "in consequence of the above tax the company's charge for conveying the mail between Liverpool and Manchester would be three-halfpence per mile, instead of one penny as heretofore." For a long period the above impost was maintained. It pressed, as taxation too often does, with more force upon the poor than the rich; upon the artizan by the third than on the peer by the first class. It was unjust in principle, and unwise in practice.

It is now necessary to turn to that Great Western railway which has been truly termed "the most gigantic work, not only in Great Britain, not only in Europe, but in the entire world." The prospectus of this vast undertaking was first issued to the public in 1833, at which time it was proposed to go no further than Reading. The capital then named was £3,000,000; but, as if this were too alarming for the money power of England, its projectors reduced the amount in the following year to £2,500,000. The first application of the company for its Act

of Parliament was in 1834, and the opposition
which had been shown to other lines was extended
to this.   The usual objection that it was the speculation of engineers, attorneys, and capitalists, was
urged with the usual shallowness.   The facilities of
the railway could not be compared with those of
the river.   The people would be smothered in tunnels,
and those that escaped suffocation would be burned
in the carriages.   Slopes were magnified into precipices, engines were to be upset, necks were to be
broken.   Eton College opposed it because it would be
injurious to the discipline of the school, and dangerous to the morals of the pupils; and it was added,
" anybody who knew the nature of Eton boys, would
know that they could not be kept from the railway."
A farmer objected to it because his cows might
be killed in passing under an archway.   A gentleman objected because no public benefit could com-
pensate for destroying the beauties of his estate.
The water in the Thames, remarked one, would
be decreased, and the supply for Windsor Castle
be destroyed.   And though the general saving of carriage may be estimated from the fact that one person
alone said it would be a saving to him of £1,200

annually; though the deterioration on cattle coming to London was estimated at £12,000 a year; though the suffering of the animal could only be measured by the brutality of the drover; though the distance would be diminished, and the speed increased; though its public benefit was proved and its private annoyances would be compensated, the bill was thrown out through the interest of its opponents. Some show of reason was not wanting to justify the rejection; it was declared to be a half measure. It was said that a western railway to stop at Reading was simply absurd, and that the promoters must either have a complete western railway or none.

The rejection was regarded by its opponents as fatal. The Most Noble the Marquis of Chandos presided at a public meeting at Salthill to commemorate its defeat. The fellows of Eton College, with men who by virtue of their names and attainments should have been at the head of this national enterprise, were there in the pride of their hearts to rejoice in its overthrow; and the question was naturally asked, Where were the memories of the men whose names were in the records of that ancient college? Where were the names which had become eminent in every branch of science, which had aided by their patronage or adorned by their pursuit, every path of literature ? whose works and words should have softened the feelings, if they could not heighten the conception, of those who stood in the van of an ineffectual opposition.

When it was found that this opposition was useless, it was said, " The Great Western, though it may reach as far as Bath from Bristol, after having, like a mole, explored its way through tunnels long and deep, the shareholders who travel by it will be so heartily sick, what with foul air, smoke, and sulphur, that the very mention of a railway will be worse than ipecacuanha."

A renewed application for the line from London to Bath and Bristol was soon made. The vigour of the company was unbounded ; their resources were large, their liberality was great, their determination fixed ; and in spite of provosts opposing and colleges demurring, of the privacy of Windsor being destroyed and the Eton scholars being demoralised, the bill was passed by the end of the session of 1835, authorising a capital of £2,500,000 to be raised on stock, with a loan of £833,333.

The mode by which the opposition of landholders was neutralised, bears the same sad character as with other railways. Every passenger who goes by the Great Western pays an additional fare to meet the interest on this most unjust charge ; and every shareholder in this, as in other lines, receives a less dividend than he is entitled to from the same cause. Nor does the blame rest with the conductors of the railway. They were the agents of the shareholders ; and were bound to forward their interests. The principle of the case to them was nothing. They were bound to get the Act at the cheapest possible rate, and if the law gave their rich opponents the power of practically stopping the progress of the line, and those opponents chose to avail themselves of the law, the shame rests with the proprietor of the soil, and not with the promoter of the rail. Fancy prices were given for fancy prospects, in proportion to the power of the landowner. Noblemen were persuaded to allow their castles to be desecrated for a consideration. There can be no doubt—it was, indeed, all but demonstrated—that offers were made to, and accepted by, influential parties to withdraw their opposition to a bill which they had declared would ruin them, while the smaller and more numerous complainants were paid such prices as should actually buy off a series of long and tedious litigations.*

Various other and amended Acts were passed; in 1837 two additional bills were obtained, relating to alterations and to terminus, and in 1839, a fifth Act received the royal sanction, empowering the company to raise an additional stock of £1,250,000, and by loan £416,000.

The favourite project of Mr. Brunel, the engineer to this novel railway, was the broad guage, and that question—to be referred to in 1846, in its struggle with the narrow guage—was opened in the first act of the Great Western.

Previous to the renewal of that vehement parliamentary contest, which is yet remembered by those who witnessed it, and which is still a legend of the elder railway world, Mr. Brunel conceived the idea of changing the width of the rail. The scheme

* "Nothing less than golden arguments of the purest mint," says Mr. Sidney, "would induce noble and gentle landholders to give assent to roads which trebled their estates in value; and vast loss of money and of time was incurred in making those circuits which now excite our wonder and regret, in order to allay the fears of cities, lest contamination should attend the near approach of steam power."

was gigantic. The engineer was a plausible as well as a practical man. The directors were so far acquainted with railroads, that they expected a dividend; and when Mr. Brunel, in certain reports to the directors of the Great Western, laid down general principles, in which he proposed his change, explaining his plan, and showing its advantages, they were unwilling to reject a novelty into which they could not entirely enter. Mr. Brunel conceived that certain great lines would extend over certain districts, in which each company would reign supreme, and that the communications of these districts one with another, would be, practically, of a trifling character. The natural conclusion was, that each company might choose its own guage without the slightest reference to the guage of other lines. And this opinion of Mr. Brunel must be judged of, not by our present views, but by the information of twenty years ago. Had he then conceived the possibility of a system like that which at present prevails, he would have shared the fate of his great compatriot Mr. Stephenson, and, with more justice, been called an idle and ridiculous enthusiast. Had he deemed that the Great Western would want a

line to Birmingham, that the London and Birmingham would trench upon the rights and dues of
the Great Western; that connecting links of rails
would pass between trunk lines from north to
south, and from east to west, rendering a similarity of construction absolutely necessary for comfort and for safety; had he, indeed, surmised one-
tenth of those most extraordinary facts which the last
few years have witnessed, Mr. Brunel would probably
have smiled at his dream with unqualified wonder.
His reports were, in the existing state of things,
well worthy of consideration, and that consideration
they had. His plan, with his reasons for proposing
the change of guage from four feet eight and a-half
inches, to seven feet, was submitted to Mr. George
Stephenson, and that gentleman reported against
it. With his own directors Mr. Brunel was more
successful, and the act authorising the width of
seven feet was passed.

There was something singularly fascinating in the
proposal. The imaginative vision of the shareholders
beheld Titanic arches and vast tunnels; magnificent
bridges and fine viaducts; and the hundred miles
an hour prophesied by the engineer, exceeded the

narrow guage to an extent which promised to compel
a traffic. Their increased expenses seemed small
before their visionary dividend, and when it is remembered that the Great Western was meant to create
a demand rather than to supply it, the vague im-
aginings of the favourers of the broad guage must
be allowed for. Provincial patriotism was aroused;
the scheme of Mr. Brunel, as it has been said, was
at last patronised, and the works proceeded. This
at once necessitated a separate terminus. The London and Birmingham, which this line was to have
joined, was on the narrow guage, and the London
terminus of the Great Western was, therefore, as
inconveniently placed as could well be devised. But
that which was afterwards discovered, when the railway system was the recognised locomotion of the
land, in the break of way and all its awkward accom-
paniments, was the most striking. The seven feet
guage also entailed an increased cost in every department. Although Mr. Brunel at a later period
dec'ared that he would again lay down the broad
guage under the same circumstances, it is to be
doubted whether, placed in a similar position, and
foreseeing all that has since occurred, he would act

in a similar way, and choose a similar guage.   Enormous extra expenses were necessary, and the Great Western shareholders grew alarmed.   " The first plan," says Mr. Sidney, " on which the timbers of the road were placed was an entire failure, and were all relaid.   A bridge built over the Thames at Maidenhead, to show how the river might be crossed by two arches while the old bridge required six, fell down twice : it was again rebuilt, and stands a monument of what an engineer of genius can effect with shareholders' money."

It appears somewhat curious in a new power the essential element of which was novelty ; where works and ways and locomotives were alike strange and singular ; where all was untried and little known, that it should be thought erratic and unwise to introduce a new principle.   Such was, however, the case ; and numerous indeed were the troubles, and great was the clamour with which the enterprise of Mr. Brunel had to contend.   In addition to the construction of the railway, and to the great responsibility which rested on so magnificent an undertaking, the engineer was subjected to annoyances which assumed a purely personal form.   The railway world was against him. Failure was predicted as positive. Meetings of the board threatened his prospects; meetings of the proprietors denounced his presumption. The press, though they did not understand the question in all its bearings, were against it. The people, though they did not know how it would affect them, were afraid of it. It was called the abandonment of a principle; it was said the carriages would not run round the curves; that the axles would be broken; and, to crown all, that the shareholders would be ruined.

It was vain to tell them that it was the finest project in the world; that it would be a monument of national greatness—that foreigners would visit England to see the grandeur of the Great Western; their public spirit hid its diminished head before their private interests; they looked at the cost, and refused to be comforted.

But the high courage of Mr. Brunel supported his great capacity, and unswervingly and boldly did this gentleman uphold and carry out a theory on which his name and fame depended. Against lukewarm friends, against agitated proprietors, against avowed enemies, against the difficulty of inspiring others with his own confidence, he was successful. In another part of this work the broad guage question will be fully considered; but whatever its faults in comparison with other and narrower guages, it is right to say that it was tried, and succeeded; that Mr. Brunel reaped the fine reward of carrying out his scheme in the face of every obstacle and of every opponent, and that the plan was not unworthy the son of the genius of the Thames tunnel.

There is something marked and bold in all that belongs to Isambard Brunel. Never happier than when planning a novelty, and ever willing to expend his money on that which he believes to be sound, he is a fitting descendant of that Mark Brunel whose name is associated with the above grand idea, and was a suitable assistant against dangers which would have appalled thousands. Called " clever, but theoretical" by some, but " distinguished by the originality of his conceptions and the boldness cf his works, " according to others, said also to have " made a botch of the Bristol Docks," not being a hydraulic engineer, there are few concerning whom so wide a variety of opinion exists. George Stephenson warred to the knife against the cherished broad guage of Brunel, and thought the atmospheric, on which this gentleman spent large sums, "the greatest humbug in the world." Both these questions, however, are yet unsettled. Though the atmospheric has failed, it may still prove true : and if the broad guage has been declared inferior to the narrow, it was owing to its fortune as much as to its deserts. At any rate, it is just to record of Mr. Brunel, that he is as willing to spend his time in examining inventions as he is to spending his money in testing their promise : that he would risk his whole personal property in an untried enterprise as freely as he would spend a proprietor's deposits ; and that never so satisfied as when he can originate, he is the very spirit of progress. When he forced the broad guage on an unwilling proprietary, it required no ordinary power ; and nothing but the firmness of this resolute, determined man, could have carried the point. From the period that he was occupied with his father beneath the Thames, he has assumed an important position among the class to which he belongs. He increased the capacity of the locomotive ; he planned that great steam-ship whose loss is yet deplored; and, assisted by his friend Mr. Saunders, has maintained with a gallantry not often equalled in these degenerate days, that struggle with the powerful narrow guage interest which excited so much attention.

At the age of forty-five, a long and useful life appears before Mr. Brunel, of whom it would have been as pleasant to have been more diffuse, as it would, probably, have been unpleasant to the modesty of the engineer of that Great Western railway, the expenses of which exceeded, as usual, the cost of the estimate.

In 1839 a new Act was obtained to raise an additional capital; and in June, 1841, the whole line between London and Bristol was opened for general traffic, when for four successive weeks the receipts exceeded £14,000. The law expenses of this line were £99,091 9d., and the land cost £790,218 14s. 10d. being at the rate of £6,696 15s. 4d. a mile. These figures, although correct, are scarcely credible; and when the total expense of £56,594 6s. per mile is stated, it is curious to think that the railway has paid so well for so long a time, and not that it is now paying so ill.

It is not intended to enter thus minutely into the history of all those companies which previous to the railway mania of 1836, occupied public attention. As, however, up to that period the railroads which obtained may be regarded as ministering to a public want rather than pandering to a public desire; and as they were chiefly legitimate speculations, entered into with a view to investment, and, in this, very different from those proposed after the above period, it is important to treat them separately and independently. The reader may thus learn to moderate his intense indignation when, anathematising railways, he remembers with what unjust demands and impure claims they had to deal, and with what sad and selfish treatment it was their lot to meet. They owe nothing to the country; they owe nothing to the aristocracy. They were wronged by the former; they were contumeliously treated by the latter. They owe nothing to my Lord Brougham; they are not indebted to Colonel Sibthorp. The former made general speeches in their favour, and brought especial cases against them; while the latter has ever been a fierce though not a fatal enemy.

When, in 1832, the London and Southampton
line was presented to the notice of an intelligent
public, it was considered somewhat strange and
singular. It was natural enough to have a trunk
line between Liverpool and Manchester; it was perfectly legitimate to propose the iron way betwixt
Birmingham, which supplied the world with its
manufactures, and London, the temporary recipient
of its produce. But Southampton was in the position
of neither: it possessed no manufactures like Manchester; it was deficient in the commercial power
of Liverpool; it lacked the capitalists of Birmingham; it had not the attractions of Brighton; it
required no rapid communication with the capital;
and when its promoters first proposed to the people
of Southampton the advantages they would derive
from the rail, and Sir John Easthope explained
to the *savans* of the city the premium they would
procure from its scrip, it does not appear to have
met with a very enthusiastic reception. The energy
of its supporters, however, carried it through this
portion of its difficulties, and when Lancashire, the
home and haunt of railway enterprise, supported
it; when the shrewd Scotch followed the example,

and they of the Stock Exchange dealt in its shares, a more hopeful feeling spread throughout the body corporate.

The first estimate was between £800,000 and £900,000, and this, in the absence of that information which has since been so dearly paid for, appeared fair and feasible. It would be inconvenient to enter on the subject of its early difficulties, they were patent to all the lines, and it is sufficient to state that in July, 1834, the Act of incorporation received the royal assent. The amount authorised to be raised was £1,000,000, in 20,000 shares of £50 each, with an additional power to borrow £330,000 by loan.

A grievous error was committed, and these sums soon proved insufficient. In entering into contracts for the works, they were unhappily given in small lots to small men, at a low price, instead of being let to those who had capital and credit to lose, and upon whom full security could be placed. It was on low and unsatisfactory estimates that the bill was passed; and while the work was easy, while prices and pay remained depressed, while nothing extraordinary occurred, the work was done;

but when any engineering novelty arose, the poor
contractor was powerless. The smallest difficulty
stayed him; the slightest danger paralysed him.
He could not complete his contracts; he lacked
resources to pay the penalty; the works were often
stopped; the directors as often in despair. A second
Act was passed in 1837, empowering an additional
capital stock of £400,000, with a loan of £130,000;
and in 1839, a third Act was passed for the purpose
of constructing a branch to Gosport.

Previous to the Act of 1837, it was evident
to all connected with the line that £500,000 more
would be required, and the proprietors were startled.
The calls were difficult to be procured, the shares
were at a terrible discount, the prospects of the
company gloomy, when the gentlemen of Lancashire, who were interested, inquired into the circumstances connected with its progress. Aware of the
difficulties which had beset the paths of railways
generally, they with great promptitude appointed a
deputation to examine the accounts, to revise the
estimates, and to report on the position of the
corporation. This inquiry was satisfactory. Money
to continue the works was advanced, two of the

committee were appointed directors, and an entirely new system was adopted.   Mr. Giles resigned the engineership, the services of Mr. Locke were procured, a complete plan, showing the exact position of the work, was drawn out; everything which could assist in lessening the difficulties was adopted, and a thorough revision of traffic and expenses entered into.   Mr. Chaplin, wisely adopting the new mode of travelling as the basis of his future proceedings, joined their ranks, and to his sagacity may be traced much of the ultimate success of this railway.   He gave every information which his experience had procured; he offered every recommendation which his information could suggest; he assisted them by his counsel, and he raised them by his influence.   A fresh estimate was made of the cost of the line; much unnecessary work was avoided; £1,700,000 was regarded as the probable sum it would ultimately cost; and it will afford a significant remembrance of the difficulties which yet clung to the railroad, when it is said that the only way of procuring the money necessary to finish the undertaking was to raise £50 shares and sell them at £25, thus issuing them at a fearful discount.

Under the new management the line proceeded rapidly. Able and responsible contractors were chosen; the expenditure of one year doubled that of the three preceding years, and the line opened throughout on the 11th May, 1840. So close and cautious had been Mr. Chaplin's estimate of traffic, that within three months the receipts amounted to the sum supposed. "This," says a journalist, in 1845, "is one of the early lines, and furnishes a good example of the difficulties, discouragements, and disasters encountered by the enterprising men who, at that date, undertook the arduous duty of constructing, from private capital, these great public works, unaided, even discountenanced, by the legislature and the government; regarded with hostility, and even with hatred, by the owners of the land they were destined so materially to benefit; and considered, even by juries of their countrymen, in those days, as proper objects of unlimited and legitimate plunder. Surrounded by these difficulties without, they were met by no less formidable ones within : the infancy of the system, the inexperience of engineers, of contractors—the insufficiency of estimates—the unforeseen difficulties of works—the enormous demand for additional capital—the doubtful, or worse than doubtful, credit of the concern, evinced by shares at a discount, and without demand—discouragement, difficulty, and danger on every hand; yet did these brave men carry on their undertaking steadily, and stoutly, and manfully, with sagacity, tact, and courage of no common order, till they accomplished their great work, and brought it to its present state of excellence, prosperity, and high, yet most deserved good fortune. It is such enterprises and such men that are the honour and the strength of a country; the sources of its wealth, the causes of its prosperity; yet these are the men whom now, forgetful of past obligations, some writers, and even ministers, taunt with opprobrious epithets, and treat as narrow and selfish monopolists—as the enemies of the public and the state—and most of all, of the poor."

The cost of this line is another curiosity when compared with the estimate. The capital proposed was one million; the capital raised was two millions. The actual expenditure was £2,592,000, the land alone costing more than one-third of the entire original estimate. Thirteen thousand pounds per

mile was the supposed—more than double was the
real—cost.

It has been seen that Mr. Locke was called upon to
finish the line, and the intelligent countenance of
this gentleman, for whom all the honours due to a
high order of engineering have been claimed, is sufficiently familiar. The pupil of George Stephenson,
his fame dates from Chatmoss, over which he assisted
to form the road, and to which he owes much of
his early experience. The Grand Junction from
Liverpool to Birmingham was by him; the London
and Southampton was under his inspection. Young
and energetic, he was a valuable aid in all those
parliamentary struggles between landowners and railways which have excited so much attention, and
spent so much money. Since then he has raised
a great reputation. He formed the magnificent
viaduct and tunnel of the Manchester and Sheffield;
he introduced passenger traffic into Spain; the
principal portions of the line between Paris and
Aberdeen are by him; and to this gentleman has
been awarded the praise of keeping his works within
his estimates.

There is an easy elegance in the oratory of Mr.

Locke, which is agreeable to hear, and this is equalled by his choice of language. A member of the legislature, he speaks there with much effect, worthily representing the interest to which he is allied.

Such was the man who took the place of Mr. Giles at the time that Mr. Chaplin gave his assistance to the London and Southampton, and to none more than Mr. Chaplin was the new mode of travel important. It struck at the root of his business; it was destroying the arrangements of years; it was upsetting the combinations of a life. When, therefore, this proprietor of numerous coaches and almost innumerable horses, saw the London and Birmingham road occupied, and every other way seized on by the advocates of the locomotive; he saw also that he must take some decided course. It is not then to be wondered at that when, as already shown, that which is now known as the London and South-Western was in difficulties, Mr. Chaplin, possessing both mind and money to aid it, assisted, instead of decrying the railway; parted with his stock in trade; became one of its directors, and entered boldly and decidedly into it. His intel-

ligence and capital were recognised : he soon became
deputy chairman; was elected in 1842 to the chair
itself, and since then has maintained his position.
Like other railway men, he has entered Parliament
and is not undistinguished among that class which
owns a Stephenson, a Glyn, a Hudson, and a Locke
in our great house of legislature.

For the railway known as the London and Brighton
a fierce and factious contest ensued. During the
period of excitement five separate lines were proposed, and five contending powers disputed the
palm. The London and Brighton railway contest
is a proverb for reckless expenditure ; nor will the
following fail to surprise the reader, if not already
acquainted with the parliamentary expenses of the
competing lines. The sums spent by each company
in endeavouring to obtain an Act were :—

Rennie's line	•	•	•	•	£72,000
Stephenson's	•	•	•	•	53,750
Cundy's	•	•	•	•	•	16.500
Gibbs's	•	•	•	•	•	26,325
South-Eastern	•	•	•	•	25,000

£193,575

The most direct, but the most difficult way, was
chosen. The earth works were of an extraordinary

character; the bridges and viaducts were difficult
and numerous; the tunnels were long and expensive,
and with such a combination who can wonder that
though the first report of the directors stated the
whole cost of the undertaking would not exceed
£23,376 3s. 9d. per mile ; the actual expenditure
amounted to £37,568 17s. 6d., being an increase of
£14,192 13s. 8d. per mile.

As the first which had its commencement in the
metropolis, the London and Greenwich railway demands notice; and in looking back upon the high
hopes which accompanied its formation, on the
large dividends promised, and on the excitement it
occasioned, there is something akin to melancholy
in the knowledge that its prospects were fallacious;
that its dividends were visionary, and that its importance is now swallowed up in the South Eastern.

As a specimen of the dreams which ever accompany
new undertakings, it may be said that its arches
were to bring large rentals as warehouses ; that
pedestrians were to pay a toll; that a hundred thousand were to travel by it daily, and that the three
millions of people who yearly visited London were
to travel on it as a curiosity.

The South-Eastern railway was projected in 1833, in the form of a line between London and Dover. After a severe struggle with the North Kent and Central Kent railways, an Act was obtained on the 21st June, 1836 ; by this a joint-stock capital of £1,400,000 was authorised, with power to raise an additional £450,000 by loan. Various other Acts were afterwards passed to sanction several deviations in their route, and considerable expense was incurred in the endeavour to procure a line to Brighton.

That the utmost interest was made with senators, and that they were personally canvassed for their votes by the South-Eastern, no less than by other railways, was made evident ; and that a legislator received £300 in the shape of premiums is indisputable ; although, from the statement given by Mr. Bonham, the gentleman in question, he regarded it as a reward. It is only fair to give his own statement as at once an elucidation and a history.

" In the early part of the session of 1836 Mr. Wray, to whom I was under considerable obligations, came to me and said, ' I am very much interested in the success of the South-Eastern railway, and I wish you would give us a lift ; I want your advice

on some points.' I said, ' My dear Wray, I owe very
great obligations to you, and I will do everything I can
to serve you.' He said, ' I should be very much
obliged to you if you would.' And upon that I have
not the least hesitation in saying that I did all I could
individually to assist Mr. Wray in the object he had
in view; that is, in plain terms, I did what I could
to assist him in passing that bill, both in and out
of parliament. Mr. Wray never held out to me
one word, nor did any conversation ever take place,
as to any advantage of any kind or sort that I was
to derive from it. I considered it a great personal
advantage—I mean personal with reference to the
debt of gratitude I owed him. I considered it a
great pleasure to myself to do what I could for him.
There were some questions upon the French lines
where I gave them some advice—I will not say
assistance—because they were able to assist themselves. I never had any communication in any way
with any members of the South-Eastern railway committee ; I never had from them, directly or indirectly,
any offer of any personal advantage to myself, to be
derived from it. After that bill was passed, Mr.
Wray came to me, and stated that the South-Eastern

railway company felt that I had been of use to them—great use to them, I think he said, and that they had kept a quantity of reserved shares, which had not been disposed of, and that they had determined to appropriate one hundred shares for my benefit. Mr. Wray said, 'I know it will not be convenient for you to hold these shares— I will hold them for you; and I think I can derive some advantage from them.' Mr. Wray, I think about three weeks afterwards, came to me and said, 'I have been able to make three hundred pounds of those shares, which I will give you.'"

Thus Mr. Bonham acknowledged to have received for his services the three hundred pounds which resulted from the sale of the shares, and a committee of the Commons reported that they felt the greatest regret in being obliged to direct the attention of the House to this circumstance; but they were bound in justice to Mr. Bonham to add, that they received no evidence to show that such gratuity was the result of any previous arrangement between Mr. Bonham and the company.

It is unnecessary to detail the progress of such unimportant lines as the London and Blackwall, and the

London and Croydon. On the former the electric telegraph was first worked, and the latter is remarkable for nothing save its huge cost. They, with those already given, and with the Eastern Counties, which occupies the ensuing chapter, composed the principal lines up to 1836. Enough evidence has been adduced to prove the difficulties opposed to railways, nor will the reader find the following history deficient in similar troubles.

CHAPTER IX.

LONDON AND ESSEX RAILROAD. — FIRST PROSPECTUS OF THE EASTERN.
COUNTIES.—OPPOSITION TO IT.— ITS ESTIMATE.— LORD PETRE'S QUARREL
WITH THE DIRECTORS.—HIS TRIUMPH.—FORTUNES AND MISFORTUNES OF
THE EASTERN COUNTIES.— PERSONAL SKETCH OF SAMUEL MORTON PETO.

THOUGH last, not least of those lines which will
be treated in detail, stands the scape-goat of companies, the pariah of railways, the Eastern Counties.
Under the title of the "London and Essex railroad,"
the initiative was taken in 1831, in that undertaking
which has excited more attention, caused more alarm,
created more correspondence, and unhappily witnessed
more accidents than any other railway in the kingdom.
Arising, like all others, from the success of the
Liverpool and Manchester, the prospectus pointed to
its progress, and promised more than its profits.

Nor will the social economist be displeased to see how the promoter heralded his project :

" By the proposed railroad, places thirty or forty miles distant from London will be brought within a two hours' journey. The whole country will become contributory to the London market; the first necessaries of life will be supplied in greater abundance; competition increased, and a reduction in prices the necessary consequence. All descriptions of persons will be enabled to participate in many articles, the produce of the soil, from which the poor, and even the middling classes, in a degree, are now precluded, from high prices, occasioned by expensive cultivation in the immediate vicinity of the town."

These were some of the advantages promised; but while the luxuries of the middle class were to be augmented and the cost diminished, owners and occupiers of land were also to benefit. The entire agricultural districts were to improve in productiveness and value. Thousands of labourers temporarily, and many permanently, were to be employed; coals would be bought for comparatively nothing; and it was said with a cool intrepidity worthy the palmy days of 1845, that "every shareholder would in a few years save the cost of his share in his fuel." The fisheries, it was added, would be more abundantly employed. The supply would be large and certain. Westerly winds and opposing tides must sink into insignificance, while millions of mackarel would supply the consumer and raise the price of scrip. Holland, Hamburgh, and other parts of the continent, would avail itself of the new influence to increase our trade; foreign mails and fresh sea water; a level country and few bridges; no viaducts and no tunneling; with moderate embankments, and no "private property of particular value" to invade, formed an additional stimulus. Large dividends and "gradual return of the capital," completed a picture, which, to judge from the prospectus, only failed in procuring shareholders because it was guiltless of presidents and vice-presidents, had a blank space for the directors, and left all the other offices to be filled by the imagination of its reader. Such were a few of the items which in 1831 first declared to the people of the eastern counties of England that they required a railroad to increase their prosperity.

The next proposition bears the date of 20th September, 1834, and the Eastern Counties railway itself was before the public. A curious and most interesting document was presented :

The cost of the entire line would be	.	.	.	£1,567,000
Annual expense of working it	.	.	.	150,000
Passengers would produce	.	.	.	153,837
Merchandise and provisions	.	.	.	206,919
Agricultural produce	.	.	.	49,909
Live stock	.	.	.	157,055
Coals and manure	.	.	.	18,493
Fish	.	.	.	40,000
Traffic now in existence	.	.	.	626,213
Of which the railway would procure	.	.	.	417,475
Deduct annual expense	.	.	.	150,000
Clear annual profit of fifteen per cent.	.	.	.	267,475

This was the crude account tendered. No credit was given for an increased business, although it was stated that the communication on the Liverpool and Manchester had been multiplied six-fold, and on the Stockton and Darlington forty-fold. No allowance was made, on the other hand, for compensation to landowners, for expenses in obtaining the Act, or for a hundred of those frailties and fallibilities which the railway is heir to.

The number of acres required was calculated at

two thousand, averaging £100 an acre. Two thousand labourers were to be constantly employed during its execution; and it was thrown out as a lure, that as the Liverpool and Manchester railway paid one-fifth of the poors' rates of every parish through which it passed, the Eastern Counties might reasonably be expected to do the same. Mr. Braithwaite was acting, and Mr. Vignolles was consulting, engineer.

Opposition was not wanting for the directors. It met them in the county papers; it encountered them in pamphlets. They were assailed by letters; they were denounced in party journals. They were accused of empty assertions, and fallacious promises. The solicitors were tauntingly told that " by their own superior intelligence they had ascertained the landed and commercial interests of Norfolk, Suffolk, and Essex were quite ignorant of their own concerns." It was said that if the railway were to be carried into effect, the nursery of our best sailors would be destroyed; the foundation of our maritime decay be laid, and the downfall of England's glory—that downfall which has been preached and prophesied so often—be ensured.

The promoters were not idle. They appealed in public to " the united intelligence of the three kingdoms," and they promised money in private. They claimed the support of the commercial interests; they attacked the cupidity of peers; they assailed the philanthropy of parish rulers; they promised it should be the principal and favourite medium of transport for more than a million of people annually. There were no canals to oppose it; no railways to compete with it. It would embrace more towns than any other line, and it would convey a greater number of passengers. Above all, it would pay fifteen per cent. Notwithstanding the exertions of engineers and secretary, the scheme was abandoned for a time; while its opponents sat down to congratulate themselves on a victory, its friends prepared with renewed vigour to prepare another plan and another prospectus.

The names which graced the latter—men who bore the burden and the heat of the day—were not names belonging to our great commercial aristocracy. There were physicians from the suburbs, and gentlemen at large from the west end; there were peers who never attended the board; with

barristers who, whether briefless or not, are generally men of more words than work.   But there
were also men of business.   The name of Thomas
Gibbes, one of the oldest on the money market;
of Sir Robert Harvey, well known in the country banking interest; of Mr. Tite, who probably
joined it to become its surveyor, ; of Desanges,
of Wood, of Butler, were some guarantee that if
work were to be done it would be done well.   The
prospectus issued with the sanction of this directorate was re-written; the calculations re-modelled,
and an abstract of its contents may be interesting to the reader, evidencing, as it does, the uncertainty of railway estimates, and showing also the
progress which railways had made in popular opinion.

"The superiority of railways as a means of inland
transport, may now be considered as established
beyond all chance of refutation. . . . . It has again
and again been proved to the perfect satisfaction
of both houses of Parliament, that railways furnish
a far cheaper, safer, and more expeditious mode
of conveyance for passengers and most kind of goods,
than any other yet devised; that as soon as a railway has been opened in any district it has not

only met all the demands of the traffic existing at the time, but increased that traffic to a degree, and with a rapidity, wholly without example ; that wherever railways abound most, there the greatest rise in the value of land has been observed, and the most rapid strides been made in agricultural, manufacturing, and commercial prosperity ; that they have not only materially reduced the poor rates of every district they intersect, by furnishing profitable occupation to large numbers of the unemployed poor, but have still further relieved the old rate-payers by contributing largely towards the reduced rates, and that while thus conferring incalculable benefits on the community at large they have yielded to their proprietors a quicker return on the capital invested than was ever obtained from any other description of public undertaking."

The railways then in existence were appealed to. Their past profits and their present prospects were shown. The increase in their traffic was pointed out ; the saving of time alluded to, and it was added, " that the value of property of every description in the vicinity of railways should have risen so rapidly since their establishment, ceases

under these circumstances to be matter of surprise."
Immediately after the opening of the Liverpool and
Manchester, the value of adjacent land had arisen
generally fifty per cent., and portions of ground in
particular situations had advanced 1,400 per cent.
The philanthropist was told to look at the employment of the poor, and the diminishing of the
rates. The speculator was told to look at the
premiums and prices of existing lines. " Other
railways may be interfered with, but this never can.
As a great main line it must always stand alone,
dividing with no other railway, but receiving the
contributions of many." Nothing marks more the
crudity of the report, the credulity of the public,
and the miscalculation of the surveyors, than the
fact that the estimated expenditure for land, compensation, engineering, and parliamentary expenses
was £270,000, while the actual expenditure was
£718,765 16s. 10d.

The following is a copy of the assumed expenses
of the line by the prospectus of 1st December, 1834:

To purchase of land, 1,000 acres, at £150 .	£150,000
Compensation to owners and occupiers .	100,000
Offices, depôts, sheds, gasworks, pipes, and lamps	20,000

Excavations and embankments . . .	£200,000
Masonry, bridges, culverts, &c. . . .	200,000
Rails, chairs, keys, pins, plugs, freightage, and cartage	271,648
Blocks, sleepers, ballasting, and laying rails .	226,512
Fencing	74,000
Seven water stations	3,500
Seven pumps	700
Forty locomotive engines	40,000
Two hundred and fifty waggons . . .	7,500
Sixty coaches	9,000
Engineering and surveying, parliamentary and law expenses, canvassing proprietors and occupiers, and other incidental disbursements	20,000
	£1,322,860
Allowance for deficiencies and unforeseen expenses	277,140
	£1,600,000
Working line, per annum	200,000

The revenue calculated on was

Passengers by public conveyance . . .	£121,677
Parcels	24,335
Mail bags	5,000
Passengers by private conveyance . . .	17,962
Merchandise and provisions conveyed by land .	198,412
Corn, flour, malt, &c., conveyed coastwise .	49,909
Cattle, sheep, lambs, pigs, poultry, by land .	157,053
Coals and manure	18,493
Fish	40,000
	£632,841
Two-thirds of the above by railway . .	421,894
Working railway	200,000
	£221,894

Showing a dividend of 13 per cent. on £1,600,000

But the Eastern Counties met an animated competition from rival companies.   The Northern and
North-East line issued prospectuses, and the Grand
Northern railway occupied public attention to some
extent.   Both the preceding lines were to proceed
to Edinburgh, and " would cost," said their opponents, oracularly, " more millions than have ever
been yet subscribed, or are ever likely to be
subscribed, for any similar undertaking."   Circulars and handbills were plentiful, but the Eastern
Counties maintained its ground, while shareholders
veiled their private interests under assertions of the
public good.   On the opposition side it was said, the
new railway " ran away " from all the traffic of Norfolk, Suffolk, and Essex ; that it passed through
the poorest and least populated districts, that it would
not touch one town of importance, that it would
please few, offend many, and yield little, if any, profit.

Reasons in support of the line were gathered from
all quarters of the globe.   Oyster-beds and manufacturers, the British herring-fishery, and the East
India trade were pressed into the service.   Places
which had hitherto remained in modest obscurity,
were to be places of note.   And it was added,

" the benefits which will result from this railway will not become merely local and national; it will become the great highway to the British metropolis from Scotland, Holland, Germany, Hamburg, and Lubeck." Scientific men wrote in scientific journals with energy and eloquence of the advantages of the new undertaking. Daily papers were called in to assist it. The progress of the locomotive was dwelt on by some with regard to its social influence : its pecuniary advantages were blazoned by others.

" So many and so various are the schemes for railways," said a writer at this period, " that one can hardly take up a newspaper, but some new project, gilded with an assurance of twenty or thirty per cent. profit, stares him in the face. Twenty-seven of these projects are now in progress, to exercise the wisdom and exhaust the patience of our legislators. Whether they will turn out profitable to the shareholders, is a knot time alone can untie. There is, however, no question that the state of society needs and must have this new species of transit, and that railways will go on progressing for many a year, until every link of the chain of internal communication is completed. Some think the present prejudice of the public in favour of rail-

ways, is a mania. It is a mania like the astrono-
mical madness of Copernicus, the more it is known,
the more it will be approved and the better it will be
supported : for it is a mania whose cause is necessity,
utility the effect, and mankind the party to be benefited. It will therefore continue, the public being
generally too wise to neglect what is found to be
advantageous." Need it be added that an eulogium
on the Eastern Counties followed ?

" Hardly a day passes," wrote an evening paper, in
October, 1835, and the writer deems no picture so true
as those chronicles which reflect the fears and the
feelings of the times, " but we have to record some
additions to the number of railroads already in progress, or proposed to be carried into effect. . . . .
The superiority of the railroad over every other
mode of inland conveyance, has been proved by
such a weight of evidence, that it seems almost
a work of supererogation to recommend it to the
public favour. The advocate of improvement, however, is ill-qualified for his office if he flatters himself
that his task is finished when he has demonstrated
the utility of any of those plans of amelioration
which the spirit of enterprise, now so actively

engaged in developing the national resources, is constantly bringing forward. He must not forget that the obstacles which lie in his path cannot be surmounted but by unwearied perseverance. He must return to the charge again and again, not disdaining to combat the oft-refuted objection, and labouring to weaken, if he cannot remove, the prejudice which clings to the old ways. He must not lose his temper when a timid old gentleman tells him that to travel at a speed of twenty miles an hour smacks of revolution. And when the wisdom of our ancestors is pleaded against the rapid movement, it becomes him to prove that the slow pace of our forefathers had no hand in rendering them the glory of the world and the envy of surrounding nations."

It was said with justice that the unprincipled opposition to the railway had been in some degree beneficial. That it had proved to the legislature, and to the world, the great advantages derived from it; it had decided that in cheapness, safety, and expedition, no mode of conveyance could compete with it; that wherever it was introduced it increased the traffic of the district; raised the value of land ; gave a new and powerful impulse to agriculture, manufactures, and commerce ; reduced the poor-rates, and promised a high but rapid profit to those who invested, " combining by a happy union, public with private interest." Shall we say the Eastern Counties was said to promise more than all these great and glorious benefits.

The transaction of Lord Petre with the Eastern Counties directors, stands almost unparalleled in the history of railway adventure ; but it would appear, so far as the writer has been able to ascertain the facts, that if his lordship clung to that which the law allowed him ; if, like Shylock, he exacted his bond, it was owing to certain unwise and undignified irritations to which he had been subjected. Previous to obtaining the bill, a secret engagement was entered into with his lordship by the provisional committee, who engaged to pay him the sum of £120,000 nominally for the land through which the rail was to pass, but really for the withdrawal of an opposition which might have been disastrous. When the bill was passed there appears to have been some objection to fulfilling the contract on the pretended ground of misrepresentation. Nor did the directors hesitate to assert that to fulfil it would be a fraud on the proprietors, the legislature, and the public. But if the company were unwilling to pay the money, his lordship was equally unwilling to give it up. He obtained an injunction against them ; he opposed and prevented them from passing through his grounds ; he harrassed and irritated them as they had irritated him, and with far more effect. But the stake was too great to yield quietly. In addition to the money involved, it has been said Lord Petre's pride was raised. The engineer and secretary—in what manner it does not appear—had offended his dignity. The board was urged by these gentlemen to oppose him. They were told that his claim was invalid ; that their opposition must be successful, and when an amended bill— hereafter to be alluded to—was brought before the commons, Lord Petre was enabled to oppose them with great effect.

The company, wishing to be safe, appointed seven eminent surveyors to report as to the damage likely to be caused to his lordship's estate ; copies of their reports were forwarded to Lord Petre, and an offer

was made to use them as the basis of an amicable
arrangement. His lordship, however, positively declined any change in the terms of the bond. All
his influence, with that of Mr. Labouchere, whose
estate was also to be invaded, was used to oppose
the progress of the line ; and so strong was the
feeling, that the directors consented to stay the progress of the bill, and, seeing the folly of their proceedings, to refer the claim to arbitration. Lord
Petre, however, refused all such interference, and
the company was emphatically grounded. If they
resisted their opponent in the house, the bill would
be lost and proceedings delayed for a year. If
they resisted him in the law courts, the result would
be the same. If the bill were abandoned, the compulsory power of the company by its first Act
would soon cease to exist ; and if they even gained
a chancery suit and annulled the contract, their
opponent might refuse to sell his land at all, and
thus a gap of six unfinished miles grace the line.

There only remained, therefore, for the company
to pay the money. His lordship beat the board,
and exacted the full amount of his bond : £120,000
with interest, was paid for land which was even

then said to be only worth £5,000, and which at the present time is perhaps improved by the change. It is due to the directors to add that though they regretted the payment of so large a sum, time, which has modified their wrath, has made them equally regret the spirit with which they opposed it.

Three years had by this time elapsed since the design of the Eastern Counties was first given to the public. The various interests which had tended to delay its progress had prevented it from being fairly developed, until about ten months previous to its incorporation in July 1836, and when the provisional committee was formed, there remained only a few weeks for operations which usually occupied many months. The energy with which the project was proceeded with, during this brief period, was irresistible. The sections and surveys of one hundred and twenty-six miles were formed in six weeks. The proprietors were canvassed for the breadth of half a mile along the whole line. Essex, Suffolk, and Norfolk, were travelled by a deputation of the committee; public meetings were called wherever they went; private representations were made to influential individuals; part of the monied interest aided the scheme, and before the second reading of the bill, the greater portion of the capital was subscribed. Shares were taken by the inhabitants of the principal commercial towns; and without the help of the men of Manchester, Birmingham, and Liverpool, who subscribed for many thousand shares, the scheme must have fallen. With their aid the bill passed the House of Commons, a committee of which reported "that the Eastern Counties railway between the termini would traverse the most populous and most cultivated parts of the counties through which it was intended to be carried, and that great benefit would be given to trade and agriculture by its adoption."

When the bill had passed the Lower House, its opponents, stimulated, perhaps, by the thought of Lord Petre's one hundred and twenty thousand pounds, endeavoured to injure it in the Upper; " but," said the first report, " the directors, by meeting the parties with the same promptness and in the same fair spirit which had carried them successfully through their previous negociations, effected amicable arrangements with them."

What these " amicable arrangements " were, may

be traced in the history of all selfish opposition, and may be judged from the fact that they formed an excuse for the large preliminary expenses which swelled the accounts presented to the proprietary. It produced, however, an unquestionable effect. Those who had received money supported the company most strenuously, while those who hoped to receive it, were yet stronger in their expression of opinion.

The Eastern Counties railway was received as the line to be supported, and after a most extraordinary opposition with as extraordinary methods to subdue it, the company was incorporated, and a career commenced which will long make that corporation marked and memorable. The first meeting of the shareholders shortly followed, and it is scarcely possible to read unmoved the glowing orations of the speakers, or to think without a sigh that "Ichabod, Ichabod, the glory is departed!" is written on the heart and saddens the brow of every shareholder. But it is necessary to follow the prospects of this fine line, and equally so to show the elation which glowed in the heart, and was uttered from the lips of chairman and of proprietor.

"You are here assembled in such numbers and

with such cordiality of feeling, because you see in the new means of communication which we are about to open between the metropolis and the various cities, towns, and ports on our eastern coast, a prospect of one of the proudest triumphs of the march of science, because you feel assured that by it the stream of traffic and correspondence in this quarter of the kingdom will be preserved in the same channel in which it has run for ages, re-invigorated and redoubled; because in countless ways it must stimulate the industry of every place through which it passes or goes near, or becomes connected with; because the agriculture, now depressed, and the manufactures of the eastern counties will be both eminently promoted by the means which it will afford of cheap and speedy transmission to the greatest mart in the world, of the produce of the ploughshare and the fabrics of the loom; because from that mart will flow in return to the eastern counties ample supplies of every commodity, foreign or domestic, of which it is the great storehouse; because the fisheries of our eastern shores, freed from every restraint on their abundance, will become ten times more productive than ever;

because the ports of the eastern counties will once more be rendered the favourite ports of ingress; because this railway must bring with it whatever can give vigour to industry, make commerce active, or render a people happy."

Yarmouth, it was added, would renew her youth and fill her harbour with commerce, while every port near which the railway passed would be prosperous. It was a picture which many enterprises present in their youth, and it was a portraiture of the sanguine character of companies ere they have spent their cash, lost their credit, and find how difficult it is to make shareholders respond to calls.

A peculiar fortune, or misfortune, seemed to follow the Eastern Counties railway. Although a line of much importance, it carried no weight in the money market. Although **its** engineers calculated on no great difficulty, they found their calculations erring. Although the directors judged the land would present no obstacle in its owners, they found themselves hampered with an engagement to one of the lords of the soil, which they could with difficulty pay. Although they expected to receive their calls in proper time, they found the panics of the

money-market interfering with their expectations.
The extension of the powers of the company was
opposed. The owners and occupiers of land resisted
it by precept and by example; while, to conclude
this agreeable picture, some of the shareholders were
arrayed against others in the Court of Chancery
to prevent the remainder from carrying out their
plans.

That money was not forthcoming with the necessary rapidity may be judged from the fact, that
in July 1837, it was proposed to the proprietors
voluntarily to advance £600,000 at 4 per cent., and
so satisfied were the directors that the line must
pay 10 per cent., they recommended the shareholders to divide, when the line should be opened,
a dividend at that rate on the whole of the paid
up capital.

In 1837, 61,000 out of 64,000 shares were registered; half were held by the men of Liverpool
and Manchester, and there were 1,410 shareholders
altogether.

Some of these, however, refused to pay the calls.
They had subscribed in expectation of a premium,
and they objected strongly to advancing their cash

when shares were at a discount. Letters were written to defaulters that their shares would be forfeited, but they paid no attention. Advertisements were published to remind the defaulters that the works must stop; but they refused to notice them, until a new and more alarming mode was devised to recal the delinquents to their duty.

"It is painful to the directors," says a letter, bearing date July, 1839, "to have been obliged to resort to legal proceedings to enforce the calls; but in justice to the shareholders who have paid, and considering that the works must stop unless the arrears be promptly settled, the directors have had no other alternative but to compel payment by legal means."

As legal measures are slow, however, and capital was required immediately, the directors continued to make further calls, while the others remained unpaid, and the effect which this had upon a money-market already depressed, may be imagined.

The funds of the company being exhausted in past and prospective engagements, the shares being at 50 per cent. discount, the capital being difficult to collect, the compulsory power to purchase land shortly ceasing, the directors deemed it necessary to apply to parliament in the session of 1838, for power to raise by loan a sum equal to one-third of the capital, together with a prolongation of their powers. After the opposition of Lord Petre and Mr. Labouchere, already detailed, was negatived, the bill was obtained, and on 27th July, 1838, it received the royal assent.

The following is a list of the provisional committee to whom the promotion of the line is due; and the career of this company will be resumed at a future period in detailing the position occupied by the Railway King in its councils, and the effect he produced on its interests.

PROVISIONAL COMMITTEE OF THE EASTERN COUNTIES RAILWAY.

Sir Robert Alexander	Thomas Gibbes
Henry Bosanquet	William Gunston
Cornelius Butler	Charles Thomas Holcombe
Reverend John Chevallier	Col. Sir Robert Harvey
George Clapham	Charles Hood
John Cobbold	Henry Luard
W. C. Crawford	Joseph Marriage
Louis Desanges	Thomas Robertson
Lord Charles Fitzroy	William Tite
Thomas B. Tyler	W. Collings Wells.

The Cambridge portion of this line, now known as the Eastern Counties, was constructed by Mr. Samuel Morton Peto, about 1843; and to the railway contractor who has arisen with the railway power, this gentleman should be an example and a type. Born of that great middle class to which England owes so much of her grandeur, leaving school at an early age to serve an apprenticeship, it is to his honour that, determined to attain a practical knowledge of the work to which he was devoted, the future legislator handled the trowel of the mason, and worked with the chisel of the carpenter, with characteristic energy.

Apprenticed to his uncle, one of the largest builders in England, he had scarcely emerged from his servitude, when he became that uncle's successor; yet he did not forget that labour is the lot of life, nor did he shrink from the responsibility which his position entailed. The firm of which he became a partner by his relative's death, increased in business importance, and, apart from the ordinary branches of the builders' craft, formed large contracts. The members of it devised Hungerford-market and re-built the Houses of Parliament; they erected clubs, and formed model-prisons; contracted for theatres, built castles, and constructed docks of the most perfect character in the kingdom. When, therefore, in 1834, the new mode of locomotion had forced itself on public notice, Mr. Peto, seeing at once its power and the position it must give to those who forwarded in it the material progress of England, dissolved his connexion with the building firm, and became a "railway contractor." From his first work —the Wharncliffe viaduct—he has been prominent among those whose life is on the rail. He has been first and foremost in singly taking contracts at which companies would once have hesitated; and he has been one of the few who, holding a moral and physical sway over thousands, have not betrayed their trust.

It is little to the public that Samuel Morton Peto has prospered in the pursuit he embraced; it is little to them that seven hundred miles of railway have been formed by him; that from north to south, and from east to west, his contracts have extended; or that the success of these contracts has made him one of our many *millionaires*; but it is much to the public that in the words of one who knows him well, " It has been Mr. Peto's maxim through life, that all who shared with him his toils and labours, should have their full share of his rewards." It is a principle which the writer rejoices to relate, and it is a principle which, in itself peculiarly honourable, is a proof also, that his mental are equalled by his moral qualifications. Identified with the people, he acts as if he were one of them. He feels that property has its duties as well as its dues; its responsibilities as well as its rights. When placed over a large body of rude, illiterate men, he treated them as brothers, and not as brutes; he did not pay them at long intervals, leaving them in the interim to the mercy of usurers; he has ever repudiated the truck system; he has never made twenty-five per cent. of their daily bread; and the night of payment with those under him, therefore, has not been a scene of disgraceful strife.

But these are negative qualities. Mr. Peto has been a positive benefactor to the railway labourer. Believing that the 14,000 navigators—the average number he employed for several years—had minds as well as bodies, he acted up to that creed. He supplied them with books, and engaged for them teachers. He formed sick-clubs, introduced benefit-societies, and taught them the use of saving-banks. He built temporary cottages, and let them at a proper price. He took care that the apartments should be tenanted with due regard to decency; and the consequence was that, in the words of Bishop Stanley, "the gin-shops were deserted, and the schools were full." He personally superintended his works as much as their vast extent would permit, and if not physically, he was morally ubiquitous. Wherever his men were gathered in numbers, there a large room arose, in which, when heavy rains obstructed the work, it was no unpicturesque sight to view the hard, athletic navigator listening with grave attention to some volume which, striking at once his reason and his fancy, kept him from drink and saved him from debauchery. Many a man, before his engagement with Mr. Peto in utter ignorance of everything, has been taught to read at his master's expense. These things—in such an eager pursuit of gain as this volume records—are as gratifying to the philanthropist as they are important to the politician; and Mr. Peto has met with his reward. He has been complimented by bishops; he has been honoured in the orations of deans;* parliamentary committees have reported his

---

* "Mr. Peto was a dissenter," said Dr. Stanley; "and he envied the sect to which he belonged the possession of such a man, and he would gladly purchase him at his own price; and heartily he prayed that he would ere long become a

worth; the lamented protectionist leader bore testimony to his benefits; the press has done justice to his benevolence; senators have delighted to do him honour; the projector of the broad guage thought few could act as Mr. Peto had acted; and all these things prove that Bishop Stanley was right when he so eloquently enlarged upon the Christian virtues of Mr. Peto. This gentleman was born to a fortune, which is not the case with many of the powerful class to which he belongs, who, beginning life as navigators, have become contractors; who, having saved money, have become "gangers," realised capital, and formed contracts, first for thousands and then for hundreds of thousands. These are almost a caste by

member of the Church of England. He (Bishop Stanley) was a churchman, and holding a high office in the church, and believed that in that church was the purest faith; but he was still a catholic Christian, and as such he would hold it a dereliction of his duty if he did not express his approbation, respect, and regard for the exertions used for the moral benefit of railway labourers by Mr. Peto. All down the line he had met with his agents, and had found them not merely giving directions and instructions, but also giving to the men religious and school books for the education of themselves and their children; and thus showing them that education can civilise the mind, reform the habits, and elevate the understanding. The gin shops were left deserted, and the schools were full. The good and exemplary conduct of Mr. Peto's railway labourers under this system deserved to be a tale told three times three with one cheer more; and let it be recorded as a fact of which there could be no denial, not one labourer in the Norwich district had been guilty of misconduct that made him amenable to the law."

themselves. They make ,ortunes, and purchase landed estates. Many a fine property has passed from some improvident possessor to a railway labourer ; and some of the most beautiful country seats in England belong to men who trundled the barrow, who delved with the spade, who smote with the pick-axe, and blasted the rock.

To these Mr. Peto is an exception. The name was known in connexion with some of our most splendid edifices long before railways were thought of. But it may be truly said that although to this peculiar class Mr. Peto is alien, yet in forming a tenth part of the railroads of the United Kingdom, he has converted an ample into a princely fortune. He has purchased the estates, and rebuilt for his own use the family mansions, of peers ; he was as ready a few months since to undertake the entire construction of a railway, as he was a few years before to erect a theatre in thirteen weeks ; and he who, much less than a quarter of a century previous, handled the trowel or hammered the nail, might have been heard seconding the address on a queen's speech, listened to by gentlemen and applauded by scholars.

There is one more particular to relate of Mr. Peto, and with it the writer will conclude the present sketch. It is in the memory of all that the prospects of that which is known as the Great Exhibition, however triumphant now, wore at the close of 1849 a dark and doubtful aspect. Money was scarce, and croakers were plentiful. The Gurneys and the Barings of the city had not yet come forward, and men found it more pleasant to frame excuses than to pay subscriptions. Its very existence was jeopardised, when Mr. Peto set an example so noble that others were ashamed not to follow it; and it is very characteristic of this gentleman that when he offered the princely sum of £50,000 to meet any deficiency, he begged also as a favour that the fact might not be reported by the commissioners.

CHAPTER X.

THE first attempt to legislate by a general bill for railways was made in 1836 by Mr. Morrison, who then moved "that in all such bills it be made a condition that the dividends be limited to a certain rate, and that Parliament reserve to itself the power of fixing periodically the tolls on passengers and goods;" thus attempting to impress on the house a due sense of the magnitude of the change, which, in his own prophetic words, was likely "at no distant period to transfer our chief public conveyances from the king's highways to a number of joint-stock railway companies."

That Mr. Morrison was correct in his premises

there can be no doubt. The history of the past has taught commercial men to little purpose, if it has not convinced them that when a company is prosperous, the directors are indifferent. A share in the New River company is a moderate man's income; but the water is indifferent, and the price high. The discovery to which Winsor devoted a life has produced fortunes, and paid fine dividends; but the charge to the public is exorbitant. The water corporations of the metropolis, after a fierce contention, divided the public between them, and left that public to mourn. The canals had already taught the manufacturing world that an ill-regulated monopoly was ruinous to its subjects. The management of Life Assurance associations was an additional proof that powerful companies required controul or competition. With such examples before the House, it was evident that railways required legislation. The period, too, was propitious. The Great Western was not yet opened; the London and Birmingham but partially so; the bills for other lines had only just been passed; and the entire interest was unable to make any effective demonstration.

The reasons of Mr. Morrison were such as should
have addressed themselves to a body of intelligent
gentlemen.   He said it was important to a mercantile and manufacturing people that the conveyance
of goods should be as perfect as possible ; that it was
difficult to estimate the result of late improvements
on the country ; that competition had lowered prices
in our larger towns, and visited even our villages ;
that the facilities of travelling had promoted the
remarkable movement in our internal industry with
which all were familiar.   Hitherto, he remarked, a
perfect competition had existed in our public roads ;
every improvement was at once made use of, but in
the many railway Acts then before the House no
endeavour was made to secure improvement.   Another
danger was in the prospect of opposition lines ; and
Mr. Morrison stated in 1836 what is very noticeable in 1850, that the London and Birmingham
railway, after spending many millions in its construction, might find a rival rising by its side to
compete with its traffic and eat into its profits.
The best comment on this remark is the Great
Northern.

The principle for which Mr. Morrison then contended was practically allowed by the government; when it limited the profits of the railways, and in many other instances it had received the sanction of the legislature. "For these and a variety of reasons," continued the above gentleman, "I am clearly of opinion that parliament should, when it establishes companies for the formation of canals, railroads, or similar undertakings, invariably reserve to itself the power to make such periodical revisions of the rates of charges as it may deem expedient. It should have the power to examine into the whole management and affairs of each company, to correct what may have been amiss in the former, and to fix the rates of charges for another period of years, always taking care that the proprietors are allowed a fair return for the original outlay of capital, as well as compensation for the risk to which such undertakings are more or less subject." These remarks Mr. Morrison closed by moving: "That in all bills for railways, or other public works of that description, it be made a condition, with a view to the protection of the public interests which might otherwise be seriously compromised, that the dividends be limited to a certain rate, or that power be reserved to parliament of revising and fixing at the end of every twenty years the tolls chargeable on passengers and goods conveyed.

The proposition was generally well received, and the " honourable gentleman " was called on to move at once for leave to bring in a bill to effect the proposed object. This was done; the bill was read a first time; but before a second reading could take place, Mr. Morrison became sensible of the hopelessness of his task. It was said that no man would purchase a share with such an avalanche hanging over him; that it would ruin all those who were in possession of railway property; that it would create a panic; that everybody would try to sell, and that nobody would buy. It was added, and with some degree of truth, that if the state had done nothing to help, it ought to do nothing to injure them. "What have the government done to promote railways?" said Mr. Herapath. "Have they done a single thing? I am not conscious of one. Have they removed a single impediment?— not to my knowledge; but they have raised several. Have they contributed a single shilling? Rather, I believe, by the intolerable and vexatious oppositions permitted in passing the bills, have been the cause of spending many hundreds of thousands, which, like another national debt, will prey to the end of time on the vitals of public industry." These were the opinions of one well capable of forming a judgment, and must be received with deference. Sir Robert Peel declared himself decidedly opposed to it. In presenting a petition against the Periodical Revision of Tolls bill, this statesman said, " Such a measure should not be postponed from day to day, and kept up in the shape of a menace against railway speculations. The effect was, that many were deterred from purchasing in railways, that the transfer of shares in most of them had come to a stand-still, and that, in fact, this branch of public commerce was injured and almost paralysed."

Mr. Morrison's reasons for abandoning a bill so important to the well-being of railways, is to be found in the fact " that before the time of the second reading arrived, doubts were entertained in high quarters as to the adviseableness of interfering with new undertakings, by which capitalists might be deterred from embarking in them; and he could look for no support where support was necessary to success."

The question appears plain; and averse as the

writer is to legislative controul over commercial companies, there can be no doubt that in the present exceptional case great good would have resulted to the people and to the proprietary. With such a periodical search, the public would have been safe. However advantageous the competitive principle may be, a sound co-operative principle is far more so. The law which exists for the tradesman, holds good for the company; and a malevolent competition carried on between two great corporations, must be mischievous to both. Monopoly is the cant word of the day; but the public is now stronger than any monopoly; and had the bill of Mr. Morrison been carried into operation, it is difficult to calculate its effects. The whole of the railway companies might have been banded together; railway potentates might have been as self-important as canal magnates; they might have fixed their fares and arranged their times as arrogantly as they pleased; but they would have been powerless to injure the public, while the advantages to their proprietary would have been inestimable. Trains would not have been run at prices which did not pay for the grease used in the wheels; similar hours would not have been chosen by two lines running into each other's dominions; a Western railway would not have intruded on a North-Western; nor a Great Northern swept away the profits of a Midland. Competitions, contemptible save in their results, would not have been attempted at the expense of millions; lines would not have been made, for which, to use the words of Mr. Robert Stephenson, "there was no more occasion than a coach has for five wheels;" lawyers would not have obtained a bad eminence; surveyors would have remained in their pristine insignificance; useless works would not have been formed; and sixty or seventy millions sterling would have been saved.

In addition to the above abortive attempt, a motion was made by Mr. Harvey, that a committee should be appointed, to which any application for railways having a termination within seven miles of the Royal Exchange should be referred; and that before any such bill was read a second time, the committee should report on the directness of the communication, the probable expenditure, the safety of the public, and the effect upon private property. This, however, was withdrawn.

The scene was occasionally enlivened by some honourable member's alarm for his character. Thus, in the same session, Sir C. Burrell complained that Mr. Cundy, engineer to one of the Brighton competing lines, had used his name in a most reprehensible way. Nor was the charge unworthy rebutting, as Mr. Cundy was accused of stating that Sir Charles had voted for Stephenson's line, because £15,000 had been awarded him for land not worth so many hundreds. " Such an imputation was totally untrue," said Sir Charles, indignantly. Various members gave varying opinions on the subject ; Captain Pechell believing " such a trumpery case had never been brought before the House before ;" while Mr. Wynn was of opinion " that charges of so grave a nature should not pass unnoticed." Mr. Nicholas Wilcox Cundy was in consequence summoned before the bar of the House, and an investigation was instituted. It appeared, however, that Mr. Cundy had not made the statement on his own authority, but that he had quoted it from a Brighton journal. Mr. Cundy was, therefore, released from his unpleasant position, and the House proceeded to graver affairs.

In the session of 1836, no fewer than thirty-five railway bills passed the legislature, six being for alterations only, while twenty-nine were for new lines, the total length of which was nine hundred and ninety-four miles, at an estimate of £17,595,000.

By 1837 it was discovered that railways had produced the effect of sending a great number of stage coaches from the turnpike-roads. The post-office was placed in unparalleled difficulty. Contractors, disappointed in the passengers they hoped to carry, were unable to fulfil their agreements. The government advertised, but could obtain no offer for places between which they wished to establish a communication, excepting at an increased cost of four hundred per cent. Many villages which demanded postal connexion were compelled to suffer great social evils arising from its absence. When the London and Birmingham railway was opened, seven mails were at once abolished because the contractor could not maintain his engagement. Colonel Maberley, very illiberally, said the railways possessed an entire monopoly against the post-office, and that they seemed inclined to exact what terms they pleased. The question was important, and a

select committee of the House of Commons came
to the resolution that as railway companies have
it in their power to prevent the transmission of
post-office correspondence, the legislature should
not only have its attention constantly directed to
the subject, but that a bill should be immediately
submitted to the house, compelling them to perform all services required by the postmaster-general;
and in the event of disagreement as to terms, to
submit the case to arbitration.

The bill founded on this contained some very
obnoxious clauses; by one of which the post-office
authorities might run their own trains on any line
without paying any toll; by another, they might
remove all obstacles in the shape of passenger or
other carriages out of their way; by a third, pains
and penalties were denounced on the companies'
servants if they disobeyed the government; and by
a fourth, the aid of the railway plant and the railway officials was commanded; all these benefits
to be remunerated by a consideration for the wear
and tear on the rails.

The various companies rose in defence of their
privileges. It was in vain they were told that the

mails travelled on the ordinary roads toll free ; they very naturally replied " they could not see the analogy, that a common road being common property, paid for by the public, the public had a right to use it. But on the contrary the railroad was formed by private enterprise and maintained by private individuals. The queen had no right over a canal ; what right had she over a railway ? If troops passed over a private bridge, they were paid for as private persons, why then should a railway be placed in a different position?" And it was added, that "if the crown had certain rights on the highway, it was by virtue of clauses in their Acts of Parliament, but such clauses were absent in railway bills." When the measure was proposed to the House, it met with continued opposition.

Mr. Labouchere said the country was at the mercy of these companies ; that they had bound the land in bonds of iron ; and that, if the railroads had cost extravagant sums, the country had no right to pay for the mistakes of engineers and speculators.

Lord Sandon put the question on the broad principle of whether the post-office had a right to take possession of railroads and use them without remuneration.

Mr. Rice warned all railroad directors to beware of opposing the bill, threatening them with more stringent measures if they were so ill-advised.

Sir Robert Peel said—and therein rested the truth of the question—that they were now called upon to repair an enormous omission. The legislature had established a monopoly with which there could be no future competition. The legislature had said to landowners, "you must, for a great public benefit, forego your own will and discretion, and dispose of your lands to these companies;" and Parliament had now the same right to say to railway proprietors, "for a great public benefit you must, to some extent, give up your rights of private property."

The companies were naturally jealous of their prerogatives, without exactly knowing how far those prerogatives went. The government, with the ordinary desire of all weak governments to achieve a petty economy, were disposed to claim rights which no corporation could fairly allow. They wanted to send the letters thrice as quick and thrice as often, for less than the amount which they had paid by mail. They wished to avail themselves of roads formed at an expense of £50,000 a mile, and maintained at an annual cost of £2,000 or £3,000 a mile without paying any toll. And, however commercially important it may be that letters should be forwarded as rapidly as possible ; it is also morally important that the large mass of railway proprietors should not be rendered discontented, and that the government of a great country should not be parties to an arrangement at variance with justice.

Mr. Glyn stated that of all the monstrous measures he had ever read, the bill for the conveyance of mails on railways, as originally proposed, was the most striking : but, that government having listened to the representations made to them, he trusted the measure would now work effectually for the good of all.

The bill eventually passed contained enactments by which railway companies were bound to convey mails at such hours as the postmaster-general should direct ; if required, they were to apply separate carriages exclusively to their conveyance ; remuneration was to be according to agreement between the directors and the postmaster, and any difference between them was to be settled by arbitration. Mr. Labouchere distinctly stated that though he had given up his own views in deference to those of the railway companies, yet, if the directors should not afford every facility for the transmission of correspondence, he should introduce a measure to compel compliance. Such was one difficulty besetting the interest in 1838, and for the result of which the proprietors are indebted to the resolute remonstrance of that power which public men, to suit a party purpose, or to raise a party cry, are pleased to term a monopoly.

The memory of those months which range from 1836 to 1837, will long be remembered by commercial men. Companies which engrossed the care and the capital of thousands, were projected. Eleven years had passed since the excitement of 1825; the resources of the country had increased; the only loan which had absorbed her savings had been that of twenty millions for our West Indian colonies; money was lying comparatively idle; the four per cents. had not long been reduced; the current rate of interest was from three and a-half to four per cent.; illegitimate sources of profit were sought for; the inventor used his arts to excite the rich; companies were once more the fashion, and once more the whole city rejoiced in what it was pleased to deem a sure and solid prosperity. Until July, 1836, with the exception of the London and Birmingham, the Carlisle and Newcastle, the Southampton, the Great Western, and those which have been already chronicled, but few undertakings had been entered into. A host of proposals followed this calm; "and," said the *Edinburgh Review*, "there is scarcely, in fact, a practicable line between two considerable places, however remote, that has not been occupied by a company. Frequently two, three, or four rival lines have started simultaneously." With this increase in the number of new railway propositions, there was an equally sudden rise in the price of the shares of most of the established companies, and the scrip in the greater number of the new projects was either brought out at, or speedily commanded a premium. Unemployed engineers and attorneys, with the whole tribe of jobbers and speculators, were not slow to perceive the advantages they might derive. Public attention had been much occupied by the London and Birmingham and other great lines. The most exaggerated accounts were disseminated of the wonderful advantages the railways would confer on proprietors. The shares in all continued rapidly to advance; the cupidity of the people was inflamed; the multitude were tempted; the fever extended on all sides; numbers of undigested prospectuses were produced, and with them that extraordinary demand for shares of any sort by which the first six months of July, 1836, were distinguished. The notice attracted by those already in course of construction assisted to draw the attention of capitalists to this new power, and a desire for companies was common.

The press supported the mania; the government sanctioned it; the people paid for it. Railways were at once a fashion and a frenzy. England was mapped out for iron roads. The profits and per centage of the Liverpool and Manchester were largely quoted. The prospects and the power of the London and Birmingham were as freely prophecied. Company after company arose; line after line was projected; million after million was demanded. To this period we owe the success of many of our most important undertakings. Competing lines were the order of the day, and for the Brighton no fewer than five claimants excited the attention of the town. To doubt the profits of railways was ignorance ; to deny their success was madness. They were all called safe and stable investments. They were all sure to pay a large per centage. The convenience and comfort of this mode of travelling were addressed to the public notice. The facilities of communication ; the increase of commerce ; the bringing mind and mind together ; the creating demands for knowledge ; the cultivation of the mental capabilities, and the improvement of the physical powers, were ordinary topics of the press and of society. It was said in 1836, in the House of Commons, " there was no subject of a domestic nature which so largely occupied the public attention as that of railways. A greater number of persons was enlisted in their advocacy or in opposition to them ; a larger amount of capital was embarked in their furtherance ; a vaster extent of property was involved in their prosecution, than in any one other subject." Colonel Sibthorp, with the self-devotion which distinguishes him in the senate, said he considered all railways as public frauds and as private robberies. The clergy of Hampshire petitioned against the new power, because the rustics kept away from church to see the train pass by; and Mr. Morrison, it has been seen, wisely proposed to the legislature in 1836, that the dividends should not only be limited, but that parliament should be allowed the privilege of revising the tolls every twenty years.

"Our very language begins to be affected by it," wrote one. "Men talk of 'getting up the steam,' of 'railway speed,' and reckon distances by hours and minutes." The story of a gentleman who left Manchester in the morning, who went thence to Liverpool, purchased and took back with him one hundred and fifty tons of cotton, and having sold it, returned to Liverpool on a similar errand with similar success, was a stereotyped story for the press.

"It is not the promoters, but the opponents of railways, who are the madmen. If it is a mania, it is a mania which is like the air we breathe."

Our commerce was to be magnified by the Greenwich railway. The London and Blackwall was to ruin the St. Katherine and destroy the London docks. The Greenwich, in the hour of its excitement, proposed to tunnel the park and to build marble arches adorned with marble busts, while the Commercial, now known as the Blackwall railway, talked, in the plenitude of its audacity, of making the East India House a station for its four projected miles. Three distinct lines were proposed to Norwich. Surrey was entirely mapped and marked out. All the opposition lines to Brighton were at a premium. In one parish of a metropolitan borough, sixteen schemes were afloat, and upwards of one thousand two hundred houses scheduled to be taken down. With some of the most evident bubbles the names of senators were connected. Railroads were advertised to places where no coaches ran. The Marquis of Londonderry stated that in Durham three railroads had been attempted by one projector, all running in parallel lines. One was at par, another was bankrupt, and he believed the third would never pay. The wildest schemes were calmly entertained. One projector proposed sails to propel his engine, and induced a company to try them. Another offered to propel his locomotives with rockets, confidently promising one hundred miles an hour. A third invented a wooden line, to be raised many feet from the ground to allow a free and uninterrupted intercourse beneath. Railways to carry invalids to bed were advertised, and a safety railway out of reach of injury was proposed. Competition was carried into villages hitherto contented with all which had contented their rude forefathers. The smaller towns exhibited an unwonted business and bustle. High prices could no more be demanded for bad goods; and the tradesman availing himself of railway speed could visit the warehouse of the manufacturer, or the counting-house of the merchant; obtain better articles at less expense, and contribute in a remarkable degree to develope the internal industry of the nation, no less than to excite a general spirit of enterprise.

The ordinary laxity of principle which ever distinguishes such epochs was displayed. Those who had property through which one line was to pass, were told that if they opposed the bill their compensation would be reduced to the lowest possible amount, but that if they petitioned for it, they would be liberally compensated. One gentleman was waited on at his private residence and offered £1,000 not to resist a particular bill. Nor were peers wanting in an ungenerous opposition. The estate of a nobleman was near a proposed line. He was proud of his park, and great was his resentment. In vain was it proved that the road would not come within six miles of his house, that the highway lay between, that a tunnel would hide the inelegance. He resisted all overture on the plea of his feelings, until £30,000 was offered. The route was, however, afterwards changed. A new line was marked out which would not even approach his domain; and, enraged at the prospect of losing the £30,000, he resisted it as strenuously as the other.

The projectors generally, however, were not allowed to proceed on their path rejoicingly. They met with the opposition they deserved. The political economist wrote essays to prove that railways would absorb too much of the national capital, and divert it from its more legitimate channels. The bondholders in turnpike roads petitioned that any deficiency in their profits should be paid out of railway receipts. The senator said the demand for labour would be so great as to raise wages and increase prices. The Blackwall railway was opposed because it crossed the road. The coach-owners petitioned against it because it would lessen their profits. Invention was brought to decry the railway when truth was insufficient. One company, it was said, could not proceed for want of money. Another was deeply in debt to the contractor. The Greenwich was often reported to have fallen in, and as often was it asserted that the whole property was seized under an execution. The country gentleman, it was added, required protection, and not the companies. The tunnelling of Shakespeare's cliff was objected to by the antiquarian as a desecration; but still the projector continued to project, and the public to purchase shares; the engineer continued to make profits, and directors continued to make premiums.

"A needy adventurer takes it into his head," wrote Mr. Herapath, "that a line of railway from the town A. to the town B. is a matter of great public utility, because out of it he may get a great private benefit. He procures an ordnance map and a directory. On the first he sketches out a line between the two towns, prettily curving here and there, and calls it a survey. The gazetteer, directory, and coachman supply him with a statement of revenue, which never fails to be less than fifteen or thirty per cent. He inveigles a secretary with a few hundred pounds, and induces a solicitor out of practice to join him."

The tricks were as ingenious, if not so plentiful, as at a later period; and innumerable inventions of artful knaves disgraced the supporters, many of whom were men of substance. When it became necessary to have a subscription to the amount of half the estimates, any or everybody was asked to sign who came in the way. The managing directors told the secretaries to apply to any person they thought proper; and one man, enjoying a salary of £60, signed for £35,000; while a second signed it who neither knew nor cared what it bound him to do. By one railway, signatures were procured at ten shillings a-head. The Deptford and Dover contract was signed at four shillings each. A third, being deficient £80,000 of the subscriptions necessary to complete the standing orders, borrowed the amount, and paid it in on account of the company.

In another which obtained an Act of parliament, only £235 was subscribed; and not one of the directors had paid a single shilling on the shares which qualified them for their seats at the board.

The Clarence railway required £200,000, and the sum was procured. The directors found it necessary to borrow £190,000 more, the entire expense being £380,000 for a work which yielded £2,500 a year, or about fifteen shillings per cent.

Another difficulty which beset railroads was the parliamentary contests. In one case £100,000 was spent without any result. In a second, six counsel and twenty solicitors were employed at an expense of £57,000. In a third, where five competing lines obtained, the committee, after being occupied the whole of one session and one month of the succeeding, at an expense of hundreds of thousands, in despair of coming to a just conclusion with evidence which was very conflicting, referred the whole to a military engineer.

The large demands of landowners and leaseholders was another source of trouble. In one instance the removal of a line a very short distance would enable the company to avoid a tunnel, at the expense of £50,000. "Give us," it was said, "the price of that tunnel, and we will withdraw our opposition." Thirty thousand pounds was the reward of this cunning. Hundreds were constantly awarded where thousands were demanded. A man who claimed £8,000 absolutely accepted £80; and it was forcibly said that no other term than plunderer was due to him who asked whatever he chose, but took whatever he could get.

In the four years which elapsed from 1832 to 1836, about 450 miles of railway were completed, and 350 miles were in progress. The demand for engineers skilled in the iron way was difficult to supply. Great works fell necessarily under the superintendence of persons deficient in the required knowledge. Fantastic novelties were consequently adopted. The rashness of ignorance was often displayed in attempting notoriety. Endeavours to improve were often more fatal than favourable; and the consequence was felt in large calls, heavy loans, and small dividends. The prices and prospects of railways in 1837 may be judged from the fact already stated in this history, that the London and South-Western, with £40 paid up, was then at a discount of £27, and to raise money was compelled to create shares at fifty per cent. discount. The cheques of the Great Western were returned. In the Bristol and Exeter, when £10 was paid, premiums were offered with the shares to any one who would accept them; the London and Birmingham were more than once at a discount, and one line which afterwards reached £50 premium, was for three years giving away on the stock-exchange. The government in the meantime were singularly supine. The various bills were laboriously contested by promoters and opposers, and the necessary consequence was litigation, extortion, jobbing, bribery, and extravagance, disgraceful in principle and deplorable in practice.

The time of reaction was at hand. Money became scarce; the eyes of the people were open to their folly; and shares of every description fell. Then came that terrible revulsion, when ruin visits the social board, and sorrow desolates the domestic hearth. Men who had lifted their heads in the pride of presumed riches, mourned their recklessness, and women wept that which they could not prevent.

In the city the panic was great. The rate of discount was raised to five per cent. The interest was increased on exchequer bills from three-halfpence to two-pence-halfpenny a day; but they fell to ten per cent. discount. The banking-house of Esdaile & Co.

stopped payment. Consols fell four per cent., and mercantile commodities forty. Merchants with high characters, and worth more than twenty shillings in the pound, could neither sell the goods which loaded their warehouses, or discount the bills which filled their strong-box. But the misery was felt all over England. Distress and suffering in their worst and most protracted forms spread throughout the provinces. The greatest houses were brought to the brink of ruin; others sunk beneath the struggle. The manufacturer found his produce depreciated one-half. The receipts of the custom-house sunk nearly one million in a single quarter. Half the cotton mills of the country were shut up. The skilled artisan and operative were distressed to an unprecedented degree. In Manchester and its vicinity, 50,000 hands were unemployed for six months. At Paisley and its neighbourhood 20,000 workmen were idle. At Glasgow nearly half the labouring classes were starving, and thousands were only kept alive by bounty and benevolence. If these facts are painful to record, how much more painful must they have been to the class whose sufferings are recorded?

The more important cities of England were not behind the metropolis; and York, with its neighbourhood, witnessed an equally undisciplined spirit. It need not be said that in the latter Mr. Hudson was the presiding genius. The inhabitants of Scarborough and Bridlington also attempted a railway; but failed. They of Whitby and Pickering succeeded. Mr. Cundy and Mr. Gibbs endeavoured to form a line between York and London, but both Mr. Cundy and Mr. Gibbs proved unsuccessful. The inhabitants of the former regarded the movements with anxious interest; and as a communication with the capital was very desirable, made attempts which at first produced more meetings than money.

In 1835, Mr. Stephenson projected a railway from Leeds to Derby; and from Derby a further line was proposed to Rugby, by which a railway route would be obtained from Leeds to London.

The citizens of York, with Mr. Hudson at their head, projected and formed another line, which, called the York and North-Midland Company, gave a railway route to London from York; and so energetic were the directors, that in 1839, York

was united with Milford, amidst great rejoicings.
The rise and progress of Mr. Hudson is so inti-
mately connected with the railways of the north, and
his public career belongs so thoroughly to a later
period, that it is unnecessary at present to allude
to this interesting portion of railway history more particularly than to indicate that he was laying the
foundation of that name and fortune, which, for
good or for ill, produced so marked an effect in
succeeding years.

[NOTE]. The panic of which record has just been
made, procured an inquiry into the law of limited
responsibility. This most important commercial subject was reported on with great skill ; and the opinions
expressed by various members of the interest it
affects, are briefly given, because it is a question
which is gaining great consideration, and because

it has been deemed by competent authorities, very uncertain whether England would have suffered so severely or so frequently from such excitements as those
of 1825, 1836, and 1845, under a different system.
In France the law of partnership, " *en commandité*,"
exists, enabling the master and his assistants to
work together. The former often gives the latter
small shares in the business, knowing that, while
there is no risk to himself, he secures the earnest
though selfish assistance of his subordinates. Habits
of thrift and temperance are thus encouraged; a
system of kindly co-operation is insured; and the
moral effect is ever found to be gratifying. In
New York any person may contribute any sum
without risking the remainder of his fortune; being
responsible only to the amount he has jeopardised.
In Ireland a similar partnership Act also existed,
under the title of " An Act to promote trade and
manufacture, by regulating and encouraging partnerships," by which it was arranged that " anonymous
partners should not be subject to bankrupt laws,
or to any greater loss than the amount of their
subscriptions." In our own colony of the Mau-
ritius also, the same law is in being, and is found

to work well, and to the contentment of all. The chief objections arrayed against this custom are,

1. That it would give rise to fraud.

2. That it would lead to overtrading.

3. That it is not required in this country, where capital is readily found for every profitable under-taking, and credit for all who deserve it.

The opinions of commercial men differed on the topic. Mr. Thomas Tooke allowed that the diffi-culties of the present system constituted a serious evil; but that "the leaning of his opinion was on the whole against the expediency of introducing the law of *commandité* into this country."

Mr. George Warde Norman "was disposed to take the affirmative side."

Mr. Samuel Jones Loyd thought the present state of the law of partnership very imperfect, and believed also that in the peculiar condition of this country "the advantages of the *commandité* system would be less and the evils greater, than in most other countries."

It is a vexed question, into which it is difficult calmly to enter. But it is one which affects our large middle class very seriously; and there are various evils it would alleviate. It would encourage a legitimate spirit of commercial enterprise; it would enable a man to lend a portion of his savings without risking all. And more than this, and that which, perhaps, is more pertinent to the present work, is the fact that it would empower every man in England to subscribe a small amount of his capital in sound co-operative or joint-stock speculations, without the constant dread of confiscating every penny of which he is possessed. It has been seen that the railway and other companies of 1836 bore terrible witness to the destruction which the absence of limited partnership occasions. It was given in evidence that where a man of substance was morally only responsible for a few hundreds, he was glad to give thousands to another person to take from him the risk he had legally incurred. It was the fear of this law which both then and at a future period led the public to act in so fraudulent a manner. It was this law which induced gentlemen to write in other persons' names, with other persons' signatures. It was this law which produced applications for shares in the names of minors; it was this which made clergymen responsible for amounts they were not capable of paying; which made the annuitant part from his annuity, and which produced most of those serious evils that ever result from speculative excitements, and the feverish alarm which follows them. Whether the abrogation of the present system, and the introduction of a new law of limited partnership into this country would be beneficial to commerce, is doubtful; but that it would mitigate the evils which flow from the present plan of railway and other Joint Stock companies—previous to their incorporation—cannot admit of a moment's doubt.

The opinions in favour of the law of limited partnership were as follows :—

Lord Ashburton thought it would bring additional capital into commerce.

Mr. Norman believed that the unequal distribution of capital in this country required it.

Mr. Senior asserted that it would cause much capital to be judiciously employed.

Mr. Bothamley believed it would induce respectable persons to join Joint Stock companies.

Mr. Duncan, who, perhaps, has been more extensively engaged in these companies than any other person, stated his strong impression that "Joint Stock companies *never would be respectable generally, or respected,* until the law was altered to allow companies to be formed of the nature of the *commandité* and *anonyme* partnership in France."

END OF VOL. I.

A HISTORY

OF THE

ENGLISH RAILWAY.

A HISTORY

OF THE

ENGLISH RAILWAY;

ITS SOCIAL RELATIONS AND REVELATIONS.

1820—1845.

BY JOHN FRANCIS;

AUTHOR OF "THE HISTORY OF THE BANK OF ENGLAND; ITS TIMES AND TRADITIONS;" AND
"CHRONICLES AND CHARACTERS OF THE STOCK EXCHANGE."

VOL. II.

LONDON:
LONGMAN, BROWN, GREEN, & LONGMANS.

MDCCCLI.

CONTENTS OF VOL. II.

viii   CONTENTS.

HISTORY

ENGLISH RAILWAY.

CHAPTER I.

ALTERATION OF THE LAW WITH REGARD TO RAILWAY DEPOSITS.—ITS EF-
FECT.—PERSONAL SKETCH OF MR. GLYN.— BLUE BOOKS OF 1840.—MR.
HUMPHERY AND THE LONDON AND BLACKWALL RAILWAY.—VIRTUOUS IN-
DIGNATION OF PROPRIETORS.—CHARGES AND COUNTER-CHARGES.—TRIUM-
PHANT DEFENCE OF MR. HUMPHERY.—ATTEMPT TO LEGISLATE.—LORD
SEYMOUR'S BILL AND ITS ENACTMENTS.—LIST OF RAILWAYS.—PROGRESS OF
THE COUNTRY.

ONE circumstance which had increased the number
of companies in 1836, was the law with regard to
deposits, which pressing heavily on honest speculations, was valueless against those of a fraudulent
character. The examination of a committee of the
House of Commons in 1837 into railway ras-
calities was searching and successful. Previous to

the inquiry, as no deposit was required, it was in-incumbent on promoters to prove a *bonâ fide* sub-scription, and this gave rise to expensive contests. To prevent these it was ordered that one-tenth portion of the amount of capital should be de-posited with government authorities, and that the period of notice for any new line should be ex-tended from one to two years. These regulations proved at first very effective. No new railway was asked for in 1838, and the ten per cent. was sup-posed to act beneficially. Nor is there any doubt that it prevented many from joining projects which bound them to so large a payment. "Before the new law," said one, "it was astonishing what a number of ladies and clergymen signed bubble sub-scription lists, and classes of persons who could not, from their want of knowledge of the world, be on their guard against fraud, or gambling specu-lations in these matters. A large proportion were, indeed, at one time, women, and other classes who, from their designation and residence, were evidently persons unable to judge of the probability of a company being remunerative."

The effect of this large deposit will be found in

the proceedings of 1844 and 1845. It must ever
be difficult to prevent that speculative tendency
which, in spite of legislative enactment and Bank
Charter acts, breaks forth in proportion to the calm
which has preceded it; and it is only by an examination of similar periods, and a comparison of
the past with the present, that any benefit can be
gained or any conclusion deduced.

The year 1837, which witnessed the accession of
Mr. Glyn to the chairmanship of the London and
Birmingham Railway company, appears the proper
period to introduce one of the most important actors
in the railway drama.

Foreseeing at an early period the importance of the
discovery; joining it at a time when most men regarded it suspiciously; giving it the sanction of a
house high in the world of banking; the name of
George Carr Glyn stood prominently forward in
that interest of which, at a later and more remarkable period, he was the chief moral aid and
ally; and there was probably no other man throughout broad England better adapted to champion the
power whose interests he advocated.

When Mr. Solly, the first chairman of the London

and Birmingham, left his important position, Mr. Glyn was naturally regarded as his successor, and fortunate was it for the shareholders that he accepted the trust. It must be remembered that when this gentleman first joined the railway world it was entirely new ; that its promoters had to deal with elements which baffled all their calculations ; that one estimate was falsified by a freak of nature ; that another was upset by an interested combination ; that everything was strange, and everything untried. The result was that the directors were generally at fault. They were very good governors of a dock corporation, and they were capital managers of an assurance company ; but they too often made the mistake of thinking that railways required a new mode of business. Mr. Glyn himself —and no one appreciates his peculiar capacity more than the writer—was no heaven-born director any more than he was a heaven-born banker ; he only, when others sought to apply novel principles to the novel power, applied the ordinary rules of business to the railway, and was rewarded by success. In the early portion of its history he was its dexterous chief ; in the later part of its career he was its determined safeguard. When ten per cent. was its current dividend; when a price of 250 was paid for its stock; and when shareholders waxed presumptuous, he checked their presumption.* When the dark hour was on railway property, he stimulated hope and soothed depression. When balance-sheets were menacingly demanded; when accounts were examined with audacious eagerness; when men watched his look as he entered the room, and hung on his words as the words of their oracle, he met that mixed tumultuous throng with a countenance as decided and a brow as unruffled as when he had delighted their willing ears with premiums and amalgamations.

The proper place to see Mr. Glyn, is as chair-

---

* It has been a principle with the directors never to conceal anything from their proprietors; and it is right, therefore, that in these early days I should make you acquainted with my own individual feelings on this point. It will, of course, be some time before this new capital can be brought into operation; and it is impossible, looking at the skill, the enterprise, and the industry of this country, to say what may not in the interim take place. Many of my colleagues are sanguine in their hope that even with the great increase which we propose to-day, we may be able to keep up the present dividend. *This, I repeat, is not my opinion.—Speech of Mr. Glyn.*

It is worthy of remark that with a most gigantic system of gambling around him, and with every opportunity of creating a colossal fortune in his power, Mr. Glyn has yet scrupulously abstained from the Stock Exchange, and upon principle avoided the share market.

man in that noble room, where, with an earnest multitude around him, with the representative of every class and caste before him, with Jew and Gentile ready to carp at and criticise his statements, he yet moves them at his pleasure and leads them at his will. And perhaps the ascendancy of one man over many is seldom more agreeably seen than when, standing before a huge expectant audience, he enlivens the platitude of one with some light epigrammatic touch, answers another with a clear tabular statement, or replies to a third with some fallacy so like a fact that the recipient sits contentedly down, about as wise as he was before. Whether Mr. Glyn was denying the assertion of a marquis,* or repudiating all interference by the

---

* I allude particularly to a declaration made some time back in the House of Lords by Lord Clanricarde; and I must say that it seems strange, if charges are to be preferred, common courtesy is not extended towards public companies, that they may have an opportunity of having a defence ready. . . . Lord Clanricarde said that it would be a singular inquiry how far the London and Birmingham Company had carried out their pledge to the public, and whether they had not, for the sake of increasing their dividend, added very much to their charges. . . . Lord Clanricarde and other members of the legislature may say that ten per cent. is too high a dividend; it is, however, the dividend uniformly fixed in the acts of parliament, and I would appeal to any one whether, considering the great experiment which we undertook and the chances of failure which we ran, the return which we now have is, in point of fact, anything more than a fair one.—*Speech of Mr. Glyn.*

state,* whether he was exposing the injustice of a government tax,† or denouncing the iniquity of parish rates,‡ he was ever firm in maintaining the interests of his great corporation; and the only drawback to the thorough enjoyment of this gentleman when thus employed, is the remembrance that there is a wear and tear upon his intelligent brain which no personal gratification can counteract, and a demand upon his physical power which only repose can satisfy. Such, the writer believes, is the true character of Mr. Glyn in con-

* A question of paramount importance, not only to this company but to all railways,— I allude to the special meeting on the Audit bill then before parliament. The almost unanimous vote which that meeting arrived at, expressive as it was of the strong opposition to the proposed measure of the government, had, I am certain, a very great effect in what subsequently took place with respect to that bill. . . . I can speak confidently upon the part of those who attended the meetings most diligently that they had but one object in view, that object being to defeat the measure of the government which would take from you that which, at your special meetings here, you said you would not surrender.—*Speech of Mr. Glyn.*

† There was another point upon which he would touch, which was of the highest importance to their interest; he meant the bill for the conveyance of mails on railways. Of all the monstrous measures he had ever read, the bill in question was the most striking.—*Ibid.*

‡ Then comes the last item of local taxes and parochial rates; these, gentlemen, we do take exception to. . . . The county assessors, and the parties to whom appeal from them is made, seem actuated by one principle; namely, to extract every farthing they can from the railway property. We ask no boon, we ask for no favour from government on this subject; but we do ask for justice.—*Ibid.*

nexion with railways; and with a brief *resumé* of his more private and personal career, the sketch will be concluded.

The banking-house of Mr. Glyn employs a greater number of clerks and does more business, especially with Railway balances, than any in the city. Mr. Glyn himself is no unfair representative of that large class to which he belongs, and among whom the directorates of all the chief companies are divided. Not only chairman of one extensive railway, but director also of a dock company, and active in the management of an insurance office, trusteeships, and commissionerships help to occupy his time, and render necessary all that personal and mental activity which his very look denotes. The son of a baronet, educated at Westminster, member of parliament for Kendal, and—if his constituents are grateful—the most popular man there, as the accent of the railway subordinates suggests—known as a liberal, an avowed and " decided free-trader ; " member of the club which, arising with reform, taught its opponents the importance of the men who composed it ; married to the daughter of that Pascoe Grenfell whose name was once a word of dread to bank directors, the father of future railway kings, and arrived at the mature age of fifty-three; these are the portions of Mr. Glyn's life which belong to the public, and such is Mr. Glyn himself, the chairman and the champion of the London and North-Western Railway.

The blue book of 1840, known as the "five reports on railway communication," excited much attention. In that volume the committee entered into every question which could affect the interest they examined; and the enquiries they made into the past were brought to bear on the present. When the railway was first sanctioned, it was scarcely understood; and, considering it in the light of a canal, the way was left open for all. To this the promoters not only consented, but declared it was not their wish, as it could not be their benefit, to convey passengers or goods, and that they were only anxious to be toll proprietors. The legislature had, therefore, enacted that any person might run his own trains by paying certain tolls. Owners and occupiers of adjoining lands also were empowered to make branch lines and have free access to the railway. Lords of manors and others might erect wharfs and use that portion of tramroads which went through their own lands, without paying for the privilege.

These powers were soon discovered to be more dangerous than desirable. Some private gentlemen saw no advantage in running a locomotive at the risk of life; others declined to place their capital where they had little controul; and it was soon found that if the tram were used like a turnpike road, accidents would be plentiful and passengers few. It was consequently recommended that this plan should be abolished, it being incidentally mentioned that the cost of providing locomotive power might be considered at the rate of a farthing per mile per passenger.

The next point was the tax on travelling which had caused much disapprobation. It has been stated, and the fact has been previously commented on, that in 1832, government with singular short-sightedness fixed the impost on railway travelling at one half-penny per mile for every four passengers, without reference to first, second, or third class carriages. It was found that the poor were, as usual, the chief sufferers; that the more railway communication extended, the worse it would be; and that while one great reason for enlarging it was to promote the "health and enjoyment of the mechanics, artisans, and poor inhabitants of the large towns," it absolutely negatived the object, and where it was felt the most, it benefited the revenue the least.

On a line of one hundred and twenty miles, where the first class was thirty, the second twenty, and the third ten shillings, the duty on each passenger was fifteen pence; thus pressing but slightly on the gentleman who travelled with a full purse and a light heart, but heavily on the operative who sought some new field for employment, and who in that sad speculation had, perhaps, pledged his furniture and embarked his all. In the one case it was nothing, in the other it was everything.

Some curious information was elicited on the advantage of the railroad to the weavers in the neighbourhood of Manchester; and the amelioration of the troubles of this intelligent class was at once a gratification and a proof of the inequality of the tax. Before the railway was formed, one day in six was spent in procuring and in carrying back their work. When the trains enabled them to ride, they walked four miles to the station with their twenty-eight pounds of work, travelled by the third-class, and, unable to pay for another ride, walked back the whole of the way with the silk or cotton which was to occupy their next weeks' labour. They then combined: three of them gave their goods to one who, riding to Manchester and back, saved both money and time. But railway managers are political economists; and they stopped this for a period by allowing one person to carry only one pack. The weavers were indignant; and sooner than submit to what they termed very harsh, and which certainly was very hard, they walked the whole way as before. The feeling spread very wide; the defection of third-class passengers was great; and the directors, compelled to make a virtue of necessity, returned to their old regulations. If the grievance of railway taxation was great for the proprietors, the reader may judge how great it must have been for such passengers as these. While the rich man travelling in the first-class train for pleasure paid to the state three and a-half per cent. upon his fare, the poor man hurrying on the business which supported his household, paid twelve and a-half. It will be seen that such evidence was not ineffective when placed before the senate.

The increase in the duty on railway passengers was curious. In 1835 it amounted to £6,852, in 1836 it reached £8,693, in 1837 it was £10,296, while in 1838 it was £16,892. In 1839 again, a rapid stride was perceptible, the sum received being £39,570, while in 1840 it reached £72,716.

The first specimen of public quarrel between railway proprietors occurred in 1841, and demands, therefore, to be briefly recorded. In July of that year it was whispered in railway circles that a great discovery had been made; and a paragraph appeared in the newspapers that a director of the London and Blackwall railway company had been guilty of jobbing to a large extent in its shares. The virtue of the public was aroused, the indignation of share-holders excited, and reports were numerous. Thousands of shares were said to have been jobbed; thousands of pounds were said to have been made; the character of the company was declared to be ruined, the value of the property reduced, and Mr. Humphery, as senator and as citizen, was boldly impeached; while, as a public and party man, " he paid the penalty of being great," in the assertions which prevailed and the stories which were invented.

A general meeting of the company—convened for other purposes—was held about this time; the subject was mooted, and a fierce and fiery attack made on the worthy alderman. The chairman acknowledged that one of their body had sold shares he did not possess; that a meeting of the board had been called; and that the resignation of Mr. alderman Humphery was the consequence; kindly adding, "to what extent the interests of the proprietors had been affected by it, was impossible to say."

The invective of the proprietary was amusing. "Mr. alderman Humphery, as a director, has abandoned his trust," said one of them, with praiseworthy indignation; "he has been guilty of trafficking in shares with the view of depreciating the profits of his constituents. I have not words to express my contempt for such conduct." He was unworthy to be director of a railway company, a member of Parliament, or an alderman. Mr. Salomons followed in the same strain; a torrent of truisms was poured forth by others; resolutions were proposed; discussions were entered into; charges were made; Mr. Humphery was abused for not attending a meeting he had no right to attend, and the shareholders retired, righteously thankful they were not as this alderman.

They had condemned without hearing. Statements and counter-statements passed between the contending parties. Mr. Humphery said he had been attacked by Mr. Rennie at the instigation of a director, because he had resisted a job, and opposed by Mr. Salomons because they were antagonistic in the city. The directors took refuge in their dignity, and came to the "unanimous determination not to enter into any controversy with that gentleman." Mr. Humphery, at the next general meeting proved that the number of shares in which he had "trafficked" was only one hundred, and carried the war into the enemy's camp with a vigour which astonished them. He said that they confiscated the shares of private proprietors for being, like Mr. Salomons and other directors, in arrears with their calls; that great loss had been experienced from not attending to his advice; that he had sold openly and honourably, fairly adding, that if it had proved injurious to the interests of the company, he would be glad to repair it.

The accusation thus reduced to its true proportions was abandoned, the directors fell back upon principle, the accusers withdrew the charge, and it is curious to look back to a period when the time bargain of a railway director, to the extent of one hundred shares, created so great an effect, and when the interests of a railway company were so keenly looked after as they were in 1841. That which Mr. alderman Humphery did was no impeachment of his honour, no taint upon his integrity ; he had done only as hundreds had done before, and as thousands after him ; and if it involved his discretion, it involved far more the wisdom of those who at a public meeting accused a public man of dishonourable practices, without being able to substantiate their charge.

A further legislative enactment was made in 1840, the speeches concerning which were only worthy notice, that, while Mr. Muntz, a name now well known in railway records, thanked heaven he never had possessed, nor did he ever mean to possess, a share in any line ; in another the important fact was elicited that railroads were of no service to his grace of Wellington, as he was obliged to maintain a stage coach at his own expence. The measure introduced, now generally known as Lord Seymour's bill, was entitled " An Act for Regulating Railroads," and demands special notice, because it first placed in the hands of the board of trade a certain power which has increased with the increase of railways, and which by a constant supervision and by suggestions which emanate from an unprejudiced body, have been and are likely to be of no little service. The following are the clauses chiefly worthy of notice :—

The board of trade to be at liberty to authorise any person or persons to inspect any railway, and at all reasonable times to enter upon and examine the said railway stations, works, carriages, &c. ; no person to be eligible to such appointment who within one year should have been a director, or have held any office of trust or profit under any railway company.

All bye laws of all companies to be placed before the board for inspection.

Persons obstructing railways or endangering the safety of passengers, guilty of a misdemeanor and liable to imprisonment for two years.

The general progress of railways in England from

1825 to 1840 was by no means unimportant. They
had become the recognised mode of locomotion.
Although the excitement of 1836 had been followed
by a natural calm, yet it had sufficed to give them
an impetus which could not easily pass away. By
the following list it is evident that by 1840 nearly
every important district might be reached by the
new mode of travel ; that a large capital was
invested ; that year after year witnessed an increased
number of Acts; and it was generally understood
that the stagnation which was then evident in the
railway world was not likely to endure. It will
be seen that the state recognised the railways as a
power to minister to its necessities, and was as eager
to claim its services, as it was willing to influence
its destinies. The struggle of the legislature with
new interests is always note-worthy. Leaving them
to rise or fall according to their natural buoyancy,
never venturing to acknowledge them, for fear recog-
nition should be construed into assistance, it waits
till they have acquired sufficient strength to bear
an impost or to yield a benefit.

The following important list of railways for which
Acts had been granted between 1826 and 1840, will

account for the difficulty which the claims of government experienced when those claims were deemed unjust or impolitic :—

1826. The Heck Bridge and Wentbridge railway, for the conveyance of stone in the West Riding of Yorkshire, from Snaith to Kirksmeaton. Distance seven and a-half miles. Capital £21,700.

1826. Ballochney railway, for coal, iron, stone, and passengers, from Arbuckle to Kippbyres. Distance four and a-half miles. Capital £93,333.

1826. Liverpool and Manchester railway, for general traffic. Distance thirty-one miles. Capital £1,832,375.

1826. Edinburgh and Dalkeith railway, for coal, merchandise, and passengers. Distance fifteen miles. Capital £208,753.

1826. Manchester and Oldham railway. Capital £95,000.

1826. Hereford railway, for coal, corn, &c. Distance twelve and a quarter miles. Capital £35,000.

1826. Dundee and Newtyle railway, for passengers and general merchandise. Distance ten and a-half miles. Capital £170,000.

1826. Dulais railway; for minerals, &c. Distance eight and three-quarter miles. Capital £14,000.

1826. Garnkirk and Glasgow railway; for coal and passengers. Distance eight and a-quarter miles. Capital £169,195.

1826. Limerick and Waterford railway. Capital £600,000.

1827. Johnstone and Ardrossan railway; for coal, passengers, &c. Distance twenty-two and a-half miles. Capital £106,666.

1828. Clarence railway; for coal, passengers, &c. Distance thirty-six miles. Capital £500,000.

1828. Llanelly railway; for coal and other minerals. Distance twenty-six miles. Capital £270,000.

1828. Bridgend railway; for minerals. Distance four and a-half miles. Capital £10,000.

1828. Bristol and Gloucestershire railway; for coal, stone, &c. Distance nine miles. Capital £77,000.

1828. Avon and Gloucestershire Railway, to connect quarries and collieries with the Avon. Distance four and a-half miles. Capital, £31,000.

1829. Kenyon and Leigh junction railway. Distance two and a-half miles. Capital, £46,000

1829. Warrington and Newton railway for passengers and general traffic. Distance four and a-quarter miles. Capital £93,000.

1829. Newcastle and Carlisle railway, for passengers and general traffic. Distance sixty-one miles. Capital £950,000.

1829. Wishaw and Coltness railway, for minerals, &c. Distance thirteen miles. Capital £160,000.

1829. Saundersfoot railway for coal, &c. Capital £25,500.

1830. Wigan Branch railway for passengers and general traffic. Distance seven miles. Capital £87,500.

1830. Leicester and Swannington railway, for coal, lime, and passengers, &c. Length sixteen miles. Capital £175,000.

1830. Leeds and Selby railway, for passengers and general traffic. Distance twenty miles. Capital £340,000.

1830. St. Helens and Runcorn Gap railway, for coal and passengers. Distance twelve miles. Capital £220,000.

1830. Polloc and Govan railway, for the conveyance of coal. Capital £66,000.

1831. Preston and Wigan railway, for passengers

and general traffic. Distance fifteen and a-half miles. Capital £333,000.

1831. Rutherglen railway, for coal. Capital £20,000.

1831. Sheffield and Manchester railway. Capital £706,000.

1831. Manchester and Bolton railway, for passengers and general traffic. Distance ten miles. Capital £650,000.

1831. Dublin and Kingstown railway, for passengers and general traffic. Distance five miles. Capital £270,000.

1832. Belfast and Cavehill railway, for the conveyance of stone. Distance two miles. Capital £38,200.

1832. Bodmin and Wadebridge railway, for minerals, passengers, &c. Distance twelve miles. Capital £35,500.

1832. Festiniog railway, for the conveyance of slates. Distance thirteen and a-quarter miles. Capital £50,185.

1832. Hartlepool railway, chiefly for coal. Distance fifteen miles. Capital £492,000.

1832. Exeter and Crediton railway. Capital £47,000.

1833. Grand Junction railway, for passengers and general traffic. Distance eighty-two and a-half miles. Capital £1,957,800.

1833. Whitby and Pickering railway, for passengers and general traffic. Distance twenty-four miles. Capital £135,000.

1833. London and Birmingham railway, for passengers, and general traffic. Distance one hundred and twelve and a-half miles. Capital £5,500,000.

1833. London and Greenwich railway, chiefly for passengers. Distance three and three-quarter miles. Capital £993,000.

1833. Coleorton railway, for the conveyance of coal. Capital £31,000.

1834. Blaydon, Gateshead, and Hebburn railway. Capital £80,000.

1834. Durham Junction railway, chiefly for coal, passengers, &c. Capital £130,000.

1834. Hayle railway, for the conveyance of minerals. Distance twelve miles. Capital £80,000.

1834. London and Southampton railway, for passengers and general traffic. Distance seventy-six and three-quarter miles. Capital £1,860,000.

1834. Durham and Sunderland railway, chiefly for coal. Distance sixteen miles. Capital £256,000.

1835. London and Croydon railway, for passengers and general traffic. Distance eight and three-quarter miles. Capital £741,000.

1835. Slamannan railway, chiefly for minerals. Distance twelve and a-half miles. Capital £186,666.

1835. Preston and Wyre railway, for passengers and general traffic. Capital £400,000.

1835. Brandling Junction railway, for passengers, coal, &c. Distance fifteen and a-quarter miles. Capital £400,000.

1835. Newtyle and Coupar Angus railway, for passengers and general traffic. Distance five and a-quarter miles. Capital £40,200.

1835. Paisley and Renfrew railway, for passengers to steam-boats. Distance three and a-quarter miles. Capital £33,000.

1835. Newtyle and Glammis railway, for passengers and general traffic. Capital £26,600.

1835. Great Western railway, for passengers and general traffic. Distance one hundred and seventeen and a-half miles. Capital £4,999,999.

1836. Birmingham and Gloucester railway, for

passengers and general traffic. Distance forty-five miles. Capital £1,266,666.

1836. Dundee and Arbroath railway, for passengers and general traffic. Distance sixteen and three-quarter miles. Capital £140,000.

1836. Ulster railway, for passengers and general traffic. Distance thirty-six miles. Capital £800,000.

1836. Arbroath and Forfar railway, for passengers and general traffic. Distance fifteen and a-quarter miles. Capital £160,000.

1836. Birmingham and Derby Junction, for passengers and general traffic. Distance forty-eight and a-half miles. Capital £1,056,666.

1836. Bristol and Exeter railway, for passengers and general traffic. Distance seventy-five and a-half miles. Capital £2,000,000.

1836. Aylesbury railway, for passengers and general traffic. Distance seven miles. Capital £66,000.

1836. Deptford Pier Junction railway, for passengers. Distance seven hundred and eighty-three yards. Capital £120,000.

1836. South-Eastern railway, for passengers and general traffic. Distance sixty-six miles. Capital £1,850,000.

1836. Newcastle and North Shields railway, chiefly for passengers. Distance six and three-quarter miles. Capital £320,000.

1836. Cheltenham and Great Western Union railway, for passengers and general traffic. Distance forty-three and a half miles. Capital £1,000,000.

1836. Midland Counties railway, for passengers and general traffic. Distance fifty-seven miles. Capital £1,333,000.

1836. Birmingham, Bristol, and Thames Junction railway. Distance three miles. Capital £280,000.

1836. Hull and Selby railway, for passengers and general traffic. Distance thirty and three-quarter miles. Capital £533,333.

1836. York and North Midland railway, for passengers and general traffic. Distance twenty-three and a-half miles. Capital £446,666.

1836. Taff Vale railway, for minerals, merchandise, and passengers. Distance twenty-four and a-half miles. Capital £620,000.

1836. Northern and Eastern railway, for passengers and general traffic. Distance thirty miles. Capital £960,000.

1836. London Grand Junction railway. Distance two and a-half miles. Capital £800,000.

1836. Great North of England railway, for passengers and general traffic. Distance seventy-six miles. Capital £1,330,000.

1836. Eastern Counties railway, for passengers and general traffic. Distance one hundred and twenty-six miles. Capital £2,133,333.

1836. North Midland railway, for passengers and general traffic. Distance seventy-two and a-quarter miles. Capital £3,000,000.

1836. Thames Haven railway, for coal, merchandise, and passengers. Distance fifteen and a-half miles. Capital £600,000.

1836. Sheffield and Rotherham railway, for passengers and general traffic. Distance five and a-quarter miles. Capital £200,000.

1836. Manchester and Leeds railway, for passengers and general traffic. Distance fifty and a-half miles. Capital £2,599,000.

1836. Preston and Longridge railway, for the conveyance of Longridge stone, goods, &c. Distance seven miles. Capital £40,000.

1836. Commercial railway, for passengers and

general traffic. Distance three and a-half miles. Capital £800,000.

1836. Launceston and Victoria railway. Distance sixteen and three-quarter miles. Capital £220,000.

1836. Edinburgh, Leith, and Newhaven railway, for passengers, goods, &c. Distance two and a-quarter miles. Capital £140,000.

1836. Dublin and Drogheda railway, for passengers and general traffic. Distance thirty-two miles. Capital £600,000.

1837. Sheffield, Ashton, and Manchester railway, for passengers and general traffic. Distance forty miles. Capital £933,000.

1837. Lancaster and Preston Junction railway, for passengers and general traffic. Distance twenty and a-half miles. Capital £488,000.

1837. Chester and Crewe railway, for passengers and general traffic. Distance twenty and a-half miles. Capital £458,333.

1837. Manchester and Birmingham railway, for passengers and general traffic. Distance thirty-eight and a-half miles. Capital £2,800,000.

1837. Great North of England, Clarence, and

Hartlepool Junction railway. Distance seven and three-quarter miles. Capital £70,000.

1837. Dundalk Western railway, for passengers, &c. Distance twenty-four miles. Capital £132,000.

1837. Maryport and Carlisle railway, for passengers and general traffic. Distance twenty-eight miles. Capital £240,000.

1837. Great Leinster and Munster railway, for passengers and general traffic. Distance seventy-three and a-half miles. Capital £1,065,000.

1837. Chester and Birkenhead railway, for passengers and general traffic. Distance fourteen and a-half miles. Capital £499,999.

1837. Cork and Passage railway, for passengers. Distance six and a-quarter miles. Capital £266,000.

1837. Glasgow, Paisley, and Greenock railway, for passengers and general traffic. Distance twenty-two and a-half miles. Capital £533,333.

1837. Glasgow, Paisley, Kilmarnock, and Ayr railway, for passengers and general traffic. Distance forty miles. Capital £833,000.

1837. London and Brighton railway, for passengers and general traffic. Distance forty-one and a-half miles. Capital £2,400,000.

1837. Bolton and Preston railway, for passengers and general traffic. Distance fourteen and a-half miles. Capital £506,000.

1837. Bishop Auckland and Weardale railway, for coal, passengers, &c. Capital £96,000.

1838. Taw Vale railway, for passengers, merchandise, &c. Distance two and a-quarter miles. Capital £20,000.

1838. Edinburgh and Glasgow railway, for passengers and general traffic. Distance forty-six miles. Capital £1,200,000.

1839. Gosport branch railway, for passengers and general traffic. Distance fifteen and three-quarter miles. Capital £400,000.

1839. Bristol and Gloucester railway, for passengers and general traffic. Distance twenty-two miles. Capital £533,000.

1839. West Durham railway, chiefly for minerals. Distance five and a-half miles. Capital £45,230.

These claims on the capital of the empire had not been made without the power to meet them. There is no country in the world in which similar strides have been made in so short a space of time; and history fails to show any people who, having within half a century made such struggles for the welfare of the land at such a pecuniary sacrifice, have yet found in the end that their wealth more than kept pace with their endeavours. All that was required, or felt to be required, was an increased speed, and a greater power of carriage. For this efforts had been made; nor is it much to say that they were almost in keeping with the enlarged importance of England. Had the soil increased its supply instead of the manufactory, and had the capital of the country been invested in an augmented production of grain, the demand for rapid transit would not, probably, have been so great, and the railway movement which most of us have witnessed, would have been in the future. But the reverse was the case; and it was absolutely said in 1833, before a committee of the House of Commons, that in consequence of the landed gentlemen trusting to protection to procure a profit, the annual produce of the soil was falling off in quantity. But the mill and the manufactory had prospered. The astute genius of the people and the nature of the climate were both favourable to their development; and the property invested in the production of goods

for which England was literally the mart of the
world, was enormous and increasing. From 1820
to 1824, the average annual export of woollen goods
was 1,064,000 pieces; from 1835 to 1839, it was
1,429,000 pieces. The steam-power newly provided
in 1835, in the cotton districts of Lancashire, was
seventeen times greater than the entire steam power
in use at the beginning of the century. From 1835
to 1839, the number of persons employed in woollen
worsted factories only, increased by upwards of
15,000. Small towns sprung into importance, and
new ones were created; each of which required
a rapid communication with the capital, or with
a sea-port. Thus in Bradford, the population between 1801 and 1841 rose from 29,000 to 105,000.
In one year only, 700 new houses were added to
it. In the West Riding of Yorkshire, again—the
very heart of woollen manufactures—the population
augmented 104 per cent.

The increase of the manufacturing interest—and
it must be borne in mind most distinctly that to
this increase we owe the railway—was yet more
evident in cotton. In 1801 the official value of these
goods which were exported was seven millions; in

1840 it was seventy-three millions. For this the world was indebted to Arkwright, whose invention, when generally adopted, trebled the manufacture in fifteen years. The cotton trade alone furnished subsistence for about a million and a quarter persons, most of whom were dependent on the railway for their maintenance. The population of England progressed with great rapidity : while from 1770 to 1800, it had increased only twenty-seven per cent., from 1801 to 1831 it had augmented fifty-six per cent. In the first year of the present century the United Kingdom numbered 16,338,000 ; in 1841 it was 26,895,000. The revenue was equally progressive. The customs produced £255,000 in 1801, in 1841 it rose to £1,160,000. In the corresponding years the excise increased from £435,000 to £784,000. In 1800 taxation produced thirty-four millions; in 1841 forty-eight millions were levied. The personal property of the kingdom was estimated to have risen from £1,200,000,000 to £2,000,000,000, being an augmentation of 800 millions from 1814 to 1841. The yearly value of the land also may be assumed to have increased, as that which was assessed in 1841, exceeded by nineteen millions that which was assessed in 1815, and the value of property in the form of rent from the soil, had doubled between 1790-1840.

Our shipping was not behind-hand. In 1802, 10,803 vessels only were cleared for foreign markets; in 1841 the number had increased to 28,250, and it must not be forgotten that few of these left the port from whence they sailed without carrying some article which had been expedited by the rail or delayed for the want of it. And when this truth is remembered, and it is further borne in mind that the entire exports of the empire, which in 1801 amounted only to £24,927,684, reached £102,180,517 in 1841, and that these amounts represented interests which were influenced more or less by locomotion—the vast increase of this power will not be wondered at. It would have been more surprising had it failed. Such interests as these were not to be sacrificed for a feeling or abandoned for a fancy.

Up to 1840, therefore, it is clear that England had only embarked a proper amount in a sound and safe investment, which, though it might not immediately pay the expected dividend, contributed to the comfort and increased the capital of the country.

CHAPTER II.

NEW RAILWAY BILL.—OBJECTIONS TO IT.—OPINIONS OF MEMBERS.—LEGIS-
LATION FOR THE SUNDAY.—OPPOSITION TO IT.—REPORTS ON THE PAS-
SENGER TAX.—OBJECTIONS TO IT.—ITS ALTERATION.—RISE AND PROGRESS
OF THE RAILWAY CLEARING HOUSE.—OPPOSITION TO IT.—SUPPORTED BY
MR. GLYN.—ITS ULTIMATE SUCCESS.

In 1842 the legislature again interfered with railways, a bill being introduced by Mr. Gladstone which,
backed by ministerial power and ministerial majorities,
was eventually carried. In introducing the measure,
Mr. Gladstone remarked that the functions of the
board of trade having operated with success, it would
be unnecessary to give the executive any extraordinary control. The experience of the past year
justified this; and although Colonel Sibthorp, thinking the public had received no advantages from
railways, did not agree with Mr. Gladstone, the latter

remained unchanged in his opinion. As to licensing engine-drivers, no such provision would be proposed, it being better for public opinion to act upon railway directors. By the proposed bill there would be a more efficient inspection of new lines before they were opened, and there would be the power of postponing the opening. The board of trade would also have authority to obtain returns connected with railway accidents. Various minor topics were broached to which the reader's attention will not be called, the only other provision of importance being that which provided a punishment for the misconduct of those employed on railways.

It need not be said that a warm discussion ensued. Colonel Sibthorp said he would have been greatly pleased if the right honourable gentleman had brought in a bill to annihilate railways altogether. The present measure was a milk-and-water measure; he, if no one else would do so, would apply for the return of killed and wounded on railways, which ought to be under government controul. The state ought to tax them, and thus make them of some use to the public revenue; for when they relinquished the old modes of travelling, they adopted a system which constantly placed the lives of the people in jeopardy. This remarkable gentleman, after commenting in a similar strain on the great injury done to that most respectable class of persons, the proprietors of stage-coaches and the owners of inns, concluded by expressing his determination to oppose the bill—a bill which at least ameliorated the evils of the rail he detested—in all its stages.

Mr. Wakley considered the measure was not stringent enough. He thought the controul of railways ought to be given to government; and, in humble imitation of Sidney Smith, added, that if three or four lords or members of parliament were killed, something more would be done. He then diverted himself with a general tirade against Whig measures and Whig ministers; and concluded by alluding to an accident on the Great Western, which he attributed to the managers of that line.

Sir Robert Peel said—and the speech is given entire, because, on a topic which yet engrosses much attention, the opinions of such a man should be placed on record :

" I think, considering the nature of such establishments as railways—establishments conducted by

large companies with great capital, and superseding,
to some considerable extent, other modes of travelling
—if the legislature think right to interfere, to see that
proper precautions are taken to prevent the occurrence
of accidents, they would be perfectly justified in doing
so; and I am sure that there is no influence of
the railway proprietors in this House which could
stand for a moment against the sense and justice
of applying a remedy the moment the necessity
was proved to exist. Indeed, I have reason to doubt
very much whether all the railway companies and
railway proprietors in the country would have the
power to prevent parliament from adopting any
effectual regulations they thought fit the moment
it was shown that these regulations had a tendency
to prevent accidents. But, whilst I admit the power
and right of parliament to interfere, nobody can
deprecate more than I do the interference of parliament carried beyond proper limits. I am sure that
such interference would not tend to the security of
the public, and that it would be impossible for
the parliament, or the government, or any department of the government, to undertake too minute
an interference; or that, if they did undertake it,

it would be productive of any great increase of security. In the first place, it is the interest of the railway companies to do all in their power to prevent accidents. Whenever accidents occur, a diminution of railway travelling is the consequence, from the preference consequently given to other modes of travelling. Before any gentleman forms his opinion on this point, I would recommend him to read the evidence given last year upon this subject. That evidence is very interesting in itself, and will show that to undertake an interference of the kind suggested would only lessen the responsibility of the railway directors, and would not increase the public security. With respect to the suggestion that a certain interval should exist between the railway carriage and the engine, I think that any interference of the kind would tend rather to increase the risk than to diminish it. The railway companies would be glad to shelter themselves under the responsibility of the government. They would say that these regulations were forced on them by the government, and they would, in consequence of the government interference, be released from the responsibility which would otherwise attach to them. It seems to me,

that if you interfere by legislation, you take some
of the responsibility from the railway companies, and
assume it yourselves. All the evidence is perfectly
conclusive, that any attempt to regulate the speed
at which the train was to travel, would be beyond the
authority of the government to effect; and so far as
the safety of persons is concerned, by such interference it would rather be lessened than increased."

During the progress of this important measure
through the House, various amendments were proposed. Many of the companies petitioned, but in
vain; as the board of trade declined to admit any
amendment which could possibly affect the safety
of the public. "And," said the *Railway Times*,
"so far as we can make out from the extremely
ill-worded memorial, what it is that is asked for,
we think the answer of the board of trade a most
proper one."

A committee of the various companies was employed to watch the progress of the bill, which in
committee received much attention. One member—
Mr. Howard—objected to a clause which required
a policeman at every gate along a line, because the
police would have nothing to do but fall asleep

or get drunk. Another gentleman proposed an amendment to diminish danger, which every practical person declared would increase it. A third senator made it his especial business to inquire whether proper care was taken of her most gracious Majesty's person when she travelled ; while others were disposed to enter into the most minute particulars, and legislate for the fastening to a door or the opening of a window.

The unhappy accident on the Versailles line greatly occupied public attention, and it was the desire of many members to make it imperative on companies not to lock the door.

The debate was· enlivened when Mr. Phillips proposed a test to discover public opinion on the subject, by Mr. Escott suggesting that the honourable member was scarcely an impartial witness, inasmuch, if he were upset and the door were locked, he was too large to get out of the window. Mr. Phillips retorted that once when in that unfortunate position with two gentlemen of the size of Mr. Escott, they attempted to get out together, but could not get out at all.

Sir Robert Peel said, if it were necessary to legislate

thus minutely, the next casualty which occurred would be met by a bill to prevent accidents altogether; and that if there were any old ladies or ecclesiastics afraid of being locked up, the railway directors would settle it with them.

An amendment was also proposed by Mr. Plumptre, a representative of the class that

> Compounds for sins which they are blind to,
> By damning those they have no mind to.

The alteration was to the effect that "no railway shall be used on any part of the Lord's day," and a considerable agitation was got up by those who recognised Mr. Plumptre as their champion, and Sir Andrew Agnew as their saint. The Versailles accident was a great assistance to them. It was made use of to frighten the recusant, and stimulate the lukewarm. One gentleman, by courtesy termed reverend, called all railway excursions on Sunday, "trips to hell, at seven shillings and sixpence per head." Awful denunciations were uttered on the sin of enjoying the Sabbath. Hand-bills, of which the following is a copy, disgraceful to the cause they were meant to serve, and disreputable to those who circulated them, were sent about the streets, and thrust into the wayfarers' hands :—

" Solemn warning for Sabbath-breakers ! God coming in judgment ! !" so ran this Christian document, " as revealed by the sudden destruction of nearly one hundred immortal beings on the Paris and Versailles railway, on Sabbath the 8th instant ; and also in the destruction by fire of the Sabbath-breaking town of Hamburgh !"

Such things as these are difficult to treat with temper. It is a great error to confound the Jewish with the Christian Sabbath. They who lived nearest to the time of Christ made no such mistake. The apostles did not enjoin their followers to refrain from labour. Peter is considered to have worked at his tents on a Sunday. During the first three centuries it was not regarded as a Sabbath ; and the initiative step was only taken in the fourth by the half pagan Constantine closing the courts of law—meant, probably, as a relaxation for the higher order of labour—as the peasant and artisan were still seen at work. The most erudite researches have shown that previous to this era there was no law binding to its strict observance. Eight hundred and twenty-nine years after Christ, it was determined by a council solemnly convened for the purpose, that the keeping of the Lord's day had no other ground but mere custom ; and more than a thousand years after Christ elapsed, before this day was distinguished from the gaieties of church feasts and church festivals. And if this were the case when labour was light and the labourer was not taxed beyond his power, how much more necessary is it now that one day in seven should recruit the frame which supports his family, and renew the strength which gains his bread? The benefit of a railway on the Sunday is incalculable. It takes the workman from his loathsome neighbourhood to the purest haunts of nature ; it gives a glimpse of that beauty to which for six weary days he is an utter stranger ; it purifies the body ; it invigorates the mind ; and for that one day passed with those he loves, he is a better man, and, what is of more political note, he is a better subject. Let those who thus endeavour to force their peculiar tenets on the legislation of the country ; who, " dealing damnation round the land," righteously thank heaven they are not as other men, remember the unanswerable argument of Mr. Macaulay, that "they have no right to indulge in that mode of travel which is pleasant to themselves, while they prohibit that which is necessary to others." A fatal antagonism of classes may arrive soon enough, without its being hastened by an unworthy legislation. Fortunately the bill was carried, undisgraced by Mr. Plumptre's enactment.

By the Act every railway company, within forty-eight hours after the occurrence of any accident attended with serious personal injury to the public, was bound to give notice to the lords of the committee of the board of trade.

The lords of the said committee were empowered to order any railway company to deliver returns of serious accidents occurring in the course of the public traffic, whether attended with personal injury or not, in such form as they might require.

Disputes between railway companies having a common terminus, or a portion of the same line of rails in common, to be settled by the board of trade.

The opinion of Mr. Glyn on this measure will tend to give an idea of its true character. "There

has been presented to Parliament," said that gentleman, "for the further regulation of railways, a bill
which I do not hesitate to say is on the whole
calculated to do the interests of railways very considerable service."

In this bill an alteration of the tax on passengers
was introduced. Nor was the alteration uncalled
for. The tax hitherto levied on each was one-eighth
of a penny per mile, and though this at first view
may appear unlikely to interfere with the traffic,
yet practically its operation was most unequal. At
one period the companies were allowed to compound
with government, but when this principle was
abandoned, the directors raised the fares ; the traffic
was diminished ; the public were deprived of their
customary convenience ; and, to crown all, the financial position of the railway was lowered. Previous
to 1839 the government had remitted sixty per cent.
of one line, and eighty per cent. of another ; but
the abandonment of the composition produced petitions for an alteration from the directors of various
lines. These were referred to the select committee,
who reported that the tax was unequal ; that it
"fell more heavily on the railways in the poorer

districts of the country where the passengers were labourers and mechanics, than on the great lines where a number of travellers paid the highest fare," and the committee added, "the subject was well deserving the consideration of the legislature."

For a long time no enactment followed. Various petitions again made their appearance. Again was a select committee referred to, and again and again was it reported, "that it was inexpedient to continue a system of taxation which tended to separate the interests of the railway companies and the public, and which would gradually exclude a great number of persons from the benefit of cheap conveyance." The committee also recommended that a gradual scale of taxation should be adopted proportionate to the fare, and that the alteration should be carried into effect with as little delay as possible. The recommendation was disregarded, and in 1842 the agitation was renewed. Petitions once more poured in for an alteration, and facts were not wanting to prove that one company paid twenty-five per cent. on their gross receipts, and that wherever the population was rich and fares were high, the duty was not felt, but where the contrary was the case, the tax was oppressive.

The Great Western, the London and Birmingham, and the Grand Junction opposed any change. They begged to submit that it would be unjustifiable; that it would be in direct contravention of a sound and enlightened policy; that it would be attended with immediate injury to the public; that it would be highly inexpedient, and manifestly injurious to themselves; with various other phrases expressive of the memorialists' love of a good dividend. They carried their grievances to the feet of the Chancellor; and whether the arguments by which he was assailed, or the importance of the deputation affected him, he appears to have proposed to the House a smaller amount of duty than was feared by the disaffected lines in the early portion of their alarm.

Five per cent. upon their gross receipts is the sum annually paid by railway companies for the privilege of increasing the commercial prosperity of the country. The view for the legislature to take should be, not "how much they can get," but "how little they can do with." And though in a highly-taxed country the question is difficult to treat abstractedly, yet the less an impost presses upon communication, the better it is for that commerce which is the support of England.

The banking clearing-house in Lombard-street has been established about three-quarters of a century, and its aids and uses are well known in that great metropolis to whose purposes it ministers. The railway clearing-house, constituted to a certain extent on the same principle, was commenced in 1842. In the early annals of railroads a new difficulty had arisen, and the completion of the line from London to Liverpool proved to the railway manager that the facilitation of the through passage, at the points where the three railways joined, would be necessary.*

It was found desirable that the passenger who wished to pass between the above places should not be annoyed by changing his carriage, and watch-

* Not only must passengers be permitted to perform any journey within the limits to which continuous communication by railway extended, without being required to change their carriage, but that a similar principle must pervade the arrangements for working every description of through traffic if the public were to be conciliated, and the resources of the railway system developed to their full extent. The expediency of taking this course in relation to the through traffic, became still more evident at a subsequent period, when the chain of railways which connect the metropolis and York was opened throughout.— *Morison.*

ing his luggage ; and that the goods of the merchant
should not be shifted from one vehicle to another,
with loss of time and risk of damage. It was a
difficulty which had arisen with the increase of railways, and the public ever ready to find fault, used
all its energy to procure an amelioration. Those
who scarcely had any other mode of travelling,
declared they would rather patronise the old coaching
system than be thus inconvenienced. Others dilated
on the possible nuisance in eloquent epistles to
newspapers, and vituperative epistles to directors;
but all had one peroration composed of the " supine-
ness of railways," the " evils of the system," and
the " results of monopoly." It was the old cry in
a new form. But it produced its effect, and an
attempt to remedy the evil was made, which, like
many first attempts in the shape of reform, met
with much difficulty. It is true the directors of
some lines acknowledged the wisdom of the proposition and endeavoured to make it subservient
to their interests, but the same lamentable want
of justice which has been so evident in every portion of this history, followed one company in its
dealings with another.

That there were various modes of keeping accounts, which involved mutual difficulties in agreeing them, was natural enough; that this difficulty should create great confusion, was also to be expected; natural enough, too, was it that officials grew very angry, and that disputes arose in the settlement of accounts; but what shall be said to the most shameful fact, and what excuse shall be made for those most unprincipled persons, who, entering into an agreement to render accurate returns, and pay a fixed rate for the use they made of each others vehicles, should, in violation of faith, and utter disregard of right, make an unacknowledged use of the waggons of other lines to an extent which was a positive grievance, and with an absence of justice which was a positive infamy? It has been the writer's painful duty on more than one occasion to speak plainly of the evil done by great men and great bodies; and it is now his further duty to affirm that a wrong like that he has recorded was disgraceful to those who committed it, and disreputable to those who connived at it. The simple rule of right is the best mode of governing, and no paltry or contemptible expedients can ever fail of recoiling alike on those who plan and on those who profit by them.

Connected with the London and Birmingham railway as auditor, was one who, greatly interested in the welfare of railways, came, after much consideration, to the conclusion that a central office, carried out on the plan of the banking clearing-house, but modified to meet the requirements of railways, would at once furnish a remedy. And fortunate was it for this idea that at the head of the London and Birmingham railway was a man not likely to pooh-pooh it, because it was the proposal of another; but who, with characteristic clearness saw its advantages, adopted and aided it, gave the great weight of his name and sanction to it, and who, if he did not originate, at least assisted the infancy of that fine system, which, suggested by Mr. Morison, has under his watchful guidance attained an almost perfect form; which, commencing with four clerks, now employs two hundred; which then employed by four railways, is now employed by fifty-three, and which embracing then a territory of 418 miles, has increased it in nine years to 4,596 miles.

The difficulties to be obviated were, however, very numerous. All those who saw their dishonest gains were likely to be curtailed, fought vigorously against it. Some who thought that it might bring an increase of trouble, were at least lukewarm. Many who believed it might open the door to deception, opposed it from principle; while the superior officers of some of the railways had an insuperable objection, either because it was new, or because it might be an annoyance. Time would fail the writer to dilate on all the past and petty troubles of the period; or how Mr. Glyn, more and more convinced of its necessity, agitated, argued, and almost battled, for the child he was determined to rear. Nor should the support of Mr. Hudson be omitted. His name is indelibly recorded in the prosperity of the railway system, and on this occasion he gave his sanction and support when it was most required.

On the second of January, 1842, from London to Darlington and from Manchester to Hull, was the operation of the system begun; on that day the railway clearing-house commenced its career, and from that day it has increased more and more in importance; it has augmented more and more the comfort and contentment of the public, while it has not diminished the dividend of the proprietor."

"It was soon adopted," says Mr. Morison, its most able manager, "by the companies whose railways extend from Darlington to Carlisle, Sunderland, Hartlepool, and Scarborough, and from Birmingham to Manchester." The main principles of the system so widely diffused are, that passengers by paying one fare may go to any place or any distance without changing carriage; that horses and cattle shall be similarly treated, and that goods shall be carried through without being shifted or re-assorted. Each company pays a fixed rate per mile for those vehicles which it uses not being its own property, and no direct settlement takes place between any company when the accounts are passed through the railway clearing-house.

To enter the building with its various offices; to see the number of books and papers which constitute its contents; to note the many officials occupied in arranging them; to glance at the curious, and, to an unpractised eye, extraordinary documents

which appear to litter its desks, is, even to one
not wholly unacquainted with great accounts, somewhat bewildering. But to enter into the detail,
to watch the working of the office, and to see how
simply and beautifully the plan adopted bears on
each peculiarity, how the accounts are simplified,
fraud prevented, and error detected, is exceedingly
interesting. Every ticket which the companies issue
is sent to the clearing-house, examined, and returned
to the railway which issued it; the number of tickets
thus sorted being about 12,000 weekly. The returns
received from the 1300 stations are placed in the
hands of juniors to arrange and classify, in order
to save the more valuable time of the senior clerks,
who, to economise labour, have adopted every
plan, hieroglyphical or tabular, that experience can
suggest.

The office is divided into the goods, mileage
coaching, and accountants' departments; these again
are subdivided into sections, and where the number employed exceeds twenty, every section has
a chief clerk and accountant; where it is practicable,
two of these gentlemen work together, each being
responsible for those errors which all experienced

men know must creep into large accounts ; while, to procure a thorough mastery over their business, they are kept in the same department and occupied with the same work, each, be it remembered, being first educated in the mysteries of railway geography. The accounts between the clearing-house and the companies are settled monthly ; and monthly, therefore, are 16,500 gigantic sheets of paper, covered with financial statements worthy a chancellor of the exchequer, prepared for the various railways. As it is necessary, however, to send triplicates, it follows that 49,500 of these sheets monthly, or 594,000 yearly, leave the clearing-house, bearing on them those results which, arrived at with much labour, are necessary for the arrangement of the relative accounts, and connected with which is the fact that they are copied at home during the leisure hours of the gentlemen employed in the clearing-house, and paid for independently of their yearly income.

From each of the stations the London office receives daily :—

1. A return of passengers booked through.

2. A return of horses, private carriages, and cattle booked through.

3. A return of parcels booked through.

4. A return of carriages, waggons, &c., which have arrived or been despatched, either loaded or empty.

These returns are analysed, examined, and compared; other returns are prepared in the clearing-house, exhibiting that portion of the receipts of the through traffic to which each company is entitled, with the liabilities it has incurred by using the vehicles of other companies. In the monthly settlement it acts on the system of differences, a system which has been recognised by the banking clearing-house for three-quarters of a century, which is now acted upon by the Bank of England in arranging its half-yearly balances, and which is acknowledged as the proper principle of business throughout the mercantile world. Thus the balances of one company with another amount to hundreds, while the business itself amounts to thousands : £2,600,000 is the annual amount of business : £400,000 only is the sum annually paid. The committee of the railway clearing-house is composed of the chairmen of all the railway companies included in its arrangements, Mr. Glyn being chairman of the entire body. Among them is divided, according to the business of each, the expense of carrying out the plan. In the six months ending 31st December, 1850, the amount balanced was £1,320,000, and the expense of management only £8,700.

An Act of Parliament has been passed to enable them to act with more security; an office has been erected suitable to their requirements, and as the advantages which follow in the wake of this system are already numerous, so must they indefinitely increase.

" The great, the crowning achievements of the clearing system," says Mr. Morrison, " is the facility, the economy, and the expedition with which it enables the companies to work the through traffic. The advantages of the clearing system, in relation to the influence which railways exert on all the great national interests, cannot be over estimated. It has grown with the growth of the railway system, and unless the public accommodation be restricted, and the exigencies of the commercial, manufacturing, and agricultural interests disregarded, it must advance to the limits to which continuous communication by railway extends."

The advent of this institution proves that a rail-

way combination is sometimes to the advantage of
the public, and it is an evidence also that railway
directors sometimes act upon the established fact that
to benefit their customers is to benefit themselves.

There was something very satisfactory in the
reports of the railway department of the board of
trade. It need not be said that occasionally a sad
loss of life occurred. The engine went over an
embankment, or trains came in collision, and the
news spread far and wide. A " dreadful loss of life
on railways " was a stereotyped line ; the casualties
were always exaggerated, and for a long time it
was the custom to treat of railway travelling as
very dangerous compared with that by coaches.
Men never thought of judging for themselves, and
sometimes in the pulpit, and sometimes out of it,
railway accidents were treated as special judgments
on the sins of the people. There is after this something almost ludicrous in the proportional statement
of railway and stage-coach accidents.

" If, then," wrote Mr. Laing, " stage-coaches were
attended with as little personal injury to the public
as railways, the following would be near the proportional number of casualties :—

Passengers killed from causes beyond their own control	1 in 833 years.
Killed from their own folly, negligence or misconduct	1 in 1250 years.
Persons run over in the road	1 in 500 years.
Coach servants	1 in 125 years.

The subject was settled in every reasonable mind, and the following extract from one of the reports did much to influence public opinion : " A comparison of the number of accidents attended with death or injury to passengers, with the number of passengers conveyed by railway during the same period, which, from the returns made to this department, appears to be upwards of 18,000,000, would seem to indicate that the science of locomotion has, as far as the public safety is concerned, arrived at a very high degree of perfection : of more than 18,000,000 of passengers conveyed by railway in 1842, only one having been killed while riding in the train, and observing the proper degree of caution."

The report from the officers of the above department in 1843 is not the least important of these documents, nor is the year which witnessed the establishment of an atmospheric railway undistinguished in the era of the iron way. The notion of applying the air to the propulsion of carriages is by no means new. In 1812, Mr. Medhurst, a London engineer, published " Remarks on the Practicability of Conveying Goods and Letters by Air." Twelve years after this Mr. Vallance took out a patent for a system of locomotion upon the same principle, by which a tunnel large enough to contain a train of carriages was to be exhausted of air and the whole train impelled onward. In 1827, Mr. Medhurst issued a pamphlet which he entitled " A new System of Inland Conveyance for Goods and Passengers." By this, an " aerial tube " was to be made air tight; the carriage was to be of the size and form of the tube, and to be propelled with whatever force the atmosphere would give. But the idea of forming part of a charge for a huge air gun did not meet the views of the public, and no result ensued.

Still the idea was not dropped, and in 1834 and 1826, Mr. Pinkus procured patents for a railway on the pneumatic plan; but, being imperfect, the principle made no further progress until Mr. Clegg took out a patent, which, when modified by an invention of M. Hallette and Mr. Hay, was seriously considered during that demand for railways when whatever was new was sure to be encouraged. Models were exhibited in London. A branch of the Dublin and Kingstown railway applied to government for monetary assistance to form an atmospheric railway, and a government loan of £25,000 was accorded. A good deal of attention was attracted, and scientific men examined it. Mr. Brunel favoured the principle. Mr. Stephenson was opposed to it. Other engineers took different sides, according to their interest or their inclination. When it was understood, therefore, that Major-General Pasley had reported on the subject, his opinions were looked forward to with anxiety, and read with interest. Those opinions were impartial, but decisive. The experiments he witnessed on the Kingstown and Dalkey railway, he said " were very judicious; and," he continued, " being in progress I witnessed several of them, and others were tried next day at my request, which satisfied me as to the efficiency and safety of this railway." " Of the efficiency of the atmospheric railway there can be no longer any doubt; and it may be pronounced less liable to accidents, because no following train can possibly overtake another, nor can two trains meet each other so as to cause collision." This opinion increased the confidence of those who supported the new proposition, and led to further attempts at a future period.

Another subject on which the report of 1843 touched was that of accidents; and the list given is a curious specimen of the difficulty of avoiding them. Trespassing on the rails was one cause; leaping off a train in full motion was a second; the most inveterate obstinacy caused a third. In some cases the public, being warned of the danger, would cross, though a train was moving towards them. In many instances life was lost trying to rob the company of a ride. Intoxication was not wanting to add to this list of calamities, which, however, when reduced to its true proportions, assumed a trifling appearance. In 1841, twenty-four persons were killed without inadvertence on their parts. In 1842, the number was reduced to five; and in 1843, only three of the public lost their lives.

The determination to introduce railways into Ireland re-opened in the above year the gauge question; and Major-General Pasley addressed a communication

to the leading engineers to the following purport :
—" Supposing that there were no railways in England,
and that a system of new ones were proposed, to
embrace the most important communications all
over the country, what would you, with your present
experience, recommend as being the best uniform
gauge to be adopted for the whole of them, so
that they might all work together in such a manner
that the locomotive engines and carriages of any one
railway might travel on all the others ?"

The replies were almost as various as the writers.
Mr. George Stephenson "unhesitatingly expressed
his opinion that the four feet eight and a-half inches
gauge was most economical in construction, not
only as regarded the engines and carriages, but more
particularly of the railway itself."

This gentleman, however, owned to having once
considered that a gauge of five feet two inches
would be preferable; but "having discussed the
subject fully with his son, he had again changed
his opinion."   Mr. Robert Stephenson maintained
the same views; while Mr. Rennie thought that
" a width of five feet, which was the width originally
recommended by him for the Liverpool and Man-

chester railway, might be an improvement." Mr.
Braithwaite " saw no reason to alter his former
views of a five feet gauge, and unhesitatingly recommended it as the best and most economical." Mr.
Bury, again, believed that with five feet three inches
" any reasonable speed could be obtained ;" and Mr.
Cubitt also considered that a similar gauge would
be "the most useful and economical." And when
it is added that Mr. Miller " did not think that
a gauge above five feet six inches was necessary to
produce a good locomotive engine ;" that Mr. Gooch
" was not inclined to recommend a greater gauge
than six feet ;" while Mr. Gray was of opinion that
" a uniform gauge of five feet six inches would have
been a great improvement in the railways of Great
Britain,"—it need not be said that the public
greatly wondered at the difference of opinion. It is
to be supposed that Mr. Brunel was not asked on
account of his decided and well-known opinion on
the subject.

Mr. George Stephenson and his son were alone
in their preference for a gauge of four feet eight
and a-half inches. It must, however, be remembered that a natural prejudice clung to these gen-

tlemen in favour of the width they had introduced : but the very fact that so firm a man as the engineer of the Liverpool and Manchester had once changed his mind, argues in favour of an alteration. A perusal of the remarks made by the chief men of the day, given dispassionately and after due consideration to a government officer, appears to prove that Mr. Stephenson and his son were wrong, and that an increase of the width of the gauge would enable the engineer to improve the locomotive.

CHAPTER III.

THE RAILWAY LABOURERS.—THEIR ORIGIN, CHARACTER, AND TREATMENT.—THE
DREAD THEY INSPIRED.—THEIR DWELLINGS.—EFFECT ON COUNTRY LIFE.
—THE RAILWAY CONTRACTOR.—EFFORTS OF MR. CHADWICK IN THEIR BE-
HALF.—HIS SUCCESS.

A CHAPTER devoted to the railway labourer may
be regarded as intrusive by some, and as gossipping
by others ; by a third class it may be considered
as repulsive. But the " navigator " is necessary to
the rail. He is an important portion of this new
system of political economy. He risks life and
limb to form the works which we admire. He
braves all weather, he dares all danger, he labours
with a power and a purpose which demand attention.
For years he was disregarded by those who, availing
themselves of his strength and skill, left him, when
his daily task was done, to his own pleasures and
his own resources. Rude, rugged, and uncultivated,

possessed of great animal strength, collected in large
numbers, living and working entirely together, they
are a class and a community by themselves. Before
the time of that great duke who called inland
navigation into existence, this class was unknown;
and in the works which bear witness to his forethought, the "navigator" gained his title. The canal
manias which ensued created a demand and increased
the body; the great architectural works of the
kingdom continued it; and when the rail first began
to spread its iron road through England, the labourer
attracted no attention from politician or philosopher,
from statistician or from statesman; he had joined
no important body, he had not made himself an
object of dread. Rough alike in morals and in
manners, collected from the wild hills of Yorkshire
and of Lancashire, coming in troops from the fens
of Lincolnshire, and afterwards pouring in masses
from every county in the empire; displaying an
unbending vigour and an independent bearing; mostly
dwelling apart from the villagers near whom they
worked; with all the strong propensities of an
untaught, undisciplined nature; unable to read and
unwilling to be taught; impetuous, impulsive, and

brute-like; regarded as the pariahs of private life, herding together like beasts of the field, owning no moral law and feeling no social tie, they increased with an increased demand, and from thousands grew to hundreds of thousands. They lived but for the present; they cared not for the past; they were indifferent to the future. They were a wandering people, who only spoke of God to wonder why he had made some so rich and others so poor; and only heard of a coming state to hope that there they might cease to be railway labourers. They were heathens in the heart of a Christian people; savages in the midst of civilisation: and it is scarcely an exaggeration to say, that a feeling something akin to that which awed the luxurious Roman when the Goth was at his gates, fell on the minds of those English citizens near whom the railway labourer pitched his tent.

"A perfect dread," said one witness before a committee of the House of Commons, "was on the minds of the people of the town near which the railway labourer was expected." Nor was it until this period, when they became an element of the power of England; when their numbers made

them feared by the rich who avoided them, and
a curse to the poor who associated with them, that
the Chadwicks of the nineteenth century could
compel the attention they deserved

The inquiry instituted by parliament elicited information which surprised some and revolted all. The
mode in which they herded together was melancholy ;
and if the homes of the people be an index to their
civilisation, the home of the railway labourer was
significant enough. They earned high wages, and
they spent them. They worked hard, and they
lived well. The waste of power which their daily
labour necessitated, was supplied by an absorption
of stimulant and nourishment perfectly astounding.
Bread, beef, bacon, and beer, were the staple of their
food. They drank ardent spirits if they had money,
credit, or craft to procure it; for "there was not
an atom's worth of honesty among them." They
devoured as earnestly as they worked; they drank
whisky by the tumbler, and called it "white beer:"
and they proved what open air and hard labour
would do in the disposal of their food. They were
in a state of utter barbarism. They made their
homes where they got their work. Some slept

in huts constructed of damp turf, cut from the wet grass, too low to stand upright in; while small sticks, covered with straw, served as rafters. Barns were better places than the best railway labourer's dwellings. Others formed a room of stones without mortar, placed thatch or flags across the roof, and took possession of it with their families, often making it a source of profit by lodging as many of their fellow-workmen as they could crowd into it. It mattered not to them that the rain beat through the roof, and that the wind swept through the holes. If they caught a fever, they died; if they took an infectious complaint, they wandered in the open air, spreading the disease wherever they went. In these huts they lived; with the space over-crowded; with man, woman, and child mixing in promiscuous guilt; with no possible separation of the sexes; in summer wasted by unwholesome heats, and in winter literally hewing their way to their work through the snow. In such places from nine to fifteen hundred men were crowded for six years. "Living like brutes, they were depraved, degraded, and reckless. Drunkenness and dissoluteness of morals prevailed. There were many women, but

few wives; loathsome forms of disease were uni·
versal. Work often went on without intermission
on Sundays as well as on other days."

"Possessed of all the daring recklessness of the
smuggler," says Mr. Roscoe, and it is necessary
to quote other opinions to confirm the writer's
picture, so serious is the nature of his assertions,
"their ferocious behaviour can only be equalled
by the brutality of their language. It may be
truly said their hand is against every man's, and
before they have been long located, every man's
hand is against theirs. From being long known
to each other, they generally act in concert, and
put at defiance any local constabulary force; consequently crimes of the most atrocious character
were common, and robbery without any attempt
at concealment was an every-day occurrence." Attention was rarely paid to the day of rest, excepting
to make it a day of debauchery. Many of them
lived in a state of intoxication until their money was
spent, and they were again obliged to have recourse
to labour, to the loan ticket and the truck system.

The dread which such men as these spread
throughout a rural community, was striking; nor

was it without a cause. Depredation among the
farms and fields of the vicinity were frequent.
They injured everything they approached. From
their huts to that part of the railway at which
they worked, over corn or grass, tearing down
embankments, injuring young plantations, making
gaps in hedges, on they went, in one direct line,
without regard to damage done or property invaded.
Game disappeared from the most sacred preserves ;
game-keepers were defied ; and country gentlemen
who had imprisoned rustics by the dozen for violating
the same law, shrunk in despair from the railway
" navigator." They often committed the most out-
rageous acts in their drunken madness. Like dogs
released from a week's confinement, they ran about
and did not know what to do with themselves. They
defied the law ; broke open prisons ; released their
comrades, and slew policemen. The Scotch fought
with the Irish, and the Irish attacked the Scotch ;
while the rural peace-officers, utterly inadequate
to suppress the tumult, stood calmly by and waited
the result. When no work was required of them
on the Sunday, the most beautiful spots in England
were desecrated by their presence. Lounging in

highways and byeways, grouping together in lanes
and valleys, insolent and insulting, they were dreaded
by the good, and welcomed by the bad. They left
a sadness in the homes of many whose sons they
had vitiated and whose daughters they had dis-
honoured. Stones were thrown at passers-by; women were personally abused; and men were irritated.
On the week day, when their work was done, the
streets were void of all save their lawless visitors
and of those who associated with them. They were
regarded as savages; and when it is remembered
that large bodies of men armed with pitchforks
and scythes went out to do battle with those on
another line a few miles off, the feeling was justified
by facts. Crime of all description increased, but
offences against the person were most common. On
one occasion, hundreds of them were within five
minutes' march of each other, ere the military and
the magistrates could get between them to repress
their daring desires.

Their presence spread like a pestilence. Tempted
by the high wages they received, the hind left his
master to join them. Occasionally the inhabitants
of the district received the labourer as a lodger,

and paid for it in the impurity of character and conduct it engendered. The females of his family left their home to join the wild encampment, and were in their turn left by those who had betrayed them. Their boys aped the vices of men. They fought, smoked, swore, and reeled along the streets at an age when, in other classes, they are scarcely left by themselves. The "navigators," wanderers on the face of the earth, owning no tie and fearing no law; "were," said the Rev. St. George Sargent, "the most neglected and spiritually destitute people I ever met; ignorant of Bible religion and Gospel truth, infected with infidelity, and prone to revolutionary principles."

And for all these things were railway companies responsible. Letting large portions of their works to contractors, the latter divided their respective portions among others with smaller capital, who again subletting their part of the works to a minor class — as much labourers as contractors—engaged the workmen, assisted their operations, shared in their toils, and disregarded their welfare when the work was over. In many cases the men were paid their wages monthly; in some not so often. When

new men were engaged, they could only live by
assistance from their employers. This led to the
truck system, the advances being made by orders on
a shop, in exchange for which, the labourer received
inferior provisions at an extravagant price. Against
each man an account was kept, and on the pay
day he received the balance due. This balance
being necessarily small was soon dissipated; and
the "navigator" had no other resource. The same
demand for advances arose, the same issue of tickets
occurred, the same extortion followed. The man
was maintained by credit, and improvident habits
were continued.

The carelessness of the contractor for the welfare
of the employed is to be accounted for when it is
remembered that he often sprung from the ranks.
It has been said in the previous volume, that the
railway contractor forms a feature of the present
period. The first directors of railway companies
committed the great mistake of letting small contracts to irresponsible men, who made large profits
if they succeeded, or left the directors without a
remedy if they failed. Thus a small success led
to larger efforts; the careful "navigator" became first

an under-ganger and then a ganger ; the ganger
changed into a contractor ; and at this time there
are many men who, twenty years since, delved and
dug, and gained their bread by the sweat of their
brow, are now in possession of most valuable estates.
They have bought the places which railway speculation often sent into the market ; they possess
capital to invest in the landed property which the
operation of the corn laws may yet throw open to
the highest bidder ; they possess shrewdness which
enables them to imitate the conventional manners
of society ; they educate their family for the position
they have acquired, and their children will probably
occupy an important place in the great landed
power of the country.   There was, therefore, in too
many cases no sympathy between the employer and
the employed.   There was no confidence between
the contractor and the labourer; the system of subletting, handing the latter over to uneducated and
reckless people, who, choosing them only for their
skill and power, looked after them but to see that
their work was done.   From such as these the "navigator" found a difficulty even in procuring his wages.
Law was of no avail to him.   "There is no law,"

said the Rev. Robert Wilson, a magistrate, " which
will enforce it; if the employer has no goods on
which to levy the amount, there is no remedy."
Nor was this an uncommon circumstance. The
above gentleman stated that he had as many as
twenty-eight or thirty cases in one morning; that
within two and a-half years he had adjudicated on
a hundred; and that it frequently arose, not from
misapprehension, but because the ganger " did not
choose to pay." Sometimes a different movement was
tried. " Two labourers," said Mr. Wilson, " complained to me that they had been paid £1 short
in their wages. It was on a pay-night, the room
very much crowded, a small room; and the ganger
read from a book the sum to be paid to them;
it was £2 9s., and one of them took up the money
and went away to the other end of the table to
count it with his comrade; directly the money is
down, they are hurried away to make room for others.
When he got to the other end of the table he counted
the money and found £1 9s. instead of £2 9s. He
counted it over in the presence of his comrade and
they returned to the ganger to be paid the other
£1. He said, 'I paid you £2 9s.' The complaint

was laid before me, and the evidence on the part of the labourer was this, that one had taken up the money and gone to the table and counted it in the presence of the other. The comrade said, 'I saw him count the money;' but of course he could not say that he had slipped away one pound. The ganger merely said, in his defence, he had ordered the £2 9s. to be paid. The time-keeper, who pays the money from a basin, said he had put down £2 9s.; and another person, also in the employ of the ganger, said he was sitting near the table, and he could see that £2 9s. was put on the table and taken up by the labourer."

The truck system, originated one hundred years ago, was maintained on the greater number of the lines in formation. Under the pretence that the works were too far from the town to be supplied by its shopkeepers, the contractor often arranged with some person to open a shop near the works, where the men might have their wants supplied; and as the labourer was not paid his wages weekly, he was obliged to go to these shops, knowing that the goods he received were very dear and very bad. The feeling was strong on the subject, and

many men made it a rule never to work on lines where
there was a "tommy-shop." So sensible of the imposition were those who were obliged to take the
tickets that they would often sell them at any discount. The plan led to every sort of knavery. It
was disadvantageous also to the peace of the works.
It was contrary to the peace of the men. It prevented the circulation of money in the villages near
which the "navigators" worked. It created quarrels
with the shopkeepers. It produced exorbitant charges
for an inferior quality. It caused frequent disputes
on the night of settlement. "The men get drunk,"
said one witness, "lose their tickets, and say they
have not had them ; or they sell a two shilling
ticket for half its value, spend the money, and declare they were not paid." They never were satisfied with what they received. Unable to keep
accounts, and miscalculating the value of the goods
they had taken, they were paid less than they
imagined their due, leaving the place angry, excited,
and fit for any wild or wicked work. Bad feelings
were thus produced between the employer and the
employed. Additional scenes of drunkenness, riot,
and disorder marked the monthly payments. **Mr.**

Jackson said the men complained with great reason of the truck system ; they were most cruelly used. The Rev. Robert Wilson added that the railway labourers were induced to behave ill to their employers from the treatment they received. Mr. Speirs was of opinion that it was disadvantageous to the works, and contrary to the interests of the men.

The reverend Mr. Thompson said it led to every sort of trickery ; while, in addition to these opinions, Mr. Brunel believed it to be " a very bad system." Nor can it be sufficiently denounced. Its evils on the railway may not be so great as in Manchester. Mr. D'Israeli, in his fine story of " Sybil," has developed with great power the mode in which the principle worked there. Nor can there be a doubt that in an inferior degree the same evils were felt by the large body of men concerning whom this chapter treats. Even if the labourer, wishing to be economical, applied for cash, he could only procure it at the rate of one hundred per cent. per annum.

" If they are not unfairly dealt with," said the report of the committee, " the men suspect they are over-reached, and this engenders ill-will and

distrust towards their employers. They have little
or no means of checking the account of advances
made to them, or of ascertaining whether the balance
paid is really correct; and hence the monthly payment seems frequently an occasion for dispute, riot,
and discontent. The contractor, being interested in
the large expenditure of the men, has a strong motive
to encourage their extravagance and wastefulness,
and to induce them to anticipate their wages. In
some instances, the men cannot get employment
unless they will deal at their master's shop. Those
who live on credit are apt to be more profuse and
improvident than those who pay their way; the
less frequently the men are paid, the longer they
must live on credit; and thus the employer is induced
to pay his men at long intervals."

It must be added that all contractors were not
patrons of truck shops. To the honour of Mr.
Peto, by whom thousands of this class were employed,
some attempt was made to humanise them. He
was careful in his selection of overseers. He always
paid his wages weekly in money, and boldly avowed
that no contracter who understood his own interest
or his obligations to the men, would act otherwise.

Attention was paid to their religious instruction. Clergymen and scripture-readers were induced to visit them. He provided them with barracks to lodge in ; he introduced habits of thrift and carefulness ; he encouraged them in joining sick-clubs, and gave large sums to induce them. No one who could read was without a Bible. The consequence was, that men staid with him fourteen or fifteen years; that drunkenness was uncommon ; and that, though dissoluteness of mind and manner was impossible utterly to prevent, there was but little among the large number employed by Mr. Peto.* Nor was this gentleman alone in his endeavours. Mr. Jackson, also a large railway contractor, always paid

* In the endeavours of Mr. Peto to ameliorate the evils of the railway labourer, he met with an earnest and willing assistant in his partner, Mr. Grissell who, under the same auspices as Mr. Peto, has realised a large fortune by similar means. On the dissolution of partnership with the latter, Mr. Grissell retired from business—excepting with the contract for the Houses of Parliament—has become a landed proprietor, and co-operating with his late partner and friend, is a favourable specimen of the great railway contractor of the nineteenth century.

Mr. Grissell relates with great zest the difficulties which Mr. Peto and himself experienced in commencing as contractors. To those who know Mr. Bidder, the engineer, it need not be said that he was the last person to whom most men would have applied for information and assistance on the subject. However, to him did Mr. Peto address himself, and for a long time in vain ; nor was it until the charms or the chance of a conservatory, built in the best style of the firm, had warmed the very inaccessible Mr. Bidder, that Mr. Peto succeeded in his object.

in money. " I find," said he, " setting aside any
reference to feeling as to the comfort and condition
of the men, and looking at it in a business point
of view, that it is much more profitable, much
more comfortable, and much better in every respect,
that the men should be taken care of." He looked
after the morals of the men employed by him;
he provided for their comfort and accommodation ;
he built sixty or seventy wooden cottages; and
although the erection of these places might not
pay in a pecuniary light, they far more than repaid
in the purer feeling they created, and in the development of a moral effect previously unknown.

Mr. Chadwick first drew the attention of the
public to this class; and in a paper read before
the statistical society of Manchester, made some
statements so startling, that the House of Commons
deemed it necessary to appoint a committee to inquire
into the condition of the railway labourer; " who,"
said Mr. Chadwick, " has been detached from the
habits and influence of his home and his village, and
set to work amongst promiscuous assemblages of
men attracted from all parts; has received double
his ordinary amount of wages, and has been sur-

rounded by direct inducements to spend them in drink and debauchery. If he were a married man, little or none of his earnings have been returned to his wife and family, who in his absence have commonly obtained parochial relief, on the ground either of 'desertion by the husband,' or of his 'absence in search of work.' Whether he were married or single, the whole of the excess of money earned beyond his ordinary rate of wages has been expended under the inducements to which he has been subjected, and at the completion of the works, he has been discharged penniless, and has returned discontented, reckless, deteriorated in bodily and mental condition, or he has, with others of the same class, entered the ranks of the dangerous swarm of able-bodied mendicants, vagrants, and depredators, of whom the committals within the last few years have been so largely increased. The employment is transitory, but the evil effects have been permanent. The extra labourers available for such undertakings, the loose men unattached to any place of working, could not be expected to be of the best description of labourers; but from the absence of proper regulations, the good have been deteriorated, the indifferent made positively bad, and the bad worse."

The ills arising from the endeavour of the capitalist to employ his capital, should be counteracted as much as possible by the same agency. Instead of being an evil, the collection of these men might be made a benefit. They might be taught their responsibility; they might be shown the use of uniting; they might be introduced into the social scale which they injure; they might be raised from material to moral life; they might be educated and taught their true position; they might be treated like men, and not left to themselves, like beasts.

At war with all civilised society, the great mass glorying in Chartism, they are to be dreaded: for their thews and sinews would form no trifling element of success. It is the duty of every railway company to watch over their interests; it is the duty of every contractor to provide for them mentally as well as physically; and it is the duty of every good government to see that the power which calls them into existence also places them in that position in the state which their welfare as men demands.

No legal enactment followed the inquiry of the

committee of the House of Commons; and with the following extract the present chapter is concluded :—

"The class of the labouring population, to the state of which the inquiries of your committee have been addressed, is already large, and is likely to become very much more numerous. The rapid growth of the railway system of communication will be necessarily accompanied, for several years to come, by a vast expenditure of capital in mere construction, giving employment, probably, to not much less than 200,000 of the effective labouring population of the country.

"The great amount of outlay already thus made, its suddenness, and its temporary concentration at particular localities—often spots before but thinly inhabited—have created or developed evils, touching both the welfare of the labourers employed and the interests of society, the taint of which seems not unlikely to survive their original cause.

"It does not seem altogether unreasonable to expect that the steady employment and the high wages attained by the men engaged on railway works, added to the opportunities for their instruction, for their acquiring habits of order, of systematic industry, and of economy, as well as for bringing favourable influences to bear on them, which are afforded by the collection of large bodies of these men together, under an organised system of labour, should serve most usefully in effecting a valuable and permanent improvement of their state. Good wages, or at least such wages as secure those dependent thereon from constantly balancing on the verge of destitution, seem to be one element essential to the improvement of the labouring classes. With reference to the class your committee has had under their consideration, this element undoubtedly exists; but, besides high wages, other circumstances must be favourable, before improvement of social condition can be looked for; and if they are unfavourable, increased means of gratification may become positively harmful to the recipient as well as to society. Even the disposition and habits of the individual, the main elements in considering the prospects of improving his condition, must greatly depend on the external circumstances in which he exists; on the treatment he experiences; on the kind of life he has no choice but to lead.

"As regards the class of labourers under conside-

ration, your committee cannot but conclude, on the
evidence they have received from various parts of
the country, that the circumstances under which
their labour is carried on are too generally of a
deteriorating kind. They are brought hastily together in large bodies; no time is given for that
gradual growth of accommodation which would naturally accompany the gradual growth of numbers;
they are, therefore, crowded into unwholesome dwellings, while scarcely any provision is made for their
comfort or decency of living; they are released
from the useful influences of domestic ties and from
the habits of their former routine of life, (influences
and habits the more important, in proportion to
their want of education); they are hard worked;
they are exposed to great risk of life and limb;
they are too often hardly treated; and many inducements are presented to them to be thoughtless,
thriftless, and improvident. Under these circumstances, your committee fears that intemperance,
disorder, and demoralisation run a better chance
of growth than decency, frugality, and improvement;
and they cannot wonder at the feelings of dislike
and dismay with which the permanent inhabitants

of a neighbourhood often view the arrival of these strangers among them.

" Your committee begs to suggest that every railway company, before employing more than a small given number of labourers together, in the construction of any part of their work, should be required to notify their intention to the public board, which may be charged with the general supervision of railways, and to state the number of men likely to be employed thereupon. A competent officer should then be required by the board to proceed to the place named, and to ascertain whether there was already adequate decent lodging to be obtained for the work-people, within a reasonable distance, and to report accordingly to the board. If it should be sufficient, that then the company should be allowed at once to proceed ; otherwise, not until they have provided lodging to the satisfaction of such officer, certified by him to the board ; and these proceedings should be at the expense of the company, the exercise of whose powers might be made dependent on their being taken. The inspecting officer should be required, from time to time, to visit the works and the lodgings, and to report thereon to the board, with a power to make sanitary regulations respecting them to be observed by the company, on approval by the board.

" Facilities for instruction are little worth wherever the men are incited by their treatment to wastefulness, drunkenness, and disorder, are unjustly dealt with, defrauded, and crowded together in places where a ' humane person would hardly put a pig.' No teaching can be of much avail to counteract the ceaseless operation of such degrading and deteriorating influences."

CHAPTER IV.

IN the early part of 1844, it was found necessary
once more to consider railways, and the select committee agreed to report the following resolutions :—

1. "That in each case where bills are now pending
to authorise the construction of new lines of railway
competing with one another, such bills be respectively
referred to one committee.

2. "That the committees for the consideration of
such bills be specially constituted.

3. "That bills now pending to authorise the construction of new lines of railway which will compete

with existing railways, be in like manner referred to committees specially constituted.

4. "That such committees be composed of five members, to be nominated by the committee of selection, who shall sign a declaration that their constituents have no local interest, and that they themselves have no personal interest in the bill, or bills, referred to them, and that they will not vote on any question which may arise without having duly heard and attended to the evidence relating thereto ; and that three shall be a quorum.

5. "That a select committee be appointed to consider which of the pending railway bills shall be deemed competing bills, according to the foregoing resolutions.

6. "That such select committee be composed of five members, of whom three shall be a quorum, and that the committee have power to send for persons, papers, and records.

7. "That such cf the standing orders as relate to the composition of the committees on private bills, and the orders consequent thereon, be suspended, so far as regards competing railway bills pending in the course of the present session."

Mr. Gladstone, in proposing the above, evinced

the same knowledge of his subject which marked his other speeches on similar topics. The committee, he said, had determined to recommend the House to depart from the general rule with respect to the appointment of the committees on railway bills. They felt, in the cases of competing lines, that the number of members on the committee who were connected with, or represented the local interests, should be materially restricted, and that these local interests should be made subservient to those of the public. He should propose that the committee be formed of five gentlemen totally unconnected with the particular places in which the lines lay; and moved, therefore, that when any bills were brought in for two railways to one place, they should be referred to one committee.

The resolutions were received with much applause. It is, however, due to the firmness of Colonel Sibthorp to mention that he declared it was very well known to the country that "he had a great, an unchanged, and he rather thought an unchangeable suspicion in reference to railways." It is necessary to add that this gentleman was found in the minority of a faithful three, who lifted up their hands and voices against the measure.

In the House of Peers similar attention was paid to the subject, and Earl Fitzwilliam drew the notice of her Majesty's government to railways; "which," said the noble earl with much gravity, "are indubitably important," though he could not help thinking that importance somewhat exaggerated. "They were, however," added the earl, "when regarded as a question of political economy, of great consequence to the country." The ground occupied by the noble earl was sound, and his measure met even the support of Lord Brougham, being to the effect that a commission should be appointed to inquire into the points and places at which it was desirable to have railways, investigating the lines projected, and selecting the best.

The Duke of Wellington and Marquis of Lansdowne agreed with Earl Fitzwilliam, and Lord Brougham concurred in what his noble friend had said with regard to the desirableness of such a motion, and although it was rather late, still "it was better late than never." He hoped that the commissioners would never lose sight of the inconvenience to which individuals might be subjected, as the country houses of gentlemen, in which their forefathers had

dwelt for several generations, had been totally ruined
as residences by the immediate contiguity of railroads, which might have been avoided by the railroad taking a different course. A noble friend of
his had a magnificent mansion in the country, and
a railroad went right through his pleasure grounds.
Much was said in those projects of making sacrifices
to the public interests. It was a very easy thing
to say so; but the railway proprietors ought themselves to be required to make sacrifices also. He
would, therefore, in such cases as those, say to
them, "you must take a different line." He was
of opinion that the commissioners might render
some service to individuals, and yet not neglect
the public interests. He knew a villa which had
been frequently let for £450 and £500 a-year, not
very distant from the metropolis, but in consequence of a railway running close past it, scarcely
any rent at all could be obtained for it. The railway did not, however, actually go into the grounds,
so that the proprietor got nothing by way of compensation, although his villa was valueless. He
trusted that some measure would be adopted to prevent individuals from being subjected to such losses.

In May, 1844, a further important alteration took place. By the standing orders of the House it was necessary, previous to the presentation of a petition, to deposit ten per cent. on the proposed capital. Mr. Gladstone said, that as railway speculation proceeded by fits and starts; that as in times of prosperity they were projected in multitudes, and in periods of commercial depression few were undertaken, it was desirable during the latter season not to oppress speculation by a difficulty of raising capital. He proposed, therefore, that £5 per cent. should be the future deposit on projected railways, and that the five per cent. might be paid in money or in exchequer bills.

Mr. Hume could not see why greater facilities should be allowed to railway speculators than to others; while Mr. Labouchere and Sir Robert Peel supported the resolution, which was allowed.

The fifth blue book from the select committee on railways excited alternately the hopes and fears of proprietors and companies. It was a long and able report. It went into the subject of rating; it considered the conditions to be attached to existing companies; it specified the degree of supervision which government should exercise over future schemes, and it entered into the vexed question of facilities to be granted to the third-class passenger. This topic had already cursorily come before the House; but in such a form as the present, the railway interests saw the importance of at once joining their forces against it.

At a subsequent period Earl Dalhousie said in the House of Peers that government, having a plan of their own, would not accede to the motion previously made by Earl Fitzwilliam: adding that the third-class traffic had been a disgrace to railway companies, and if continued, would be a still greater discredit to the parliament which allowed it. The committee had recommended the House of Commons to require from all railway companies that there should be upon every line at convenient times, and with proper accommodation, carriages, with seats defended from the weather, for third-class passengers.

Some of the companies compelled third-class passengers to travel whole days without seats, making them, in a journey which might not occupy more than seven hours and a-half, stand on their feet sixteen or seventeen hours. In order to avoid such evasion as this, it was provided that the whole of the regulations as to this traffic should be under the strict superintendence of the government-board. Earl Fitzwilliam had done what he had only once before done—heard the noble Earl with the greatest pleasure and delight. He had heard, with the greatest satisfaction, that the committee which had been appointed by the other House of Parliament were likely to secure additional comforts to the labouring classes in railway travelling.

When the bill was presented, to which Lord Dalhousie alluded, it caused great public attention. An intense alarm seized upon railway shareholders at the rights it claimed and the propositions it submitted. Nor were they undeserving the attention of an expectant railway proprietary. A few of these will show that there was some cause for the alarm :—

" If, after fifteen years, any new railway shall yield ten per cent. for three years, the board of trade may, on a month's notice, reduce the tolls and fares, according to their judgment, so as to keep the profits at ten per cent.

" If the board of trade be displeased with any company on the score of management, they may inflict whatever punishment they think right on them in the shape of pecuniary deductions.

"The board of trade may in this manner repeat their revisions every seven years, or raise the tolls monthly ; but however much they may lower the fares and rates below those of the Act of Parliament under which the company undertook the enterprise, they are in no case to raise them.

"The company shall then be prohibited from any increase of capital stock, unless with the consent of the board of trade.

"The board of trade shall make the regulations for conducting the traffic, and shall inflict fines on the company for neglect or disobedience.

"At the end of fifteen years the board of trade may, if they think fit, purchase the railway.

"The board of trade may deduct from the purchase-money as much as will put the works and stock into good working order.

"The board of trade shall at all times have a right to examine and value the working stock, and deduct the depreciation from the price.

"Lines under lease to be similarly treated.

"All the books, accounts, vouchers, and other

documents of the company, to be subject to the inspection of the board of trade, and half-yearly balances transmitted to them.

" The railway to become the property of the crown.

" All leases and contracts of the company may be rendered void by one month's notice.

" All companies, in future, applying to parliament for any purpose, or having applied this session, directly or indirectly, shall provide daily third-class trains, provided with seats, and covered in, to the satisfaction of the board of trade; at hours approved by the board of trade; stopping at every station; at 1d. a mile fare; with half a hundred-weight of luggage gratis to each passenger, and more at a cheap rate. Infants gratis. Children half-price.

" The board of trade to have full discretionary control over these trains, to make orders and decide the details, with a fine of £20 a-day for dis-obedience.

" The board of trade may use their discretion to remit or alter these conditions.

" One-half only of the present and future tax to be charged on the 1d. fares.

" All railway companies in parliament in this or

future sessions to be compelled to carry troops at 1*d.* a mile, officers at 2*d.*, and stores, ammunition, and military baggage at 2*d.* per ton per mile.

" The postmaster-general may require the mails to be forwarded at any rate of speed the inspector thinks safe ; and mails may be conveyed by a guard as an ordinary passenger, without any payment to the company for the mail-bags.

" Railway companies shall allow the government the use of their line for laying down electric telegraphs.

" Where electric telegraphs exist, they shall be open to the public, with precedence to her Majesty's service, and under the superintendence of the board of trade.

" The power of the board of trade to be extended to the appointment of all officers required to exercise the new system of government superintendence.

" Issue of loan notes stopped under penalty ; past notes legalised.

" Loan notes falling due to be paid.

" Loan notes to be registered for inspection of holders and of board of trade.

" The board of trade have power to determine which are new railways, and shall publish a list in the

Gazette, and this publication shall be conclusive evidence that such line is a new railway."

The people generally were much excited by the question, and, as usual, exaggerated assertions were made. One portion of the public had flown to arms because Mr. Crawshay had jocularly talked of sending a sweep and a sootbag in the third-class train to keep respectable people out. The House of Commons was deluged with petitions about it. It was said that third-class passengers were subjected to "losses, injuries, and annoyances;" that the companies only cared to wring as much money as possible; that this class was unreasonably and purposely exposed to the inclemency of the weather; that the engine driver was ordered to linger on the journey; that the passengers were kept unnecessarily in the cold and wet; that they were made as wretched and miserable as possible; that contumely and neglect were heaped upon them; and that they were degraded as much as possible.

This question is very important, as travelling by railway is now a necessity. It is said that the facilities for transit are to the poor man greater than they ever were. Relatively they are not so.

The competition provoked is greater ; the necessity to travel is stronger ; he is compelled to join heart and hand in the conflict for daily bread, or fall to the ground. Obliged to travel by the third-class because he cannot afford the second, he is exposed unnecessarily to the weather. It is a fallacy to point to the old coaches and the travelling outside, for there is no analogy. The rate at which the train moves renders the third-class cold in the warmest atmosphere. In winter, it tests the powers of the strongest. Delicate women—delicate though poor, and valuable members of society, though belonging to the working-class—half clothed and half fed, are unable to contend with an inclement season, and often receive into their frames the seeds of indispositions which shorten their lives. The skilled artisan, too, enervated by the confined character of his labour, to whom many look for support, and on whom many hopes depend, is liable to cold, catarrh, and consumption. It is a class to which England owes much, and over the comfort of which she should watch. But railway proprietors are not social economists, and railway directors are men.

A meeting immediately took place, at which nearly all the great railways were represented. Mr. Hudson took the chair, and denounced the bill as injurious to railway property, and prejudicial to public welfare. Mr. Saunders, on behalf of the Great Western, followed, declaring his belief that the provisions affecting future lines would be brought to bear upon the old as well as the new; avowing that his directors were to a man opposed to it; while others, in the depths of their despair, saw only ruin to the railways in the clause which forced them to carry passengers comfortably and like Christians at a rational rate. That they were wrong in their deductions is now evident. A lower occasional rate has since been established; and excursion trains have proved that the present power of the rail was as little estimated by those who projected it, as its future performances are contemplated by its present managers. It is, however, scarcely possible to describe the strong feelings which then pervaded the railway world. Mutual distrust and mutual dissensions were forgotten; opposing chairman met in the same room, discussing the same interest and denouncing the same government. It was the

great question of the day; the absorbing topic of
the time. Men magnified its dangers, drew pictures
of its consequences, and trembled at the distresses
they had evoked. It was a subject on which
railway secretaries and railway chairmen waxed eloquent :—

" Let once the icy hand of power clutch the public
works of this country, and the day for glorious
enterprise and adventurous achievements—deeds as
glorious, as brave, as chivalrous, we may add,
requiring quite as high courage and noble daring
as the conquests of the field and the sword—this
spirit of independent enterprise will be congealed
and chilled down; progress will be at an end, and
the ardour of adventure to which we owe all the
great improvements of the country, will degenerate into the cold, stationary formality of official
routine."

" The railway plunder bill has been printed," said
another; " we advisedly call it by that opprobrious
designation." It was termed " flagitious injustice."
" It must be resisted and defeated *in toto*. The
bill cannot be modified : it must be defeated or withdrawn." On the second day after its appearance,

railway deputations from every part of the kingdom met in the metropolis, and after Mr. Hudson had, with characteristic shrewdness, analysed the bill, and Mr. Saunders had denounced it as unsound in principle and injurious to every railway interest, the following "reasons against the measure" were unanimously adopted; and a memorial was addressed to Sir Robert Peel praying that it might not be proceeded with during the existing session.

"Because its provisions are not called for by any complaint on the part of the public.

"Because it is introduced at so late a period of the session as to render it quite impossible that its provisions should have sufficient consideration.

"Because the bill is obviously intended to vest in government a power of interference with, and undue control over, all existing as well as future railways.

"Because such a proposal would have the effect of shaking the public confidence and security in all such undertakings, and in all privileges granted by the legislature.

"Because the exclusive application of such a bill to railways only is obviously most unjust.

" Because an unheard-of power would be vested in the government.

" Because there is no experience in this country to justify so great a change in the system of legislation with reference to railways, as that proposed.

" Because there is no pretence for such government interference arising out of misconduct by railway companies, or undue profits realised by them.

" Because if such undertakings were vested in the hands of government, and should prove unsuccessful, the loss would have to be made up by general taxation.

" Because the provisions of the bill which regulate third-class trains are inconsistent with the existing rights of railway companies.

" Because the attempt to tamper with undertakings in which property has been embarked, on the security of the legislature, tends to weaken the faith and security of the capitalist in those undertakings, and to induce him to embark his property in foreign speculations."

In the House and out of it, the railway representatives raised their voices ; deputation after deputation was appointed to resist the government. Wherever a new railway was contemplated, or an old one established, there were the promoters declaiming, and directors dictating measures against a bill, which one gentleman, more forcibly than elegantly, said, "would bring all our railways under the paws of government."

Petitions against it continued to pour into the legislature. Questions were asked with the vehemence of self-interest; the members were wearied and worried with attacks, which marked as much private virulence as they did public virtue, but still the government persisted. Every important town in the kingdom held meetings to oppose it. It was said, and with much justice, that railways were as beneficial as canals, but that, though the latter averaged thirty-three per cent., there had been no restriction on their dividends, no claim on their profits.

A deputation waited on the ministers. The representatives of twenty-nine railway companies, with fifty millions to back them, were there to persuade Sir Robert Peel and Mr. Gladstone to withdraw the bill. They were told it was injurious, uncalled-for, contrary to the spirit of English commerce, and that it had been introduced at a time when it was too late to give it due consideration. In vain, however, did Mr. Russell declaim, in vain did Mr. Glyn argue, in vain, too, did Mr. Hudson protest; they were listened to with patience, they were answered with suavity, and they were refused their request.

The government having declined to postpone the bill, fierce and fiery was the declamation which followed it to the House of Commons.

Mr. Gisborne declared it was the general feeling of the committee who had entered into the subject, that no measure should be adopted which was not supported by the railway body; and that it was not fair to proceed with a bill against which was arrayed the whole railway interest of the kingdom.

Mr. Russell said, the moment the bill became known universal alarm spread through the kingdom; memorials and petitions were presented; meetings were held, and a deputation waited on the premier to implore its postponement. In behalf of all the railway companies in the kingdom, representing eighty or one hundred millions of money, he entreated the House to interpose the exercise of its high authority to give time for the consideration of this grave and all important subject. He begged them to remember that the voluminous evidence on which it was framed had been issued in the middle of June, and could not, therefore, have been fairly considered either by railway companies, the country, or the House, at the beginning of July.

Mr. Gladstone properly and promptly replied that the proposed motion for postponement was so violent that the House could not for one moment sanction it.

An excitement very unbefitting a high legislative assembly prevailed, and after many speeches varying according to the views or interests of the speaker, Sir Robert Peel rose with the severe determination which marked him at important crises, and told the objectors though their strength might be great he would advise them to husband it; that they were afraid even to hear; that they dared not trust themselves to vote on its merits; and he ominously dilated on the power of a monopoly which tried to deprive the government, not of carrying, but of explaining a measure which they wished to introduce.

A marked effect was immediately produced; and Mr. Gladstone in a very able and a very interesting speech said, "The question of the whole bill was the purchase or option of purchase on the part of government; that their views were misrepresented, and that the parliamentary and railway agents had raised all the commotion. It was not for the proprietors of railways that secretaries and chairmen became alarmed; but it was when they advised the reference of the bill to the board of trade; it was when the committee intimated an opinion that that reference would cheapen proceedings, that opposition arose, and lobbies were crowded. The railway opposers of the bill were the unconscious instruments of maintaining a lavish, extravagant, and discreditable system of private bill legislation." He then continued, "What is the opposition to this bill? It is composed of different elements, and that is a curious and instructive part of the case. One portion of the opponents are those directors who adopt a very high tone against the interference of parliament. My hon. friend, the chairman of the Great Western, is a chieftain among this class of persons. He adopted that high tone, and was averse to any attempt to lay down general rules for railway legislation, and to applying any legislative restrictions.

Those gentlemen who have their particular mode of consoling the public on railway matters, say, ' Oh, trust to competition.' *I would no more trust the railway proprietors on railway matters, than I would Gracchus speaking of sedition !* I know of nothing more chilling than the hope which the directors of these railways hold out. If you do not shut your eyes to facts, you will draw important conclusions from what has been passing in relation to this competition, to which your attention must have been directed, and which I trust I may mention as a short episode. There has been going on during the spring a very notable affair. The London and Birmingham and the Grand Junction Railway companies have been at dreadful feud with each other; and what was the result ? There was a most flourishing prospect for the public. The public were to have the choice of a new line. The public have already a new line between Birmingham and Liverpool, and between London and Birmingham. The London and Birmingham company were engaged in the purchase of the Chester and Birkenhead railway, and they proposed to make a line from Birmingham to Shrewsbury, and, the distance from Chester not

being great, parties saw there would be a line to
Shrewsbury from that place, and then the public
were to go down to Liverpool by this route; and
this was a delightful prospect for the public. But
the Grand Junction company had as much public
spirit. They thought there would be no objection
to the two lines at the north end of the line; but
they thought that there should also be two at the
south end, and the Grand Junction proposed a line
from Stafford to Bedford, and so accomplished a
line all the way to Bedford. These companies are
now singular philanthropists, nay, they are like
lovers. No sooner had they quarrelled than recon-
ciliation followed. One of these lines, however,
has gone to the land where all things end. I state
this as an instance of the hopes which are to be
entertained from competition amongst the railway
companies. I wish to show parliament the doctrines
held by those of the high school of non-interference
on the subject of existing railway companies, and
the part which parliament ought to take with respect
to those which shall spring into future existence.
Feeling," continued the honourable gentleman with
great force, "feeling that we have right and justice

on our side, I say that although the railway companies are powerful, I do not think they have mounted so high, or that parliament has yet sunk so low, as that at their bidding you shall refuse your sanction to this bill." Mr. Gladstone concluded by saying, " It had been asserted that railway property had been shaken by it; but since the report had been produced, the price of shares had risen. They had risen, too, since the result of the deputation had been known, when a most lugubrious body of gentlemen had presented themselves, in the front rank of which stood directors and large shareholders, while behind were solicitors and agents pushing the others forward." It need not be said that Colonel Sibthorp supported Mr. Gladstone, or that Mr. Labouchere followed, declaring, " He knew no interest more recalcitrant and obdurate than that of the railway."

Sir Robert Peel could not imagine a less objectionable measure; and while he acknowledged the obligations of the country to the founders of the railway system, he could not refrain from expressing his firm belief that it was absolutely essential to the welfare of the country to adopt the measure before the House.

Every one who was interested in, or thought
he understood the question, was anxious to deliver
his sentiments; and when the second reading of
the bill was proposed, all the pens in the country
were at work.   The public were appealed to in
pamphlets; senators were threatened by their constituents; editors were inundated with letters from
correspondents; Sir Robert Peel was addressed in
an epistle from Mr. Lawrence Heyworth, in which
he talked of infatuated profligacy of principle, and
concluded by stating that manufacturers might be
dispossessed of their mills, and landowners of their
estates on the principle which produced this much
abused bill.   Mr. Gladstone received a long and
able letter from Mr. Hudson; and the whole railway
interest were engaged in making

Black not so black, nor white so very white.

The storm which surrounded the ministry produced
its effect.   They held communication with their most
active opponents, and agreed to a compromise.   An
amended bill was printed, in which the enactments
were limited to new lines, the old ones being exempted; the revision of rates was changed from

fifteen to twenty-one years, with no second revision until twenty-one years more had elapsed. New railways were not to be bought except at a fair valuation; old railways were to be exempted, and no purchases were to be made except by an express Act of parliament. These were the concessions of the state; and it is to their honour that the poorer order were not forgotten by them, but that they remained firm in demanding a third-class railway, at the rates they had proposed, which was to be conceded on remission of the tax by government.

When the modified bill was moved in committee, Mr. Morrison—a name well known in connexion with railway legislation—said government had exhibited great timidity in the way in which they had dealt with the question; while Colonel Sibthorp complained that the bill was altogether different from that which was originally brought before the notice of the House. More than one-half of its clauses had been struck out. It was partial in its operation, and left to fifty-five railway companies a licence which government intended to withhold from the new undertakings. He looked upon the alterations made as an unpardonable compromise. It gave to existing railways, which he considered gross monopolies, and not for the benefit of the public, an uncontrolled and irresponsible power. He should be sorry to see any newly-constructed railway, such as the proposed line from London to York, placed under such unjust restrictions. If the people of Lincoln would have that line, he would neither support nor oppose it. If they would cut their own throats with railway speculations, it was not his duty to assist them. He now withdrew the thanks he had at first awarded to the president of the board of trade, and would protest against the bill *in toto*.

In the House of Peers the discussions were as strong. The Sabbatical doctrine was opened by a member of the bench of bishops, who, forgetting that two thousand years ago it was emphatically said "the Sabbath was made for man, and not man for the Sabbath," would have prevented the third-class carriages from running on that day. This is scarcely the time to moot this question, but the moral and mental benefits derivable from cheap travelling on the day of rest are inestimably great. The hewers of wood and the drawers of water need a cessation from toil. The writer has met them in the vicinity of village churches which they have visited ; he has met them basking in the beauty of a Sunday summer's morning ; he has seen them plucking wild flowers with which to deck their dark dull homes, and he has ever found them thoughtful, earnest, intelligent men, who, however prejudiced in favour of a particular dogma, were generally open to conviction, and who, while they received, often imparted instruction. The world would have cried shame had any priestly or parliamentary legislation deprived them of the privilege of employing their own time after their own fashion.

In the House of Commons the subject was met as it deserved. "Why," said Mr. Thornley, logically, "should the railway be open for first and second-class and exclude third-class passengers on Sunday." Mr. Sheil said, " the question appeared to resolve itself into this, whether Dives should travel on a Sunday and Lazarus should not." Mr. Gladstone—and due respect must be paid to the opinions of the author of " The State in Relation to the Church "—took an opposite view, thinking that "the working respectable mechanic would not choose the Lord's day for travelling, and were it otherwise it would be bad policy in government to encourage such a system. The observance of the Sabbath was the main support of religion." It is melancholy to see the aberrations of so fine a mind on this subject. Place Mr. Gladstone in the position of the mechanic, let him feel the necessity of rest to the worn mind, and of free air to the enfeebled body, and that gentleman will form a very different conclusion.

The bill—one of the most important which ever affected this interest—was passed; but, as stated, in a form so modified that it was difficult to recognise the original features of the proposition. This may be considered the first important battle between government and railways, and in it most assuredly the former were beaten. A complete history of this encounter has been given, because it is an evidence of the growing power of the interest to which this work is devoted. The following are the most important clauses of an Act, the first of which empowers the lords of the treasury, if after twenty-one years from the passing of any future act for a railway, the profits shall exceed ten per cent. per annum, on an average of the preceding three years, to revise the scale of tolls and fix a new scale, so as to reduce the divisible profits to ten per cent., giving the company three months' notice thereof, with a guarantee that the annual rate of profit shall be annually made good to the amount of ten per cent. ; such revised scale and guarantee to continue for twenty-one years.

" The lords of the treasury to have the option of purchasing any future railway after the expiration of twenty-one years, upon payment of a sum equal to twenty-five years' purchase of the divisible profits, esti-mated on an average of the last three preceding years, but if the proprietors think the average below their prospects the amount to be submitted to arbitration.

" Existing railways not to be subject to the opera-tions of this Act.

" Branch or extension lines, not exceeding five miles in length, not to be considered new railways.

" No purchase under this Act to be made without first obtaining an Act of Parliament for the purpose ; of the intention to present which, three months' previous notice must be given to the company.

" Accounts of all monies paid and received to be kept for the three years preceding the expiration of the term at which the option of purchase arises, and an abstract prepared half-yearly, of which copies are to be sent to the treasury.

" All passenger railway companies which shall have been incorporated by any Act of the present session, or shall be hereafter incorporated, shall, by means of one train at the least, to travel along their railway from one end to the other of each trunk, branch, or junction line belonging to, or leased to them, once at the least each way, on every week day, except Christmas-day and Good Friday, provide for the conveyance of third-class passengers, under the following conditions :

" Such train shall start at an hour to be from time to time fixed by the directors, subject to the approval of the lords of the committee of privy council for trade and plantations.

" Such trains shall travel at an average rate of speed, not less than twelve miles an hour for the whole distance travelled on the railway, including stoppages.

" Such train shall take up and set down passengers at every passenger station which it shall pass on the line.

" The carriages to be provided with seats and protected from the weather, in a manner satisfactory to
the lords of the said committee.

" The fare for each third-class passenger not to
exceed one penny per mile.

" Each passenger by such train shall be allowed to
take with him half a hundred-weight of luggage
without extra charge.

" Children under three years of age accompanying
passengers by such train, shall be taken without any
charge, and children of three years and upwards, but
under twelve years of age, at half the charge for an
adult passenger.

" These trains to be exempt from taxation.

" Trains running on Sunday are to have carriages
attached to those which stop at the greatest number
of stations.

" The electric telegraph to be established on all
lines of railway.

" The issue of loan notes and other illegal securities
prohibited; but loan notes already issued allowed to
be renewed."

These were the principal points. And now that
the bill is viewed with unprejudiced eyes, it appears

fair and equitable. Its provision for the third-class passengers is in a kind and genial spirit, and has been of the greatest service to those it was meant to benefit. It is a pity that the railroad companies have not generally and generously improved the character of these carriages, and by making them less exposed to the weather, rendered life less perilled and health more sure. If the rich man chooses to degrade himself, the poor man should not suffer; and in the wet weather which characterises England, it is right and proper that there should be some shelter for those who, compelled to adopt this mode of travelling, feel their health is as valuable and their lives are as dear as those who travel in a covered conveyance.

The board of trade also undertook the very onerous duty of examining all departures from the usual course of railway legislation; all plans for amalgamation, or for enabling companies to exceed or deviate from the power of their several Acts; all such branch or extension schemes as might appear to impede the progress of new and legitimate enterprise, together with a general supervision over railway bills before parliament.

The report in 1844, from the select committee on Joint Stock companies, was the foundation of another bill, which affected embryo railways. This report, most interesting to commercial men, contained many facts which, bearing directly upon railways, require a detailed notice. Mr. Duncan, a competent authority, when describing these and other bubbles, said, " In the formation of a company it is usual first to issue a prospectus, *sometimes without directors' names, in the hope that parties will take up the matter and form a direction*; sometimes with directors' names inserted. . . . At other times, it is necessary to issue advertisements for subscribers; but it is surprising how dreadfully rotten the list of applications is . . . . The parties who write, do so instantly on seeing a scheme advertised; they then inquire if there be a chance of the shares coming out at a premium, however small. If that chance exist, then they use any influence they may by sidewind possess to get an allotment. Should they receive these, the common practice was, and is, to sell them for what they will fetch. I have known such letters sold at the rate of three-pence to twenty shillings a share. The practice is most disreputable. Possibly some parties may find that letters cannot be sold ; and then if there still be a chance of a small premium, they will borrow money for the deposit, and sell the shares immediately after, at a trifling profit per share. Most frequently the letters are not attended to at all, for the application of many persons are never made unless the result can bring the certainty of an immediate premium, however small. The reason why these letters can be dealt in is because the company's bankers, not knowing one from another, take money from anybody who brings a letter of appropriation, and they give a receipt. This receipt is taken to the company's office and exchanged for a scrip certificate to bearer, and then the title of the buyer of the letter is complete. If there be much risk about the company, or no great soundness, or if it be ill supported by the directory, a second call can never be obtained. The consequence is, that after from six to twelve months' duration, the company is dissolved and dies a natural death, and the deposit is found to be eaten up by expenses. Another cause for dissolution after the first deposit is, that the scrip shares have got into hands resolved to pay nothing more; who laugh at the power of forfeiture in the directors, and know that the power to sue for calls the directors have not got, as no deed of settlement has yet been signed."

The report which followed was well drawn up, and deserves to be presented in its entirety, did the limits of these volumes permit.

" Bubble companies," said this document, " may be divided into three classes :—

1. " Those which are founded on unsound cal-culations.

2. " Those which are so ill constituted as to render it probable miscarriage or failure will attend them.

3. " Those which are faulty or fraudulent.

" All the companies of the last class adopt the outward characteristics common to those of the best kind. They exhibit an array of directors and officers ; announce a large capital; adopt the style and title of a company; declare they are sanctioned by Act of parliament ; use some conspicuous place of business in a respectable situation, and employ through-out the country respectable agents and bankers.

" But many of their characteristics are fictitious. The directors have not either sanctioned the use of their names, or they are not the persons they are supposed to be. Not only is there no capital, but neither subscribers nor deed of settlement. Their purposes, though plausible, are often founded on calculations which do not admit of success, and they have not only not received the sanction or authority of parliament or of the crown, but the very statutes which are cited as conferring the authority will be found to have a very different object."

The modes adopted by the promoters of these companies to bring themselves into notice were legion; and the following sketch is very important and interesting :

" These concerns continue to accomplish their frauds by the following modes of deception—from some of which good concerns are not wholly free— and so far they sanction the adoption of them by the worst, and accustom the public not to regard them as a type or test of dishonesty.

1. " By the use of the names of persons having no existence.

2. " By the use of the names of distinguished persons, and persons of respectability and wealth, without their authority.

3. " By the use of the names of such persons as patrons and honorary directors, with their consent, while such persons have been ignorant of the nature of the concerns and of its transactions, and have exercised no control over its management.

4. " By the issue of prospectuses and advertisements containing false statements as to the authority under which it exists, as to the amount of capital of the company, or the period of its establishment.

5. " By getting reports of pretended meetings, and puffs relating thereto, inserted in the newspapers.

6. " By prospectuses fraudulently varied from time to time.

7. " By the employment throughout the country, on very tempting rates of commission, of respectable agents, whose character has cloaked the want of respectability of the company.

8. " By opening banking accounts with the Bank of England and other respectable banks.

9. " By the selection of offices in respectable situations, fitted up in a respectable manner.

10. " By the concoctors and managers living at great expense, entertaining their neighbours, and

thereby endeavouring to fortify themselves against suspicion.

11. " By the making up of fraudulent accounts.

12. " By declaring dividends out of capital, on a false representation of profit realised.

13. " By concealing the names or preventing the meeting of shareholders, and falsifying the books, by creating fictitious votes, thereby out-voting the *bona fide* shareholders.

14. " By the use of the names of respectable solicitors and counsel, deceiving the public into a belief of the soundness of the company."

It will thus be seen that previous to the great railway speculations in 1845, the country and government were sufficiently warned of the many systems of fraud in existence. The committee recommended various remedies, some of which were adopted by the House of Commons ; but, perhaps, the most important in its social bearings was that which said, " No person should act as patron, president, director, or in any similar position, who had not in his own right and behalf one or more shares."

Henceforth the creditor was safe at the expense of directors and provisional committee men. Henceforth the tradesman who trusted the company on the faith of the names which heralded it, was safe. It was meant to prevent the deceptions which up to this period had been legion ; for it was felt to be right that men should not take all the benefit without running part of the risk. But there are so many sad and sorrowful cases on which to look back ; so many painful privations to the innocent ; so many social evils which followed the decree, that the writer almost regrets the passing of an enactment which has ruined some, which has outlawed others, which has broken up entire circles, which has sent the heads of families to prison, which has changed the ownership of many an estate, which has made rich men beggars, and which has exiled peers. With such a melancholy catalogue of ills it is to be hoped that beneficial results were not wanting. It was an endeavour to stay growing speculation, or at least to make the public as secure as speculation will permit.

CHAPTER V.

IT is now necessary to treat of that great mania
which has shed a gloom for the last six years
over the domestic as well as the commercial life
of England. In 1843, railways, though depressed
in value, were regarded as good as consols. They
formed an investment for surplus capital, into which
safe men entered with a conviction of their stability.
It was a mode of transit tried and found true. It
was recognised as a novel element in our social
system. The great trunk lines from the metropolis
and from the principal towns were deemed sufficient
by the most imaginative of schemers, who never

dreamed of millions being expended on new roads
to save a few miles. Railways were, therefore, at
this period investments into which men trusted
the savings of their lives, and which had not betrayed
the trust. Of twenty-three English railway Acts
passed in 1836, four had been abandoned; three were
only partly carried out; one was not completed; and
fifteen were finished. Thirteen were at a discount;
two were leased to other companies; one was a
mineral line; three only being at a premium. The
thirteen which were below par cost the shareholders
eighteen millions, while their value in 1843 was
only eleven and a-half millions. The established
lines were conducted by men who could not have
done a mean action had they tried, and would
not have done it if they could. The monied
public felt this, and purchased freely where they
trusted fully. In 1843, twenty-four railway Acts
were passed, but this number was no more than the
public service required.

In 1844, thirty-seven additional projects received
the royal sanction. The capital stock of these was
authorised to be £13,981,000, while £4,006,000
was allowed to be raised by loan. Thus the total

amount in 1844 which received the sanction of the legislature was £17,987,000. This was, of course, only a portion of the companies projected, for in 1844 the first movement occurred in rousing the public from its quiet, and the initiative was taken in that madness which afterwards desolated England.

That some excitement would take place, that some monetary fever would ensue, was the conviction of the few who thought. The three years preceding 1845 had been remarkable for an easy state of the money market; for an increasing supply of bullion in the bank; for a large average circulation, and for discounts varying from two and a-half to three and a-half per cent. In January, 1842, the bullion in the bank coffers had been as low as £5,629,000. In January, 1845, it had increased to £14,867,000; in January, 1842, the circulation was £16,923,000; in January, 1845, it was £20,301,000. During the whole of 1844 it had averaged about the same amount. Money was very abundant. The great discount houses were full. The bank discounted at two and a-half per cent. Consols were above par, and everything promised a continuance of the golden age.

The rate of interest had indeed been gradually decreasing since 1839. From six per cent. in August of that year, to five per cent. in January 1840; from five to four, and from four to two and a-half per cent. had the value of money fallen by September, 1844. Nor is it unworthy of notice that up to that period, while railway enterprise maintained a legitimate form, the rate of discount was four per cent. But when in that month two and a-half was the published rate, it was not long before a remarkable effect occurred in the general increase of all kind of schemes and speculations; and while discounts continued thus low, and money thus plentiful, the impulse continued; but when, in November, 1845, the rate was advanced, it is in the memory of all that the panic, known as the railway panic, followed with a fierce and fatal effect.

The railway companies were proposed in 1844 with so much rapidity, that the legislature deemed it necessary to interfere; and by the Act seven and eight Victoria, bearing date 5th September, 1844, entitled a "bill for the registration, incorporation, and regulation of joint stock companies, of which an analysis has previously been given, some beneficial arrangements were made. The above act, it has been seen, provided that every person whose name appeared as one of the provisional committee should hold one or more shares, and this stringent clause rendered each of the class liable to the extent of his whole property.

Thus quietly had this great power influenced the comfort and the capital of Great Britain. Thus silently and surely had been formed an investment for the redundant wealth of the country, and thus far had the poor and the rich man been benefited by the power of the rail. The former found his weekly wages more steady, and his weekly work more sure. The latter saw the greatness of his country consolidated, and the relations of capitals increased. He saw the accumulation of wealth, which with an industrial people always outstrips the ordinary modes of investment, legitimately and justly employed in that which has ever been recognised as the first cause of a country's greatness. He saw the money which in his youth had been thrown into war loans, and in his manhood wasted on South American mines, forming roads, employing labour, and increasing business. Hitherto, in spite of some aber-

rations of the public mind, and in spite of many
deceptions of private rogues, the speculation had
been principally legitimate. There was much to
justify the early enthusiasm for the rail. Its absorption of capital was at least an absorption, if unsuccessful, in the country which had produced it. If
railroads were found unprofitable one year, they were
almost certain to improve with the commerce and
the capital of another epoch. Unlike foreign mines
and foreign loans, they could not be exhausted with
the one or be utterly valueless with the other. If
they ceased to yield a legitimate dividend, it was
but a momentary paralysis which was certain to
pass away. The mine might cease for ever to yield
its ore, the land which borrowed might cease for
ever to pay its debt; but so surely as a railway
was properly planted and fairly treated, so surely
would it force communication and compel a dividend.
It was but a question of time.

The traffic of the country had trebled within the
previous twenty-one years. Three railways, the
London and Birmingham, the Grand Junction, and
the York and North Midland, paid ten per cent.,
while a fourth, the Stockton and Darlington, divided

fifteen per cent. The safety of the locomotive had also been proved. In 1843 seventy railroads had conveyed twenty-five millions of passengers for 330 millions of miles with only three fatal accidents, and that, too, at an average cost of a penny three farthings each person.

During 1843, and the greater part of 1844, therefore, railway enterprise may be regarded as the natural effort of capital to procure a fair and proper interest. Scarcely, however, was it recognised as an object of legitimate investment than it became a subject of illegitimate speculation. The press at first fostered the excitement. It saw a great power ; it recognised a great good ; and it welcomed it. It was calculated that were 2,000 miles of the projected roads completed, 500,000 labourers would be employed for four years ; that the poor rates must necessarily diminish ; that the consumption of exciseable articles would increase ; and that the revenue of the country must improve. These points were naturally seized on. Paragraphs and essays alike dilated on the powers and properties of the rail, and the people were insensibly "led by the nose as asses are." It was expatiated on by pamphleteers, and preached on in the pulpit. Edifying sermons proved that railways were prophecied by the seers of old, and Ezekiel was expounded to sanction and to sanctify the iron way. Leading articles dilated with energy and eloquence upon its prospects. "Nor, indeed," wrote one, "can we contemplate unmoved the glorious prospect which will be opened to the world, if merely the vast and important works now in progress —works with which the useless Egyptian pyramids or the vaunted remnants of old Rome's extravagance, will not endure comparison—be carried into execution. The length of our lives, so far as regards the power of acquiring information and disseminating power, will be doubled, and we may be justified in looking for the arrival of a time when the whole world will have become as one great family, speaking one language, governed in unity by like laws, and adoring one God."

"Railways," said another, "will remain safe in the midst of panic; and though times of pressure, severe, hazardous, ruinous pressure, have been felt in this country, and unfortunately must be felt again, yet it will only prove them to be part and parcel of the genuine sources of wealth and avenues for labour, in which this country lives and moves and has its being."

Fine writing was at a premium. "Railways are the triumph of a period of peace. They are the emblems of internal confidence and prosperity. They are the prophetic announcement of an open-eyed people that they will not waste their dearest action in the tented field, but exhibit it in the mightier works of commerce." The political economist was appealed to by one. "Do the people want present employ? Railways give it to hundreds of thousands at this moment. Is it desirable that the artizan or mere labourer should at all times be able to transfer his skill or his strength to the place where he can most profitably employ either? Railways give the power to do so. Is it desirable that prices should be equalised generally through the country? Railways are the great levellers, bringing the producer and consumer into immediate contact. By railways the whole country may be, and," piously added the writer, "will be, under the blessing of divine providence, cultivated as a garden.'

Patriotism and poetry were alike resorted to. "Railways," it was said, "are the wonder of the world. Nothing during the last few years has created so marvellous a change as the great iron revolution of science. Beneath it the features of old Christendom have become changed, and its wealth and physical grandeur augmented. Other revolutions have scattered luminous influences over the world, but it remained for the new generation of railways to bring about one of the mightiest moral and social revolutions that ever hallowed the annals of any age. . . . . Omnipresence is one of the principles of their progress. Not content with making Liverpool their lineage home, and many-sounding Manchester mistress of their choice, they are throwing a girdle round the globe itself. Far-off India woos them over its waters, and China listens to the voice of the charmer. The ruined hills and broken altars of old Greece, will soon re-echo the whistle of the locomotive, or be converted to shrines sacred to commerce, by the power of those magnificent agencies by which rivers are spanned, territories traversed, commerce enfranchised, confederacies consolidated ; by which the adamantine is made divisible, and man assumes a lordship over time and space."

Such are a few specimens of the literature of

the iron road. The literature of the prospectuses is worthy a glance, from the brilliant and inviting prospects it pourtrayed. One route "would disclose a succession of picturesque scenes." Another "traversed a country of unrivalled beauty." In a third "the public interest had been the sole consideration." The direct London and Exeter was proposed partly because "it was nearly the road adopted by the Romans." The Dartmouth, Torbay, and Exeter would pay a large dividend because "its terminus was in a neighbourhood celebrated for its genial climate." The announcement of another project, it was grandiloquently said, "had been hailed with satisfaction from the north to the south;" while "the remarkable fact that in the reign of Alfred the Great the vicinity of another was the seat of an actual invasion by the Danes under Hubba" was dwelt upon with a zest more becoming the relic than the money-hunter.

Railways were to swallow up every other kind of speculation, and be the permanent deposit for all the surplus wealth of the country; "and," added the editor of the *Banker's Magazine*, too practical not to detect the absurdity which lurked in articles with more poetry than propriety, " the same authority assures us we are to have railway streets in London, with the carriages over-head and the foot-passengers and shopkeepers underneath; while in the country railway steam-engines on the atmospheric plan are not only to perform all the work of the lines, but are to employ their surplus power in impregnating the earth with carbonic acid and other gases, so that vegetation may be forced forward despite all the present ordinary vicissitudes of the weather, and corn be made to grow at railway speed."

From week to week, and from month to month, the delusion continued to spread. In January 1845, sixteen new lines were registered. The two following months saw a further increase; and in April fifty-two additional companies were added to the number. The stimulus which this gave to the prevailing fever was great, as they all bore a premium. The working railways also increased in value, and speculators pointed to their profits as a proof of prosperity. The commercial world saw high prices paid for goods generally; sales were easily and readily made; the markets were good; the chancellor of the exchequer rejoiced in his balances; the Bank

of England revelled in good bills and huge deposits ;
the private banker advanced liberally on railway
security ; our exports were large ; funds were high ;
safety and success surrounded the city, and all was
smiling.

The most cautious were deceived by this apparent
prosperity ; and men esteemed good citizens and
sound moralists were drawn into acts which avarice
urged but conscience condemned.   They saw their
neighbour's establishment increasing ; they heard the
cry of railways at every turn ; they listened to
speeches at dinners, uttered by solemn, solid men,
upon the glories of the rail ; they read of princes
mounting tenders, of peers as provisional committee
men, of marquises trundling wheelbarrows, and
of privy councillors cutting turf " on correct geome-
trical principles."   Their clerks left them to become
railway jobbers.   Their domestic servants studied
railway journals.   Men were pointed out in the
streets who had made their tens of thousands.   They
saw the whole world railway mad.   The iron road
was extolled at public meetings ; it was the object
of public worship ; it was talked of on the exchange ;
legislated for in the senate ; satirised on the stage.

It penetrated every class ; it permeated every household ; and all yielded to the temptation. Men who went to church as devoutly as to their counting-houses —men whose word had ever been as good as their bond—joined the pursuit. They entered the whirlpool, and were carried away by the vortex. They first cautiously wrote for shares in the names of their children, and sold the letters at a price which, while it consoled them for present turpitude, tempted them to fresh sin.

Their infant daughters were large subscribers; their youthful sons were down for thousands. But the care which prompted them to apply for shares in the names of irresponsible children, failed and faded before the frenzied desire for gain. Like drunken men they lost their caution and gave their signatures to everything that was offered. They bought at a premium, and sold at a profit. They forsook their business, and hung about the share-market. They became directors and provisional committee men. They pledged their purses and their persons to a great delusion : they gave the sanction of their names to shams ; and they were the men on whom the sin and the shame must rest. When careful people, who had refused the projects which were heralded by unknown names, saw the director of an established fire-office; the governor of some large joint-stock bank; the head partner in some great private establishment; or the merchant whose credit was hitherto unim-peached and unimpeachable, backing plausible but perilous schemes, they subscribed on the faith of that man's honour, and too often lost their money through their great mercantile trust.

The prosperous state of trade; the excitement of the period; the travelling from place to place and from province to province, produced a corresponding prosperity in the receipt of railways; and in the first week of 1845, the aggregate receipts of those in existence were £100,000 a week, being the large increase of £20,000 over the same period in the previous year. Nor did the journals devoted to the good cause fail to trumpet the intelligence with due importance. The great body of railway proprietors were congratulated on their prospects, with grandiloquence which persuaded some they were to maintain a large dividend, and induced others to invest their savings in the hope that it would be perpetual.

The months of May and June witnessed an increase of speculation. " The whole country from coast to coast," says Mr. Bell, " was to be traversed and dissected by iron roads. Wherever there was a hamlet or a cattle track, a market or a manufactory, there was to be a railroad; physical objects and private rights were straws under the chariot wheels of the Fire King. Mountains were to be cut through; valleys were to be lifted; the skies were to be scaled; the earth was to be tunnelled; parks, gardens, and ornamental grounds were to be broken into; the skrieking engine was to carry the riot of the town into the sylvan retreats of pastoral life; sweltering trains were to penetrate solitudes hitherto sacred to the ruins of antiquity; hissing locomotives were to rush over the tops of houses."

The advertisements indicated the mania. The daily journals realised enormous sums; the weekly papers made large profits. The established railway press was filled with names as provisional committee men, with announcements of lines never meant to be executed, with puffs, with paragraphs, with everything that could entice or allure. In one paper, there were two hundred and thirty-one columns

paid for out of the funds provided by the calls.
New railway journals were constantly appearing;
the old issued their sheets more frequently. In
one, twenty-four advertisements of a single line were
inserted. The Welsh Midland announced one hundred and sixty provisional committee men, " with
power to add to their number." Bankers, senators,
merchants, and members of the monied aristocracy,
abetted this bold and bare-faced puffing. Editors
of second-rate papers wrote to secretaries, procured
advertisements, and for inserting notices of particular
lines, realised a portion of the money so freely bestowed and so easily procured.

" Before the railway mania set in with full force,"
says Mr. Evans,* " only three railway papers existed.
As speculation progressed, others were called into
life. In 1845, as many as twenty publications
identified with the railway interest had made their
appearance. Of these, fourteen were professedly
hebdomadal; but in the height of the fever they
were issued semi-weekly; two others came out daily,
one morning and one evening, and several were
monthly publications. The morning paper, dignified

* "Commercial Crisis." Second Edition.

with the title of the *Iron Times*, flourished prodigi-
ously for months, securing vast patronage from advertisements, some, it is stated, being paid for at the rate
of two shillings a line, when honoured by a position
immediately following the leading article.   Bank-
ruptcy finally extinguished its struggles in the panic
period, and the proprietors appeared before the
commissioners in Basinghall-street.   Many of these
publications lived little longer than a few weeks.
Started expressly to get advertisements, the proprietors principally directed their attention to that
source of profit, and when advertising began to
decline, suddenly discontinued them.   Among the
multitude that sought patronage at the hands of
promoters and secretaries, were Railway Expresses,
Railway Worlds, Railway Examiners, Railway Globes,
Railway Standards, Railway Mails, Railway Engines,
Railway Telegraphs, Shareholders Advocates, Railway
Directors, Railway Registers, Railway Reviews, &c."

The daily press were thoroughly deluged with
advertisements ; double sheets did not supply space
enough for them ; double doubles were resorted
to, and then frequently insertions were delayed.   It
has been estimated that the receipts of the leading

journals averaged at one period £12,000 and £14,000 a week from this source. The railway papers on some occasions contained advertisements that must have netted from £700 to £800 on each publication. The printer, the lithographer, and the stationer, with the preparation of prospectuses, the execution of maps, and the supply of other requisites, also made a considerable harvest.

The leading engineers were necessarily at a great premium. Mr. Brunel was said to be connected with fourteen lines, Mr. Robert Stephenson with thirty-four, Mr. Locke with thirty-one, Mr. Vignolles with twenty-two, Sir John Rennie with twenty, Mr. Rastrick with seventeen, and other eminent engineers with one hundred and thirteen.

The novelist has appropriated this peculiar portion of commercial history, and describing it says, gravely and graphically, " A colony of solicitors, engineers, and seedy accountants, settled in the purlieus of Threadneedle-street. Every town and parish in the kingdom blazed out in zinc plates over the doorways. From the cellar to the roof every fragment of a room held its committee. The darkest cupboard on the stairs contained a secretary or a clerk. Men

who were never seen east of Temple-bar before
or since, were now as familiar to the pavement of
Moorgate-street* as the stock-brokers : ladies of title,
lords, members of parliament, and fashionable loun-
gers thronged the noisy passages and were jostled
by adventurers, by gamblers, rogues, and impostors."

The advantages of competition were pointed out
with the choicest phraseology. Lines which passed
by barren districts and by waste heaths, the termini
of which were in uninhabitable places, reached a high
premium. The shares of one company rose 2,400 per
cent. Everything was to pay a large dividend ; everything was to yield a large profit. One railway was
to cross the entire Principality without a single curve.

The shares of another were issued ; the company
formed, and the directors appointed, with only the
terminal points surveyed. In the Ely railway, not
one person connected with the country through
which it was to pass subscribed the title-deed.

The engineers who were examined in favour of
particular lines promised all and everything in
their evidence. It was humorously said, " They

---

* From Moorgate-street eighty-three prospectuses, demanding £90,175,000
were sent out. Gresham-street issued twenty, requiring £,17580,000.

plunge through the bowels of mountains, they undertake to drain lakes; they bridge valleys with
viaducts; their steepest gradients are gentle undu-
lations; their curves are lines of beauty; they inter-
rupt no traffic; they touch no prejudice."

Labour of all kinds increased in demand. The
price of iron rose from sixty-eight shillings to one
hundred and twenty per ton. Money remained abundant. Promoters received their tens and twenties
of thousands. Rumours of sudden fortunes were
very plentiful. Estates were purchased by those
who were content with their gains; and to crown
the whole, a grave report was circulated that North-
umberland-house with its princely remembrances
and palatial grandeur, was to be bought by the
South-Western. Many of the railways attained
prices which staggered reasonable men. The more
worthless the article, the greater seemed the struggle
to obtain it. Premiums of £5 and £6 were matters
of course, even where there were four or five
competitors for the road. One company which
contained a clause to lease it at three and a-half
per cent. for 999 years, rose to twenty premium, so
mad were the many to speculate.

Every branch of commerce participated in the advantages of an increased circulation. The chief articles of trade met with large returns; profits were regular; and all luxuries which suited an affluent community, procured an augmented sale. Banking credit remained facile; interest still kept low; money, speaking as they of the city speak, could be had for next to nothing. It was advanced on everything which bore a value, whether readily convertible or not. Bill-brokers would only allow one and a-half per cent. for cash; and what was one and a-half per cent. to men who revelled in the thought of two hundred? The exchanges remained remarkably steady. The employment of the labourer on the new lines, of the operative in the factory, of the skilled artisan in the workshop, of the clerk at the desk, tended to add to the delusive feeling, and was one of the forms in which, for a time, the population was benefited. But when the strength of the kingdom is wasted in gambling, temporary, indeed, is the good compared with the cost. Many whose money was safely invested, sold at any price to enter the share-market. Servants withdrew their hoards from the savings'-

banks. The tradesman crippled his business. The legitimate love of money became a fierce lust. The peer came from his club to his broker's; the clergyman came from his pulpit to the mart; the country gentleman forsook the calmness of his rural domain for the feverish excitement of Threadneedle-street. Voluptuous tastes were indulged in by those who were previously starving. The new men vied with the old in the luxurious adornments of their houses. Everyone smiled with contentment; every face wore a pleased expression. Some who by virtue of their unabashed impudence became provisional committee men, supported the dignity of their position in a style which raised the mirth of many and moved the envy of more. Trustees, who had no money of their own, or who had lost it, used that which was confided to them; brothers speculated with the money of sisters; sons gambled with the money of their widowed mothers; children risked their patrimony; and it is no exaggeration to say, that the funds of hundreds were surreptitiously endangered by those in whose control they were placed.

It was in vain that Mr. Glyn, with calm determination, when the spirit of speculation was at its height, positively asserted, " Railway property, as property, is in a state of great danger." It was in vain that Mr. Saunders said, " Railway property is liable to great depreciation from unnecesary competing lines." In vain Mr. Hudson warned the public against them. It was in vain that in April, 1845, Lord Brougham drew attention to the frenzy into which the community had fallen. It was in vain that Mr. Morrison brought forward motion after motion. It was in vain even that Colonel Sibthorp declared, " next to a civil war railways were the greatest curse to the country, and that they had dried up a thousand sources of labour, profit, wealth, and comfort." It was in vain that the *Edinburgh Review,* with a calmer tone and more subdued satire, wrote, " What shall we say to the railways, with their noiseless, straight-forward progress, avoiding the barren tops of our mountains, the less populous ridges of our moorlands, and forcing their way, with surveyors as their *avant couriers* and Acts of Parliament as their backers-up, through the waving wheat and green meadows of our most fertile districts, swallowing up whole acres at every hundred yards of their progress, and pausing at each intended station, only to make greater encroachments under the pretence of further accommodations?" and it was in vain that *Blackwood's Magazine* poured its merciless satire on "one counsel representing the country as abounding in mineral produce and agricultural wealth, and on the other likening it to Patmos or the stony Arabia." The reply to prophet and prognostic was unanswerable; railways were at a premium.

The name of Mr. Hudson, whose career will shortly be sketched, was very prominent during the whole of this time. It was felt that he had done much for the new power; that he was one of the men who had arisen with it; that if he had not, like Edward Pease or George Stephenson, originated the material portion of it, he had from a very early period forwarded its progress and furthered its interests. It was known all his undertakings were successful, and his actions were closely watched. "So strong is his fame felt," was it said at that time, "that you cannot take up any newspaper, whether tory, whig, or radical, whether local or metropolitan, nay, whether English or continental, without finding some article in his praise." Nor was this exaggerated. His movements were as much chronicled as those of the elder Rothschild, and as many stratagems were perpetrated to obtain his intimacy as was the case with his prototype Law. He was liberal, and therefore praised; rich, and therefore respected; the author of riches to others, and therefore worshipped. It was at this period that the subscription was opened for him which excited so much attention, and was so much satirised. That there was more selfishness than respect in it has been proved by recent occurrences. But this may be said of most testimonials, which, commenced by friends, find donors who laugh when they give their names and grumble when they give their money.*

The exertions of Mr. Hudson at this juncture were little short of astonishing. Nothing seemed to wear his mind; nothing appeared to weary his frame. He battled in parliamentary committees day by day; he argued, pleaded, and gesticulated with an earnestness which rarely failed in its object.

---

* The first railway men of the day were down to it; and when it is added that to this testimonial nearly £20,000 was subscribed, and about £16,000 absolutely received, it is pretty certain that the subscribers may be placed in two classes, namely, of those who had benefited and those who meant to benefit by of the idol they had set up.

One day in town cajoling a committee; the next persuading an archbishop. In the morning adjusting some rival claim in an obscure office; in the afternoon astonishing the Stock Exchange with some daring *coup de main*. At one time entertaining half the peerage; at another purchasing princely estates to thwart a rival. His career forms an episode which has yet to be told.

The extraordinary mania had seized on merchant and manufacturer with a power which defied control. It was condemned by parliament, and two-thirds of the members were dealers. It was condemned by the press, and editors were provisional committee men. It was condemned in the pulpit; and while a bishop was obliged to reprove his clergy, an archbishop was said to hold council with Mr. Hudson. The lord who derided it in the park, was beheld the next day in Throgmorton-street. The lady who ridiculed it in her boudoir, was seen the next hour at her broker's.

There was one fatal feature during this period which, though it may be lamented, cannot be blamed. The leading existing railways, willing enough to remain quiet, found it impossible to be so. Not only were opposition lines proposed, with pretensions which it was necessary to fight at a great expense; small branch railways were often so subtly projected that the old companies were forced to take them under their own management, and to guarantee dividends varying from three and a-half to six per cent.; and however sad the result, it seemed necessary to do so to save their own traffic.

For a time nothing but direct lines were named. The London and Birmingham, to save a few miles, was to have a rival at the expense of as many millions. The Great Western found its safety threatened by a similar opposition. "Duplicate railways," wrote Mr. Lawrence Heyworth at this period, " projected to carry the same traffic, ought not to receive the legislative sanction." The assertion of 1845 seems a platitude in 1851; but it was necessary to combat the shadows which then arose and which threatened to darken the prosperity of established companies with law expenses, or to ruin them in a competition for traffic. Only one of this kind from the metropolis was sanctioned, however; and the Great Northern is already lowering the receipts, decreasing the dividends, and increasing the dissatisfaction of those lines into whose country it enters. No railway should be sanctioned which can only pay a remunerative dividend at the expense of others.

At last the board of trade assumed the responsibility of deciding which undertakings should first meet the attention of government, and great was the consequent excitement. The usual hours of business were disregarded. Men ceased to seek their *lares* at even time. The tavern and the coffee-house saw the speculator waiting the *Gazette* with intense anxiety; for it was life or death to the reader. These reunions formed no uninstructive picture. Men of comparative importance grasped with trembling hands the authority which decided their fate. Those who failed in securing it looked with eager suspense over the others' shoulders, and sought to catch the words in the dim and wavering light. Some read aloud; others, with wild and almost wolfish eyes, followed the reader's words. "Those only who are on the spot," said the *Times*, "and witness its violence, and the general infection arising from it both within and without the walls of the Stock Exchange, can form an idea of the perilous task undertaken by the board of trade in putting forth these decisions, which are the fuel for this fire."

The days which elapsed between the issuing the *Gazettes*, were filled with rumours of the course the board would pursue with particular lines. In a few cases, by some inexplicable means, these rumours were true, and this added to the number of false reports. There is little doubt that the most fatal effects of speculation followed from the course pursued by the above board; and had government wished to encourage the mania they could not have chosen a better course. It was in truth an additional phase of the prevailing gambling, and men lost all caution and control in pursuing it.

The new powers delegated to the officers of the board of trade, in consequence of the expected pressure of railway business, were not of very long continuance, but they embraced a most important period. On 28th November, 1844, it was announced that in the exercise of the above authority, the following points would be most particularly inquired into:—

1. The ability and *bona fide* intentions of the promoters to prosecute their application to parliament in the following session.

2. The national advantages to be obtained.

3. The local advantages to the towns and districts more immediately affected.

4. The engineering circumstances of the line.

5. The estimate of cost of construction, of traffic, and of working expenses.

On 31st December in the above year, the board issued its first document concerning the schemes which had been examined, expressing an intention to report in favour of certain lines, and against others, recommending also the postponement of those which might be beneficially altered. In more elaborate papers the officers of the department stated their reasons, usually giving an opinion in favour of lines friendly to existing railways, often entering at great length into the scientific difficulties which beset competing companies. There was a general conviction at first that these opinions would decide the question, and some projects prepared for parliament were withdrawn in consequence. The recommendations were, however, soon disregarded. Men were too eager ; they had ventured too much ; they had thought, worked, risked too largely to yield while a jot of hope remained. They were laughed at when they first proposed to continue in the very face of an adverse judgment ; but speculative men are desperate men ; they proceeded with their bills, and in many instances were successful. Other schemes which had maintained a high premium because they had been warmly recommended by the board, were absolutely defeated in committee on the plea of wanting those merits for which they had been chosen. The standing orders were not complied with by many ; clerical errors were plentiful ; and it soon became evident that the railway chiefs of the board of trade were not popular with select committees or with the House. " Swayed by motives which it is difficult to fathom, the two Houses with singular unanimity agreed to reverse their wise decisions, and to give unrestricted scope to competition. Little regard was paid to the claims and interests of existing railway companies, still less to the interests of the unfortunate persons who were induced to embark in the new projects for no better reason than that they had been sanctioned by parliament. The opportunity of confining the exceptional gauge within its original territory was also for ever thrown away. By an inconceivable want of statesmanlike views and foresight no effort was made to connect the isolated railways, which then existed, by new links into one great and combined system, in the form in which they would be most subservient to the wants of the community, and to the great ends of domestic government and national defence. Further, the sudden change from one extreme of determined rejection or dilatory acquiescence, to the opposite extreme of unlimited concession, gave a powerful stimulus to the spirit of speculation, and turned nearly the whole nation into gamblers."*

The authority constituted on the 6th August, 1844, was discontinued on 10th July, 1845, and it was arranged that for the future all railway business should be transacted by the lords of the committee of privy council for trade, and that their directions and decisions should be carried into effect by the several officers of the railway department. Reports were not to be prepared for parliament favouring or condemning any particular project, but the board proposed, during the progress of the bill, to draw the notice of the House by special reports to any circumstances connected with the undertaking which might require their interference. Such reports to

* " Railway Legislation."

have reference to all questions of public safety, and to all departure from the ordinary usages of legislation. The consequence was that each company selected its own locality, and chose its own gauge. All hope of applying great general principles passed away. Every chance of directing the course of railways to form a national system of communication was lost. The statesmanlike attempts of Lord Dalhousie were thrown over; and the legislative body —to appropriate the idea of Mr. Morison—committed the mistake of converting the kingdom into a great stock exchange, and of stimulating the various members of the railway system to a deep and deadly struggle, destructive of order and fruitful of vice.

Some idea may be gathered of the increased business of those firms which affected railways, from the fact that a banker sent to the clearing-house £2,500,000. Mr. Gilbart in one of his valuable works* gives £1,700,000 as the highest amount that could be ascertained prior to the mania; the difference, therefore, between these two sums speaks volumes for the railway movement in connexion with banking.

* "Practical Treatise on Banking," fifth edition. By J. W. Gilbart,

CHAPTER VI.

GENERAL PROSPERITY.—EXTRAVAGANT PRICE FOR SCRIP.—INCREASED BUSI-
NESS OF BROKERS.—PROMOTERS,—FRAUDS IN RAILWAYS.—GAMBLING IN
THE PROVINCES.—INTERFERENCE OF THE MAGISTRATES.—INCREASED RATE
OF DISCOUNT.—PANIC IN THE SHARE MARKET.

THE government congratulated the country on the
employment of labour. The public sympathised
with the philosophical government. Dividends of
ten per cent. gratified the mental visions of investors.
Direct lines caught the imagination of the most wary.
The names of bankers of unimpeached and unimpeachable integrity, satisfied some. The names of
merchants of shrewd heads and sound hearts was
the snare for others. The *Bankers' Magazine*
preached, and the evening papers exhorted; the
" economical member for Westbury " wrote leading
articles; the daily journals honestly and heartily
proclaimed the future. Ridicule was the great reply;

cheques outweighed all argument; and premiums baffled every prophecy. The Bank of England was deified in the person of its governor for not reducing the rate of interest; consols remained high; the deposit was ordered to be increased from five to ten per cent., but still throughout July and August the number of registered schemes continued to augment. In September four hundred and fifty-seven were registered, and the beginning of October promised to maintain the people's madness. The public were thoroughly and terribly involved, and the most extravagant prices were paid for the scrip of lines which when completed could not realise their working expenses for years. A multitude of the projects had neither engineer nor surveyor. Others had only the names of those who were paid at so much the prospectus. A thousand guineas was charged by one eminent gentleman, who took no further interest and refused further responsibility.

It was found very difficult to procure really responsible names to the contracts. Fiction and fact alike testify it. " From his garret in some nameless suburb the outcast scamp; from his west-end hotel the spendthrift fop; from his dim studio the poor

artist; from his starved lodging the broken-down
gentleman; from his flying address the professional
swindler; from his fine mansion the man of notoriety,
whose life was a daily fight to keep up appearances,
poured into Moorgate-street every day."*

These were some of the " responsible men " whose
names were blazoned in prospectuses. Who that
reads cannot call to mind a representative of one
or other of these classes? But my Lord Clanricarde
confirms Mr. Bell, and the senator proves more
than the novelist asserts. " One of the names,"
said the noble marquis in his place in the upper
House, "to the deed to which he was anxious to
direct their attention, was that of a gentleman said
to reside in Finsbury-square, who had subscribed
to the amount of £25,000 ; he was informed no
such person was known at that address. There was
also in the contract deed the name of an individual
who had figured in the Dublin and Galway railway
case, who was down for £5,000, and who was
understood to be a half-pay officer in the receipt
of £54 a-year, but who appeared as a subscriber in
different railway schemes to the amount of £41,500,

* "The Ladder of Gold."

The address of another, whose name was down for £12,200, was stated to be in Watling-street, but it appeared he did not reside there. In the case of another individual down for £12,500 a false address was found to have been given. Another individual, whom he would not name, was a curate in a parish in Kent; he might be worth all the money for which he appeared responsible in various railway schemes, but his name appeared for £25,000 in different projects, and stood for £10,000 in this line. Another individual, who was down for £25,000, was represented to be in poor circumstances. A clerk in a public company was down for upwards of £50,000. There were several more cases of the same kind, but he trusted he had stated enough to establish the necessity of referring the matter to a committee. There were also two brothers, sons of a charwoman living in a garret, one of whom had signed for £12,500, and another for £25,000; these two brothers, excellent persons no doubt, but who were receiving about a guinea and a-half per week between them, were down for £37,500."

"Landowners," wrote *Fraser's Magazine*, "were kept in a constant state of anxiety by rumours of

the course each railway was likely to pursue. Young
gentlemen with theodolites and chains marched about
the fields; long white sticks with bits of paper
attached were carried ruthlessly through fields,
gardens, and sometimes even through houses." Colonel Sibthorp said, "The injuries done by the engineers
of railway companies to the property of private
individuals was most unjust. Not content with
making encroachments in the daytime, these ma-
rauders of engineers took advantage of the darkness
to commit those trespasses which their modesty
would not suffer them to do at another time. An
honourable friend of his rose one morning and actually
found a flag stuck up before his very door." There
can be no doubt that the insolent assurance of many
connected with railroads was unbounded. One proprietor, when he asked the promoters what would
be given him for the land which a line was to traverse, was informed "they would tell him when
the bill was passed into a law. That they did
not care whether he consented or not; that the
railway department of the board of trade had already
reported in favour of the line, and it would be the
worse for him if he offered opposition." Another

was told that if he objected to the rail passing near
his lawn, it would be taken through his kitchen.
Ladies of title were impudently assured that they
must get used to railways as others had done.

The proprietors of land had changed their opinions
since 1830. Instead of opposing railways they became provisional committee men, and used their
influence to enhance the price of the land they
sold. Connected with many members of the lower
House by birth and blood, they employed as much
interest to procure the passing of a bill, as formerly
they did to procure its rejection. A provisional
committee man was trebly valuable if also a senator;
and Mr. Herapath afterwards positively asserted, that
"Members had not merely been canvassed to support
a bill, but that large sums had been spent among
them, to secure their support; and that members of parliament had been known to go from
office to office and hawk their support as a pauper
would his wares." There is a growing feeling
on this subject, which was well expressed by the
Athenæum in the following words: "It is the fashion
to assume that our legislators are not now open
to pecuniary bribes. It may be so; but we must

leave that question to be decided by our children's children. *If public rumour be not more than usually scandalous and false, there are some curious revelations in store for these youngsters relating to railway bills.*" One company boasted of being able to command one hundred suffrages in the House of Commons. Nor can there be a doubt that every effort to procure votes was resorted to. Members were personally canvassed. Solicitations were made to peers. Influence of the most delicate nature was used. Promises were given to vote for special lines before the arguments were heard. Advantages in all forms and phases were proffered, to suit the circumstances of some and the temper of others. The Marquis of Salisbury said, "It was nearly impossible to bring together a jury some members of which were not interested in the railway they were about to assess." Letters of allotment were tempting, human nature was frail, and a premium on five hundred shares irresistible. Noble lords were whipped up to vote against especial bills, and prelates absent half the session made it a religious duty to oppose railways which would injure their neighbours' interest or their own prospects, and which would encourage what one who wished to be a bishop, it has been seen, called " Sunday excursions to hell at 7s. 6d. per head."

The principle of buying off opposition assumed a variety of monstrous shapes. Sums of £5,000, £6,000, £10,000, £30,000, and even £35,000 were given ostensibly for slips of land, but really to avert opposition. In one neighbourhood it was expedient to do so at a price which would compel the company to raise £15,000 additional annual toll; a sum equivalent to the fares of 100,000 third-class passengers from London to the neighbourhood in question.

The opposition of local newspapers was bought off in some instances. In others new journals were commenced to advocate particular schemes. In one place where the logic of an editor was detrimental to a line, and the honesty of the writer was equal to his logic, the directors whom he opposed determined to purchase his paper if they could not purchase him; and with all the craft which marked the period, the entire property of the journal became vested in the company. The editor refused to change his principles, and was ruthlessly dismissed.

The brokers, whether in the provinces or the

capital, could scarcely manage their business. Evening brought no leisure; the Sabbath yielded no
rest. Night was employed to examine accounts;
their sleep was broken and anxious; but though
assistance was procured, and though labour was
paid for with a lavish and liberal hand, no labour
could keep pace with the mad and frenzied public.
Mr. Morison, no ordinary man, with no ordinary
opportunity of judging, thus forcibly confirms the
writer, and expresses the facts which he witnessed.
"The subtle poison of avarice diffused itself through
every class. It infected alike the courtly and exclusive occupant of the halls of the great and the
homely inmate of the humble cottage. Duchesses
were even known to soil their fingers with scrip,
and old maids to inquire with trembling eagerness
the price of stocks. Young ladies deserted the marriage list and the obituary for the share list, and
startled their lovers with questions respecting the
operations of bulls and bears. The man of fashion
was seen more frequently at his broker's than at
his club. The man of trade left his business to look
after his shares; and in return, both his shares
and his business left him. In short, 'madness ruled

the hour,' and brought the country to the very verge of fiscal ruin."

Such was the position of railway speculation up to October; and the following form a few of the frauds which ensued. In the sketches about to be given, the names of the companies will not be mentioned, as it is with a principle the writer would deal, and he has no wish personally to indicate those who, if they have sinned, may have repented. The first specimen is somewhat curious:—A line was projected on paper. Whispers were passed through the railway world of its fine prospects. Advertisements were published to an unlimited extent. Puffs and paragraphs in newspapers were plentifully circulated. Its committee rejoiced in esquires and baronets. Its prospect of passing the House of Commons was certain. Its engineer was to be Stephenson; its potentate, Hudson; its banker, Glyn. The profits, it was modestly added, would not exceed fifteen per cent.

The plot succeeded; and when the shares were issued, 8,000 were retained for the committee, and 1,000 awarded to the public. Scarcely were the shares issued ere the panic came. There were no buyers; there was no price. But this was a state of things by no means agreeable. Stock-brokers were, therefore, sent into the market to buy with the money advanced by a few; the directors sold their own shares to their own brokers, and received the money of the depositors in exchange. The affair was wrapped in silence and secrecy. No record was in the minute-book, no names were in the cheques. False entries were made in the registries; and while some directors had signed the deeds without paying the deposits, others had neither paid the deposits nor signed the deeds.

The directors of another company placed their scrip in the hands of an agent. They then ordered the broker to buy for time all he could procure. He did so; and when the sellers wished to purchase, in order to fulfil their engagement, they were told no scrip had been issued. The penalty of the speculator was paid in the premium exacted.

A third railway had one hundred and thirty-five provisional committee men and directors;* and

* Mr. Evans in his very interesting "Commercial Crisis" vouches for the truth of the following letter, and says he could produce "scores of the kind" if it were necessary :—

as the shares came out at five premium, five hundred were given to each of them, and three hundred to each of the provisional committee men, making an aggregate of forty thousand shares out of seventy thousand, yielding a profit of £200,000. Another set of directors voted £2,200 among five of their number; and when one of them gently urged an objection, he was overruled by the modest remark that they were well worth double the money.

In another company the public were invited to send applications for shares; the number to be limited; the deposit to be twenty-two shillings each share. The directors then bought for account fifty times the number they meant to issue, and

---

"Dear ———,

"Do you want a director of your railway?—as I have lately been dealing rather extensively in such commodities, and am a director of the 'Direct ———,' advertised in the ——— and other papers. I am also a director of a Jamaica line which will be advertised next week; *and as I find railways much more profitable than law, I have cut the latter.* If you can put my name down as a director I shall be obliged.

"Yours faithfully,
"———."

"P.S. As I am intimate with several leading and influential directors, I might bring some with me if requisite."

So hungry were a great number, that one person was a director in twenty-three companies, a second in twenty-two, a third in twenty-one, and a fourth in twenty.

announced that no persons would have shares but those connected with a certain line with which their own was about to be amalgamated. The shares were at a high premium, and the unfortunate sellers were compelled to pay a price which sobered some and ruined others. One railway which failed in its first parliamentary attempt, reported itself as having spent the whole of its deposits. A proprietor in another received two hundred and fifty additional shares for procuring the name of a peer as director. Large sums of money were kept in one company's books in cypher, and cash was taken from the hands of the bankers to be lent to private persons on their mere note of hand.

In a certain company, while 11,000 shares were allotted to the public, 33,000 were reserved for the provisional committee, one of whom had 3,500 given him. They reached seven premium, and at this price was the above large amount sold. In another, five firms " of the first respectability" had 14,000 shares each, which were, or might have been, disposed of at four premium. Another company was stated by Lord Monteagle to have expended £381,000 in purchasing scrip in eleven lines. In a provincial railway,

100 shares were allotted to each provisional committee man, 10,000 were divided among the managing committee, 2,000 given to the solicitors, 200 to each of the local solicitors, 500 to bankers, and 2,000 to members of parliament; and this, of course, when the shares were at a high premium. A second allotment was made by the same company of 4,200 to the committee of management, 1,600 to the provisional committee, 1,100 to solicitors, 200 to surveyors, 300 to bankers, and 3,500 to the friends of the committee, the shares being at a premium of £5.

Three companies were started for one line. On each share of each company £2 2s. were paid. After a trifling skirmish, they amalgamated. The bill was scarcely opposed; but being lost, the directors returned out of £6 6s. paid, the sum of 15s. a share.

It need hardly be repeated that individuals entered into these speculations whose means were ludicrously disproportioned to the responsibility; and the parliamentary inquiry proved that no care had been taken to prevent it. Ticket porters were down for thousands; men with writs out against them, for tens of thousands. In one company unreal names to represent half a million of property were subscribed. Youths in the receipt of a few shillings a week signed for any and everything. One gentleman in receipt of parish alms signed for £5,000. Spinsters were down for large sums. A porter was responsible for £37,000; an officer of the British Legion in Spain subscribed for £50,000. An unbeneficed clergyman figured for half that sum. False addresses were constantly given, and fictitious names freely written.

Strangely and sadly pass these scenes before the eyes of those from whom the mania has departed. Strangely and sadly must they sound to the reader. It was no ordinary time. The pulse of the people, fierce and excited, grew by what it fed on; and as every new project unfolded its prospects, it demanded a greater stimulus and a more extended action. If the ledger was then the bible of the people of England, and if gold was then truly their god, let it be remembered that nations have their fevers as individuals; that popular delusions take all forms and features; and that in a commercial country like Great Britain, it must ever take that which agrees most with the genius of the people. Let it be remembered, also, that the base, bad acts which have been recorded, were the work of the scum on the surface; that much of the trickery and treachery which prevailed was performed by men whose very avocation was to swindle, and that, had it not assumed this form, it must have taken some other, less public but not less pernicious.

The evil which was performed was not by the men whose names belong to our merchantocracy. In the heat of the moment they joined the crowd, and the throng carried them away. But it is due to many who sanctioned the lines which bore their names, to proclaim thus publicly and positively that they could not stay the iniquities they saw; that the majority always carry the day, and that the minority were generally composed of the good men and true, to whose names the faith of the shareholders was given. Mr. Glyn expressly stated on one occasion that a particular minority, composed of London and Birmingham directors engaged in another line, were disgusted with the proceedings of the majority, but were powerless to prevent them.

These things must not be forgotten in extenuation, and allowance must be made for the frenzy which, when it seized on the nation, scarcely spared the few faithful in the city.

The gambling was as prevalent in the provinces as in the capital, but there was no method
in their madness.   In Leeds it absolutely raged.
In no town throughout the country did it attain
so fatal a form.   In no town were men more easily
duped by the falsehoods which it paid to promulgate.   In lines known to be worthless, in which
no business was doing, if a rumour were judiciously
spread that Hudson was after them, the Stock
Exchange was in a ferment, and prices rose enormously, to the loss of the holder when the contradiction come.   The same shares which were selling
in London at £21, were sold in Leeds at £25 10s., and
in one company where all the deposits were spent
and the bill was rejected, were at £4 10s. premium.
Lines which could not possibly pay more than three
per cent., and which only promised five per cent.
in their prospectuses, were at a premium, and a
price so heavy as completely to preclude all hope of
paying so good a dividend as consols.   In a third, the
construction of which had, before the parliamentary
committee, been proved to be next to impracticable, the
shares were sold at £11 premium.   While the Leeds
and West Riding Junction, rejected by the legis-

lative body, and with all its deposits expended, were freely bought at £7 10s.

The irritation was visible in the streets. The thoroughfares near the Stock Exchanges, for three of these disgraced the town, were almost impassable. The purlieus were like fairs. Crowds of anxious brokers, and yet more anxious speculators, with earnest faces and excited minds, literally ran and rushed about the place. The cautious merchant and the keen manufacturer were equally unable to resist the speculation. It spread among them like a leprosy. It ruined alike the innocent and the guilty. It perilled many a humble home ; it agitated many a princely dwelling. Men hastened to be rich, and were ruined. They bought largely ; they subscribed eagerly ; they forsook their counting-houses for companies : if successful they continued in their course, and if the reverse, they too often added to the misery of the homes they had already desolated, by destroying themselves.

The magistracy were compelled to interfere, and police were appointed to keep the streets clear. The very sharebrokers were alarmed at the excitement. The chairman of the Exchange grew sane and sensible,

and exhorted his fellow members to consider that
their risk was great, that though the amount of
their brokerage might be large and their business
profitable, their responsibility was frightful, and a
sudden reverse might produce serious consequences.
One specimen of their transactions must suffice.

After a severe contest, an amalgamation of two
lines to be called the West Riding Union railway
came out, was very popular and reached a high
premium. Another railway embracing the same district, entitled the Huddersfield, Halifax, and Bradford Union railway company was advertised; but
thought so little of that its shares were at a very
small premium, a somewhat remarkable fact during
the railway mania. The scrip was not issued, but
to the people of Leeds this was no obstacle, and a
great number of shares were sold for time at 20s.
and 30s. The company was only to consist of 15,000
shares, but five times this amount was bargained
for and sold in the full faith that so uninfluential
a line could not maintain a high price. General and
great, therefore, was the sorrow and surprise to hear
a rumour that this despised and destitute line had
amalgamated with the popular West Riding. The

rumour, at first doubted, proved a most unpleasant
fact, the shares ran up to £15 premium, and the
speculators saw themselves involved in a loss of
nearly a million. Fearful was the dismay of the
gamblers. Brokers who had guaranteed to the extent
of thousands, found themselves ruined by the inability
of their clients to redeem their bargains. Gentlemen who had been disposed to risk a portion of
their spare capital in the prevailing epidemic, paid
their differences and anathematized their folly. Men
who had varied their legitimate business with the
charms of gambling, found a heavy penalty awaited
them. A complete commercial ruin threatened a
great part of the clothing district; a week's cessation
of business was proclaimed on the Stock Exchange.
The ingenuity of the losers was taxed to escape their
appalling liability. All sorts of schemes were proposed.
A resolution was passed by some members that no
dealings could be entered into where no scrip had been
issued; but the virtue of the winners rose in arms;
they thought, naturally enough, that to repudiate
when losing, though agreeable, was unjust; and they
issued a counter declaration alleging the previous
statement to be unauthorised. It was felt to be

a very awkward question. If the shares were issued,
the differences ought to be paid. If they were not
issued, the effect would be most injurious to the company. From August to the 16th October, when the
scrip was issued, great excitement prevailed, and when
in November the Leeds committee passed a resolution to meet the difficulty, by which all time contracts were rendered null and void, it was felt that
had such a regulation been fully carried out, and
been retrospective from the commencement of the
railway mania, property to an enormous amount
would have changed hands, and speculation would
not have assumed so fearful and so frightful a form.

It became a serious consideration to know how
long this fierce excitement would continue in these
great commercial towns. Men were seen boldly
adventuring who had nothing to lose. The merchant
there, as in London, knew his clerk was as deep
in the railway speculation as himself. The manufacturer saw his workman draw his savings from his
club. The wealth of some seemed enormously increased : they boasted of their thousands and tens
of thousands. Men were pointed at in the street
as millionaires who but yesterday compounded with

their creditors. Well was it remarked by a local journal: " But the prospect becomes more serious when it is discovered in what feeble hands great masses of this speculation rest; in what manifold ways the mischief has descended through all classes of society; to how many persons a reverse will be utter ruin, not to themselves only but to helpless numbers, whom they have deceived, with whose funds they have been gaming, or to whom they owe debts that can neither be paid nor spared : with such a view before us, it is not merely the pain awakened by a single case of ruin and despair that affects us in the instance quoted above; we tremble to think how much more of the like vice and folly, now concealed under this surface of bustle and feverish excitement, may be at this moment struggling in the grasp of the same evils, and preparing other lamentable scenes of failure, shame, and madness. Nor is it for the useless object of provoking alarm that we express these apprehensions. It is with the practical honest purpose of discouraging that which, whether successful or unlucky, is thoroughly foolish, and false and vicious—the greedy pursuit of gain by unjustifiable means. This dishonesty every man commits who engages himself, in the hope of winning, in obligations which he cannot meet if the die falls on the losing hand.   It is a vice which we fear is becoming an utter plague in the land—a pestilence destructive of things infinitely more precious than even the fortunes or maintenances which it rashly hazards.   Every day brings us some new instance of its hateful effects upon private happiness and public character.   Now we are told of shameful dis- closures affecting the honour of men in office ; persons whom it was our English boast, for the last half century at least, to proclaim to the world as above the suspicion of any foul handling of lucre.   Now we are called to deplore the utter ruin of a household dashed down from decent competency into beggary and disgrace, in the frantic pursuit of sudden wealth : the next moment we hear of a pious defaulter for hundreds of thousands—and turning from him in disgust, we stumble on the body of a suicide !"

And when at a later period of this history, scrip became worse than waste paper, and provisional committee men became worse than paupers, the paroxysm was as fierce and fatal in these towns, and came home to " the business and the bosoms " of the men of Leeds and Liverpool as much as it did to the merchant and the trader of London.

A return called for by the House of Commons of the dealers in railway undertakings, forms a very remarkable blue book. The noble who in the pride of blood and birth had ever held traffic in contempt, was there blazoned as a trader. The priest who at his desk prayed to be delivered from the mammon of unrighteousness, was there revealed as seeking in the city to sell his scrip at a premium. The lawyer, who, madly risking his money, sold the property of his client to meet his losses ; the physician who perilled the savings of a life and the well-being of a family ; the chemist who forsook his laboratory for a new form of the philosopher's stone ; the banker who in the city and the senate denounced all speculation as illegitimate ; the deacon of the meeting-house ; the warden of the church ; the Jew, the Quaker, the saint, the sinner, were all down in that huge condemning volume. There were nine hundred lawyers, and there were three hundred and sixty-four persons connected with the banking interest who subscribed contracts for above £2,000. One solicitor alone risked £154,000 ; one London banker was down for £240,000, and six country bankers for £100,000; nine others for £50,000; and seventy-seven more of that large and respectable body for £10,000 each.* But this was legitimate compared with the fact that two hundred and fifty-seven "reverend" and "very reverend" clergymen signed their names to contracts, two of which were for £26,000, three for £20,000, six for £15,000, while the remainder were for sums varying from £15,000 to £2,000. There were one hundred and fifty-seven members of parliament, of whom one signed for £291,000, one for £250,000, one for £178,000, while the remainder were down for sums which must have influenced their feelings to a degree which might have influenced their votes.†

* It must be remembered that many bankers were chairmen of established companies, on whose behalf they signed their names for these enormous amounts.

† "Amongst the names are to be recognised many of the leading nobility, the largest manufacturing firms, and names familiar to most people as connected with the commerce and literature of the country. The juxtaposition of names and descriptions offers some remarkable contrasts. The same columns presenting peers and printers, vicars and vice-admirals, spinsters and half-pays, M.P.'s and special pleaders, professors and cotton-spinners, gentlemens' cooks and queen's counsel, attorneys' clerks and college scouts, waiters at Lloyd's, relieving officers and excisemen, barristers and butchers, catholic priests and coachmen, editors and engineers, dairy-men and dyers, braziers, bankers, beersellers, butlers, domestic servants, footmen and mail-guards; with a multitude of other callings unrecorded in the book of trades."—*Annual Register.*

It may thus be seen from most undeniable evidence that there has been no extravagance in the past description; and it is an unquestionable fact, that there was scarcely a family in England which was not directly or indirectly interested in the fortunes of the rail. But a change was coming. The day of triumph was over, and the night of trial was at hand.

On Thursday, 16th October, 1845, the Bank of England raised the rate of interest; and the effect was immediate. On that day men looked darkly and doubtfully at each other; on Friday there was a considerable cessation of bargains, and on Saturday the alarm commenced. The news passed from the capital to every province in the empire, that there was a panic in the share market. From London to Liverpool and from Liverpool to Edinburgh the intelligence spread. Money was scarce; the price of stock and scrip lowered; the confidence of the people was broken, and the vision of a dark future on every face. Advertisements were suddenly withdrawn from the papers; names of note were seen no more as provisional committee men; distrust followed the merchant to the mart, and the jobber to the Exchange. The new schemes ceased to be regarded ; applications ceased to be forwarded ; premiums were either lowered or ceased to exist. Bankers looked anxiously to the accounts of their customers ; bill brokers scrutinised their securities ; and every man was suspicious of his neighbour. But the distrust was not confined to projected lines. Established railways felt the shock, and were reduced in value. Consols fell one and a-half per cent. Exchequer bills declined in price, and other markets sympathised. The people had awoke from their dream, and trembled. It was a national alarm. Words are weak to express the fears and feelings which prevailed. There was no village too remote to escape the shock, and there was probably no house in town, some occupant of which did not shrink from the morrow. The statesman started to find his new bank charter so sadly and so suddenly tried. The peer who had so thoughtlessly adventured, saw ruin opening to his view. Men hurried with bated breath to their brokers. The allottee was uneasy and suspicious. The provisional committee man grew pale at his fearful responsibility. Directors ceased to boast their blushing honours, and promoters saw their expected profits evaporate. Shares which the previous week were a fortune, were the next a fatality to their owner. The reputed shareholders were not to be found when they were wanted. Provisional committee men were not more easy of access.

One railway advertised the names and addresses of thirty—none of whom were to be heard of at the residences ascribed to them. Letters were returned to the post-office day after day. Nor is this to be wondered at, when it is said that on one projected line only £60 was received for deposits which should have yielded £700,000.

It was proved in the committee of the House of Commons that one subscription list was formed of "lame ducks of the Alley;" and that in another several of the directors, including the chairman, had also altered their several subscriptions to the amount of £100,000 the very evening on which the list was deposited, and that five shillings a man was given to any one who would sign for a certain number of shares.

An immediate change was felt in every market throughout England. In Liverpool the transactions

were nominal.   At Leeds, where four share marts and
two hundred brokers had been maintained, the effect
was similar; while at most of the small towns, the
stock exchanges and the speculators shrunk into
the littleness from which they sprung.

Nothing marked more decidedly the crisis which
had arrived than the fact that every one hastened
to disown railways.   Gentlemen who had been buried
in prospectuses, whose names and descriptions had
been published under every variation that could
fascinate the public, who had figured as committee
men and received the precious guineas for their
attendance, were eager to assure the world that
they were ignorant of this great transgression.   Men
who a month before had boasted of the large sums
they had made by scrip, sent advertisements to papers
denying their responsibility, or appealed to the Lord
Mayor to protect their characters.   Members of
Parliament who had remained quiet under the in-
fliction while it was somewhat respectable, fell back
upon their privileges when they saw their purses were
in danger.   There is no doubt that an unauthorised
use of names was one feature of fraudulent companies,
and that amid a list of common names it was thought

a distinguished one might pass unnoticed. The complaints, therefore, of those who were thus unceremoniously treated were just; but the great mass of denials emanated from persons who knowingly encountered the risk, and meanly shrunk from the danger.

It is the conviction of those who are best informed that no other panic was ever so fatal to the middle class. It reached every hearth, it saddened every heart in the metropolis. Entire families were ruined. There was scarcely an important town in England but what beheld some wretched suicide. Daughters delicately nurtured went out to seek their bread. Sons were recalled from academies. Households were separated: homes were desecrated by the emissaries of the law. There was a disruption of every social tie. The debtors' jails were peopled with promoters; Whitecross-street was filled with speculators; and the Queen's Bench was full to overflowing. Men who had lived comfortably and independently found themselves suddenly responsible for sums they had no means of paying. In some cases they yielded their all, and began the world anew; in others they left the country for the continent, laughed at their creditors, and defied pursuit. One gentleman was served with four hundred writs. A peer similarly pressed, when offered to be relieved from all liabilities for £15,000, betook himself to his yacht, and forgot in the beauties of the Mediterranean the difficulties which had surrounded him. Another gentleman who, having nothing to lose, surrendered himself to his creditors, was a director of more than twenty lines. A third was provisional committee man to fifteen. A fourth, who commenced life as a printer, who became an insolvent in 1832 and a bankrupt in 1837, who had negociated partnerships, who had arranged embarrassed affairs, who had collected debts, and turned his attention to anything, did not disdain also to be a railway promoter, a railway secretary, a railway director, or to spell his name in a dozen various ways.

By the suddenness of the crisis, the cunning of promoters and provisional committee men fell upon themselves. They had delayed answering applications until it was too late to make a profit; they had meant to reserve a sufficient number to make their own fortunes; but when they saw premiums give way to discounts, when there was no price quoted for their scrip, when the public looked shy and brokers would not look at all, they were most liberal in issuing letters of allotment, and most unjust in demanding payment. Those who had requested fifty shares expecting five—about the proportion hitherto granted—found they were graciously allowed all they demanded. To pay would have been ruin. Not to pay was to be involved in law.

Such was the melancholy close of the high hopes of the memorable spring and summer of 1845. The topic is tempting, but other and equally important subjects demand attention. During the entire period the name of George Hudson was ever seen in connexion with railways; and the chapters which follow are devoted to a sketch of that man who so greatly influenced them, and whose career, necessary to the completion of a work devoted to the interest he advocated and assisted, will necessarily carry the reader to a period long antecedent to that which has just been treated.

CHAPTER VII.

THE son of a Yorkshire yeoman, with a parentage
which could be traced on the estate of Howsham
for two centuries; apprentice to a Yorkshire linendraper, and, by virtue of the same capacity which
afterwards made him the associate of peers, attaining
the position of master where he had served as apprentice; realising a capital of which the yeoman's son had
scarcely heard; George Hudson made his public *début*
in York as a member of the board of health in 1832.
In 1835 he entered into the civic councils, was soon
raised to the aldermanic dignity, and in 1837 became
Lord Mayor of the city whose interests he forwarded
and whose prosperity he promoted.

Although the fortune of the Liverpool and Manchester had attracted the attention of some, and though the ten per cent. which it paid stirred the affections of all, there was no immediate movement in favour of the rail in that fine city to which Mr. Hudson belonged.

The cost of construction was known to be heavy; the expenses of working were feared; the objectors declared the above line owed its entire success to the importance of the towns it joined, and that only such places would pay the promoters. Still a certain degree of excitement prevailed; the people of York did not see a ten per cent. dividend without wishing to appropriate it; and when the Leeds and Selby was formed in the neighbourhood, the feeling and the fervour became so much increased, that by 1832 some bold spirits conceived the idea of a line between York and certain portions of the West Riding. In 1833 this project was brought before the public, and the name of Mr. Hudson was prominently placed before the new world of railways. Preliminary and adjourned meetings were held; a committee was appointed; information was procured; surveys were made; and when, at one of the above assemblies, Mr. Hudson placed his name down for nearly all the four or five hundred shares which were subscribed in a line the very route of which was undetermined, and which, too, half the people in York said was unnecessary, it was the first bold step of a bold man in advance of his time. That its opening success was due to Mr. Hudson's energy and perseverance, is indisputable, as similar companies with equal prospects, lacking only men with the resolute determination of a George Hudson, died almost immediately they were born. Mr. Rennie surveyed the way as originally projected ; and when it was suggested that a more direct line would be desirable, the Yorkshire linendraper gave his time and spared not his trouble, explored the neighbouring districts, examined the neighbouring land, estimated its value, felt the pulse of undetermined proprietors, and became as prominent then as he was popular afterwards.

But the expense seemed frightful ; men said with alarm, and repeated with dread, that it would cost more than £7,000 a mile ; and, as the committee did not see its way clear to what was then thought so great a charge, a meeting was held to re-consider the plan. The future railway monarch and George

Stephenson then first met; and Mr. Hudson, knowing the company was not prepared to encounter parliament, believing, too, that a line might be formed at a more favourable period, not only with the West Riding, but with the South of England, recommended a delay, and that delay was willingly yielded. But Mr. Hudson only " bided his time;" and when, in 1835, a railway was proposed from Leeds to Derby, and another, the Midland Counties, to Rugby, he saw the hour had arrived, and that York, by uniting with the North Midland, might obtain a railway communication with Leeds, the West Riding, and London. From this arose the York and North Midland Railway Company, on the provisional committee of which Mr. Hudson was placed by virtue of the large number of shares for which he subscribed; and fortunate was it that he was with them, for he was its indefatigable promoter. When it was opposed by the landed proprietors, he soothed them with the most irresistible of arguments; when another interest contested its claims, he fought it step by step; when a large canal proprietary rose against him, he demonstrated the fallacy of its arguments.

The result was that in 1837 the York and North

Midland bill was passed; twelve directors were chosen to supersede the provisional committee; and Mr. Hudson assumed the proper position of chairman of that company, of which he had been, to all intents and purposes, the chief guide and guardian. He treated personally with the landed proprietors; and when, through the most vigorous exertions, it was opened on 29th May, 1839; when, with the onerous duties of the lord mayor of York upon him, he devoted to the railway interest his tact, his talent, and his zeal, he became marked in the eyes of those who associated with him as a man of no ordinary power; and it is worth noting, that while the land on the North Midland cost £5,000 a mile, that on Mr. Hudson's line averaged only £1,750.

At the conclusion of his mayoralty new honours awaited him; a testimonial, subscribed not only by the citizens of that which is no mean city, but also by the nobility of the county itself, was pre-sented in terms which spoke the feelings of his associates; and when, on the first of July, 1840, he saw the first locomotive on a line which, so much indebted to him, opened a steam communica-tion between the ancient archiepiscopal city of York and the great metropolis of the world, it is probable he felt almost contented with that which he had achieved, and gave no thought to the morrow.

It is, however, the characteristic of some minds to allow no pause; and Mr. Hudson not only procured a grant of £500 for the survey of a railway towards Scarborough, but personally visited the district, becoming confirmed in his opinion that such a line would prove most remunerative; while the fact that Sir John Rennie had failed to form a York and Scarborough railway for lack of capital was with Mr. Hudson almost a reason for attempting it. The next movement of this gentleman was bold, and beneficial to the interest he had adopted. Aware of the importance of not having the Leeds and Selby line as a rival, knowing that a movement was proposed by which it would at once have competed with the York and North Midland for the Leeds and York traffic, he, with a few of his colleagues, did not hesitate to incur the responsibility of leasing the Leeds and Selby for thirty-one years at £17,000 per annum; and at a special meeting, called to accept or reject it, so apparent was the policy and propriety of the step, that, wondering at its not occurring to their own minds, the company adopted the bargain with perfect unanimity, and gave their chairman the eulogy he deserved. Nor was that eulogy less hearty when it was found, in August 1841, that, in addition to collateral benefits, the working of the line had added to the profits and the prospects of the proprietors of the York and North Midland.

Stimulated by this, and aware, with all the world, that the Great North of England company could not complete their way to Newcastle, Mr. Hudson at once saw the advantage to the public, and seized on the great idea of three or four interested companies raising the required capital. In September 1841, the representatives of six railways attended a meeting called by Mr. Hudson, and the scheme was developed, though no positive agreement was undertaken. In October he pressed it on the attention of his own company, and as he could not then command or control the entire money market, he recommended that the requisite sum of £500,000 should be raised by certain companies leasing the new railway for ten years, and that shares should be divided in proportion to the rent they guaranteed.

The wisdom of this proposition was felt by all. The board of trade granted its approval. An eastern route to Edinburgh was a railway requirement; it was seen that the proposal of Mr. Hudson was then the only mode of procuring it, and it was hailed with pleasure.

Of this projected company—the Newcastle and Darlington—Mr. Hudson was elected chairman. The bill received the royal assent on 18th June, 1842; and not only did this gentleman evince his faith in the project by subscribing five times as much as any other director, but, to prevent anything like delay, he took upon himself a personal responsibility from which most men would have shrunk appalled, and when one of the minor companies declined to be a party to the six per cent. guarantee, Mr. Hudson, rather than peril the fine project of his brain, stepped boldly forward, and took the entire risk upon himself.

Nor were his personal exertions less striking. Though the dean and chapter of Durham opposed his plan with all the force the church could command, yet dean and chapter failed before the determination of him who met them with a resolution

as fixed as their own, and who, to his honour and
their disgrace, obtained the land for something like
twenty-five per cent. of the sum they had demanded.

In the meantime Mr. Hudson's own peculiar line,
the York and North Midland, went on and prospered. Its dividends were satisfactory, and its prospects good. He was re-chosen chairman; compli-
ments were plentiful; he was honoured by his colleagues; he was applauded by the proprietary.
The former sought his support; the latter regarded
him as a deity. When the affairs of the North
Midland waxed unfortunate, and a committee of
shareholders was appointed, it need not be said that
Mr. Hudson was the most important; and as the
dividend was diminishing, as the proprietors were
anxious, as the directors could not sufficiently reduce
expenses, it was determined that Mr. Hudson with
six others should endeavour to do so. Railway
retrenchment is a great railway difficulty. Mr.
Hudson, however, reported the astounding news
that the expenses might be reduced nearly one half,
or from £40,000 to 22,000, and great was the fever
of the men whose management was thus indirectly
impeached. A furious war arose; statements and

counter statements were plentiful; reports and re-
joinders were numerous; and when, at a meeting
met to consider the report, Mr. Hudson warmly
supported his assertions ; when with tabular and
unanswerable facts he contrasted the York and North
Midland with the North Midland ; when he proved
that he only proposed that which was in operation
on his own line ; when with a perfect mastery over
detail he evinced an equally comprehensive genius
for principles, it is no wonder that he carried his
point so triumphantly that nine of the directors
were recommended to resign ; six of whom took the
advice, leaving Mr. Hudson and his colleagues to
occupy their posts. But it was not a bed of roses ;
warm words and angry contests ensued, and it required great energy to carry out the reforms which
every one knew to be necessary. This, however,
Mr. Hudson eventually did, and that too so effectually and so fully that the shares increased greatly
in value; and though in the first half-year he had
saved £11,530, the efficiency of the management was
improved and the safety of the line was increased.
With all this accumulated trouble he did not neglect
the York and North Midland, or any other project

which demanded his attention. In 1843 he recommended a York and Scarborough line to the notice
of the York and North Midland, and obtained a
motion in favour of its construction; in the same
year, also, he induced his co-proprietors to negociate
for the purchase of the Durham Junction.

No man was more keenly alive to the evils of
competition than Mr. Hudson, and when he proposed a co-operation of the three lines which centred
in Derby he evinced his penetration. But if this
gentleman were equal to this scheme, his coadjutors
were adverse. Many opposed him from jealousy;
some from personal reasons; others from public
grounds. A few of the most influential proprietors
were against him, and though he proved that by
working various lines together, £25,000 a-year might
be saved in expenses and £20,000 added from extra
traffic, it was difficult to procure a committee to
confer on the subject. Some notion of his energy
may be formed from the fact, that on three successive days, at special and successive meetings, he
met the proprietors of three companies, answered
all their questions, and met all their objections. He
arranged conflicting interests; he soothed opposing

claims; he managed some, he quieted others; he carried his project through a stormy opposition until the great triumph was achieved, and under one management and one control he brought a capital exceeding five millions. That control and that management was George Hudson's, who, as chairman of the united directory, was virtual chief of the Midlands' railway. The first month showed an increase of £2,500 in receipts alone.

Determined to carry out his great work of taking the railway northward, he and Mr. George Stephenson purchased the Durham Junction railway between them at a cost of £88,500. He then publicly developed his scheme, and that which for years had baffled the people of Newcastle was as nothing to him who acted on railways like a fate. Intent on his old plan of reaching Edinburgh, and a projected line between Berwick and Newcastle being in want of capital, he subscribed on his own responsibility for two thousand shares of £25 each, and then—though £30,000 might have been realised by him personally—he gave them to the York and North Midland, remaining contented with the advantages obtained by the company and with a nearer

prospect of an Edinburgh railway; in furtherance
of which Mr. Hudson induced the Newcastle and
Darlington company to take the necessary steps for
continuing their line to Berwick.

On the 18th June, 1844, the heart of Mr. Hudson
was rejoiced by the opening of the line to Newcastle.   At the splendid meeting which celebrated
it, words were insufficient to speak his praises.   Corporations presented addresses, and members of parliament used their choicest oratory.   His " sagacious
mind " was dilated on.   The obligations under which
they were placed to him were said to be incalculable ;
the northern portion of England regarded him with
parasitical devotion ; and when in August, 1844,
he announced the somewhat extraordinary fact that
all the contractors on the Newcastle and Darlington line had been paid, it was considered as a note-
worthy novelty that no sooner was the line opened
than its great debts were discharged.

The competing schemes of 1844 called forth all
the power of Mr. Hudson ; and as the Midland
and York and North Midland railway found the
Great Northern company threatening their profits
and defying their power, there was no alternative

save to project those branch lines which have eaten into the receipts of trunk railways. From this arose the Scarborough and Bridlington branch, and owing to this was the purchase of the Whitby and Pickering line. But it was always contended by Mr. Hudson that a public necessity should be shown, and that local traffic should be sure, before new lines of railway were started. This gentleman—be that justice done him—saw the mischief of competition, and his principle was ever to concentrate and to co-operate. In November, 1843, he said, "there is a spirit abroad for making new lines and extending branches, some of which must injure lines already made; their traffic must depend upon what they can abstract from their neighbours."

In 1844 he declared that "all competing lines which had no local traffic were unworthy the support of parliament," and added, "he would not be connected with any line which competed with an existing railway." He refused his sanction to many because he did not think they would pay, though his name only would have sent them to a premium.

In 1845, the time of Mr. Hudson was fully occupied. The Great Northern was pressing on him

to the south.   Lord Howick was attacking him
in the north.   At this eventful moment, when the
Newcastle and Darlington company was endangered
and its property jeopardised, the Great North of
England company (York and Darlington), came
into the market.   The necessity of this line to the
well-being of the Newcastle and Darlington was
thoroughly understood by all, and they demanded
a ten per cent. guarantee, a creation of new
shares on the same terms, and the stock to be
purchased in 1850 at the rate of £250 for every
£100 share.   It was a hard and oppressive bargain.
It was felt by Mr. Hudson to be so; but George
Stephenson told him " it must be done;" and with
a reluctant hand he signed the contract.   In May,
the Great North of England shares were at £200,
a fortnight after, they were at £255.   Mr. Hudson
knew they must rise; it was a necessity consequent
on the operation he was conducting; but notwithstanding this, and although he held largely in the
companies which he unwillingly burthened with the
purchase, he did not buy or hold a single share where
he might have bought and gained thousands.

Soon after this, another great but defensive lease

was made by him of the Hull and Selby; and when
the Manchester and Leeds company endeavoured
to injure that property by a rail from Leeds to
Hull and the East Riding, Mr. Hudson, by the
magnificent purchase of Londesborough from the
Duke of Devonshire, at an immense personal cost,
at once thwarted their views and gained the victory;
and when the purchase by him of the Whitby and
Pickering line is recorded at £80,000—being £50,000
less than it cost the proprietary—this brief analysis
of his railway career to the end of 1845 is concluded;
with one exception, and that exception is his connexion with the Eastern Counties. The assistance
of this gentleman had been great to all the companies
with which he had associated; and the proprietors
of the above line—aware of the misfortunes which
had hitherto followed their directors—thought that
if any man could improve their prospects it was
the railway king. The position does not appear
to have been sought by Mr. Hudson : it was certainly
no honour to be chairman of such a company, for
it was ever in trouble; and there could be no pride
in being its head, for its profits were ever in inverse
proportion to its promises. It had no force to con-

duct it to success ; a peculiar fate seemed to shadow its path ; and its future chairman should have been aware that there was little chance of doing anything for it. It was burdened with heavy liabilities ; it was threatened by a fierce rival ; and looking back to the dangers which surrounded it, it appears strange that Mr. Hudson should have accepted a post which, bringing no honour, was equally barren of profit.

The facts which afterwards transpired, when it was found that dividends had been paid out of capital, are utterly indefensible, and they came upon the public with a shock which proved how strong a feeling existed against tampering with accounts. The excuse which has been entered for Mr. Hudson, that it was an exceptional case requiring an exceptional treatment, is insufficient.   Insufficient also the explanation that the public expected an increased dividend, and that it would have lowered the value of the stock at a critical period not to have met that expectation ; that as Mr. Hudson, by his singular railway power, had ever increased the dividends of those lines into which he had entered, it was natural that he should hope to do so with the Eastern Counties ; and that having once declared a dividend which had not been earned, the directors of the line, with those over whom they had sway, would endeavour legitimately to obtain that which had previously been illegitimately declared. It was a most unwise experiment, which even if successful would not have been justifiable. It impeached the commercial wisdom of Mr. Hudson; it proved that the irresponsible power bestowed upon him was too great; it was an error of judgment for which he has dearly paid; which he must bitterly have repented; and it is most improbable that under similar circumstances, with his present experience, his mode of action would be the same. Up to the period when he joined the Eastern Counties, however, it has been seen that he was one of the moving spirits of that world into which he had entered.

CHAPTER VIII.

THE POPULARITY OF MR. HUDSON.—HIS POSITION IN THE CITY AND THE
SENATE.—PERSONAL CHARACTER OF MR. HUDSON.—ANECDOTES OF HIM
—HIS BENEVOLENCE.—PERSONAL APPEARANCE.—ATTACK MADE ON MR.
HUDSON.—OPINIONS CONCERNING HIM.

IN little more than ten years, therefore—briefly
to sum up that which has been given in detail—
it may be seen that Mr. Hudson had originated
the York and North Midland; that he had proved
his opinion by the shares he subscribed; that he
induced a few colleagues to incur the personal
responsibility of £17,000 a-year for the line they
served; that he was the author of an Eastern route to
Edinburgh; that he carried out a reform in one
railway at a saving of twenty per cent.; that he
joined the capital of three undertakings, and effected
an enormous saving; that he bought half one railway

and subscribed 2,000 shares to forward another to Scotland ; that he largely increased the dividend of the Midland proprietary ; that through him the iron way was completed to Newcastle ; that he aided in purchasing the York and Darlington ; that he leased the Hull and Selby ; that he bought a grand estate which then was esteemed necessary to the welfare of the shareholders ; that he ever raised his voice against competition ; and that his name, moreover, was never connected with a company not meant to be carried out. His influence extended seventy-six miles over the York and North Midland ; fifty-one miles over the Hull and Selby and Leeds and Selby ; over the North Midland, Midland Counties, and another, one hundred and seventy-eight miles ; over the Newcastle and Darlington, and the Great North of England, one hundred and eleven miles ; while over the Sheffield and Rotherham, the York and Scarborough, the North British, Whitby and Pickering, it affected nearly six hundred more, making a total of 1,016 miles, all of which were successful in developing traffic, and equally successful in paying good dividends.

Success like this sanctified the power of Mr.

Hudson, and for a time no other name was heard
in the great world of railways.   In the journals
of the day men read of his wonderful doings.   The
press recorded his whereabouts ; the draughtsman
pencilled his features.   His name was connected
with preference shares and profits.   He wielded an
influence in England unparalleled and unprecedented.
Peers flattered the dispenser of scrip, and peeresses
fawned on the allotter of premiums.   It was told
with pleasure and repeated with delight that his
empire extended over a thousand miles of railway.
His fortune was computed with an almost personal
pride.   Almack's was forsaken when Albert-house
was full.   The ducal crest was seen on the carriage
at his door.   The choicest aristocracy of England
sought his presence.   Foreign potentates sued for
his society.   The coronet of the peer was vailed
before the crown of the railway king.   The minister
paid his court, and the bishop bent in homage.   The
ermine of the judge lost its dignity, and the uniform
of the officer its pride.   The Christian banker and
the Hebrew capitalist alike acknowledged his greatness.   Stories were plentiful of the fortunes he had
won, and the dividends his enterprises had paid.

"The fame of Sir Robert Peel," said a journalist,
"has given way to that of Mr. Hudson." The
réunion of the plotting statesman courted his presence, and the *soirée* of the scientific marquis was
incomplete without him. The Duke of Leeds
"esteemed his friendship, and thought his name
would be beloved for ages to come." The prince
consort was proud to be introduced to him, "shook
hands very heartily with the member, and remained in
conversation with him for some time." Men heard
of his buying estates, and they honoured him. They
read of his purchasing Londesborough, and they worshipped him. He became possessed of Newby-hall;
and the name of John Law was fondly coupled with
that of George Hudson. His alliance was sought
by patricians; his children were the companions of
peers.

If such were the position he assumed with that
class which boasts an arrogant exclusiveness, it need
not be said that in the city he was idolised. When
his name graced an advertisement, men ran to buy
the shares. He was their railway potentate; their
iron king; their golden god. His appearance on the
platform was a perfect ovation. Sober, steady-

minded men shouted with joy. Shrewd speculators supported them, and one intense, universal homage greeted the image they had set up. The thought of ten per cent. enraptured them, and the loud applause which hailed his periods would only have been justified by the oration of a Macaulay or the saxon of a Peel. Over railways and managers of railways he maintained an imperial sway. His energy bore down all opposition. When he rose in wrath, boards of directors were scattered before him ; when he spoke in anger, shareholders denied their own proposals.

There was nothing in the appearance of Mr. Hudson to justify this excessive adulation. There was nothing in his elocution to warrant this rapture. Rapid in delivery, and somewhat thick in utterance, he affected no refinement of manner ; he aimed at no grace of delivery. Plain and practical, master of his subject, he went at once to the point on which he was speaking, and said all he had to say as briefly as possible. And yet John Law, when peers, judges, bishops, and ladies waited for a fortnight in his ante-chamber to obtain an audience, was not more regarded.

If Capel-court and Belgravia did homage to him, the effect was similar in that great assembly where, it is proudly said men soon find their level. When he had been only two years in the House of Commons, having left Sir Robert Peel when Sir Robert left protection, Mr. Hudson took a place with the leaders of the opposition. He was listened to with respect on questions of national polity ; he was deferred to on all railway topics ; he was treated as a protectionist chief; and it was practically allowed that the mind which had heralded and headed the new power, which in twenty years had raised its possessor from the homestead of the yeoman to an equality with princes, and from a draper's shop to a rivalry with legislators, did not require a high education to make its influence felt on topics affecting the welfare of England.

If these things be true—and the writer defies contradiction—it is a picture from which thousands may shrink abashed. The spirit which prompted it was the spirit of mammon, and the pride which bowed before the citizen of York, was the pride of a hundred descents.

To Mr. Hudson's praise be it said, he was not

a tyrant because others were sycophants ; nor, it
may be added, did he worship the aristocracy because
the aristocracy worshipped him. Let it not be
thought that when lords courted and ladies caressed
him, he forgot those whom he had known in his
less prosperous days. To his honour he still remembered his friends ; he ever inquired kindly after their
welfare; he never refused a helping hand to their
necessities. Proud of springing from the people,
he rejoiced in being the architect of his own fortune ;
and there are anecdotes—very significant to the
student of character—confirming the kindly disposition of the man whose broad and massive frame,
whose face and figure characterised by determination
and stamped with power, might seem to argue a less
genial nature.

On one occasion, when engaged to preside at a dinner party, the guests were assembled, but Mr. Hudson
was wanting; and as he was always the most important person wherever he went, great was the
distress lest he should not come at all.

The explanation was simple. As the railway chief
drove to his appointment, his road lay by a new
line, at the various posts of which the servants were

ordered to be present. One of these was away; and, incensed at this neglect, Mr. Hudson ordered his instant dismissal. As he proceeded it occurred to him that the punishment was harsh, that the man was a poor man, that he had a large family, and he determined to annul the sentence at some future period. He proceeded yet further; and when he thought of the sorrow which the man would bear to his home, he drove back many miles to revoke the decree; and he did revoke it, though he kept his courtiers waiting at the feast.

Other circumstances are not wanting. Among his political opponents at York was one who, when riches were realised on the Stock Exchange, sought the great metropolis to make his fortune by becoming a broker. To London he came; but to be a member of the money mart two sureties are required; and he could only procure one. The difficulty continued, and great was his disappointment. In his despair he thought of the railway king; and, as a last resource, on Mr. Hudson he waited, and told his mission. "You've been no friend of mine," said the latter bluntly; "but I believe you're a good sort of fellow; call on me to-morrow." The morrow came, and, full of anxiety, he waited on the autocrat. " Well," said Mr. Hudson, " it's all settled ; I've arranged everything. Mr. —— will be your other security ; go to him ; I've told him to do it." Mr. Hudson did not add, as he might, that he had guaranteed the amount to the broker he had named, and was himself surety for the opponent he befriended.

One cause of this gentleman's success was his fine arithmetical capacity. He would throw his head on the back of his chair, cover his eyes with his hands, arrange expenses, and form the most elaborate combination of figures. In this way he would calculate the dividend of some unfinished line, and the dividend thus arrived at generally proved true. He examined personally every railway department, visited every office, and inquired into the duties of all. If too slight, he increased them ; if too onerous, he relieved them. He equalised their labour, and obtained their confidence.

In railway matters he thus was a director indeed. Not only in the board room, but every letter and every communication bore direction as to some minute detail, which the mass of directors thought beneath them.

The mental and moral nature of Mr. Hudson, as proved by deeds which, never meant to be known, cannot be specified, is as necessary to a conception of his character, as a record of his public acts is necessary to his career. He did great good by stealth; he availed himself of his riches to assist the needy; he has helped scores of persons through improvident or unfortunate undertakings; he has made loans to many without the slightest prospect of repayment. The widow—it is a bold assertion —never appealed in vain; and the orphan rarely left him unrelieved. To literary men he was peculiarly and especially kind. The poor clergyman— and, to our shame, there are too many such—found in him a fast friend; poor artists—and they form too numerous a class—were never forgotten. With a well founded case of distress the most thorough stranger was rarely, if ever, denied. Much of his munificence, like that of an Abraham Goldsmid, was spontaneous. Many an one has been benefited who never knew from whom the favour came. Many an embarrassed family has been relieved who never saw the alms-giver. He has made speculations in grain, and told his agent to give the profit away, if profit there were ; he has bought shares, and directed his broker to hand the gain to others, if gain accrued ; he has maintained in credit many who must otherwise have been ruined.   Where a ten, a twenty, or even a fifty pound note would relieve the affliction of individuals, or soothe the distress of families, it was unhesitatingly given.   Of such the cases are legion.   Nor was an application always necessary.   Without an appeal, but from natural good feeling, he has directed payments to be made to many whom he thought required it ; he has purchased shares in the market, and given them to those whom he thought were deserving. Of the labouring community he was the sincere friend, and instances are not wanting of some who, now holding an elevated position, owe it entirely to Mr. Hudson.   Those around him partook of his kindness.   It needed no intercession of others, and no interference of their own to procure a pecuniary advantage ; it is a pleasure to record that his household servants were not forgotten in the allocation of his benefits.

Nor was it in money matters only that his disposition was shown.   If he were offended, he always tried to forget it. If any one transgressed, he was always willing to forgive. His chief failing, and it is a remarkable thing to assert of such a man, is the leniency of his disposition.

The appearance of Mr. Hudson is scarcely in keeping with his character. With a large and heavy frame; with a quick, peculiar, and almost shuffling walk; with a keen grey eye which penetrates all that it regards; bearing in the day the somewhat slovenly appearance indicative of most great speculators, and at night distinguished by an expansive white waistcoat; his marked, severe, and even harsh countenance, would scarcely indicate his nature, were it not frequently mellowed by a sweet and winning smile, which entirely eradicates the first unfavourable impression.

Bearing in his grey and scanty hair the marks of half a century; carrying in his broad and wrinkled front the stamp of thought; the person of Mr. Hudson is as familiar to the denizen of the west as his name is common to the dealer in scrip, and the dweller in the city.

Such was the man and such was his position at a time when he was afterwards said to be engaged in transactions of a most questionable character; when a fierce revulsion took place in popular feeling towards him; when the public believed all that the press asserted; when tales were circulated which truth has since repudiated; when old associates shrunk from his side as from a pestilence; when but one name and one man was held up to public scorn for deeds which he and his colleagues had done, and that one was George Hudson.

At the risk of anticipating the place to which they belong in some future volume, the worst charges, and those on which he has been most severely reprobated, will now be given. The railway accusations of 1849 are yet in the reader's mind; the extravagant assertions of that period are yet in his ear; and it is difficult to divest the judgment from the strong prejudice which every man in England then held against Mr. Hudson. But it is the writer's duty to withdraw from these charges all false and all favourable colouring; to treat them dispassionately; to judge of them calmly, and to consider them by the light of that feverish mania which possessed the world in 1845, rather than by that high moral tone which belongs quite as much to quixotism as it does to commerce.   To

"Nothing extenuate, nor set down aught in malice,"

should be his motto; he desires not to be a pleader for Mr. Hudson; he is no partisan of him who was called "a stain upon the nation;" but he has entered too deeply into the bye-ways of commercial history not to be fully aware that its past records are anything but in harmony with its present purism; and that many who were most severe, were most called on to temper judgment with mercy.

In 1844 the price of iron was excedingly low; all the manufacturers were out of spirits; and though, from the prospects of railway communication being carried to every village, plenty of work was in prospect, yet each engineer having his own fancy for the pattern of his rail, the iron masters could not make for stock, and were in great want of orders to keep their men and mills in full employment. Under these circumstances Mr. Bramwell, at that time manager, now a partner in the house of Thompson and Forman, went to Mr. Hudson, and, after pointing out the prospects of the iron trade, proposed a contract with that gentleman for 20,000 tons

for a railway just proposed, called the York, Newcastle, and Berwick. The bargain was not then
concluded, and Mr. Bramwell returned without effecting his purpose. Time passed; and Mr. Hudson
seeing the probability of the price rising, drew the
attention of those who, with him, were interested
in the above railway, to the importance of securing
what they might require. Finding that his colleagues
when the bargain was proposed to them, were fearful
of so great a responsibility, Mr. Hudson contracted
on his own account, in his own name, for 10,000 tons,
stating at the same time by letter that as his colleagues declined entering into the transaction, he
would take it at his own risk.

On 30th January, 1845—it must be remembered
that Mr. Hudson's contract was in October, 1844—
the provisional committee of the York, Newcastle,
and Berwick railway, advertised for 20,000 tons of
iron. By this time the value of iron had risen
cent. per cent. Various tenders were received, and
among others Messrs. Thompsons offered to supply
20,000 tons at the market price of £12 10*s.* per
ton; a bargain was eventually concluded with them
for 14,000 tons at £12 a ton; and Mr. Hudson,

instead of selling his iron in the market, supplied 7,000 tons of that which Messrs. Thompsons had contracted to deliver. There was no loss to the company, for it was something below the market price; there was no gain to Mr. Hudson for he could have sold it easily elsewhere. It appears an indiscretion scarcely necessary to palliate, and much less necessary to defend. The worst construction that can be placed upon it is, that when Mr. Hudson induced Messrs. Thompsons to lower their price from £12 10s. to £12, he may have proposed to them the employment of his own 7,000 tons as portion of the contract, and this construction involves the fact that his interference saved the York, Newcastle, and Berwick railway company £7,000. So much was it considered in the trade as Mr. Hudson's own property, that Messrs. Crawshay—a house by no means friendly to that of Messrs. Thompsons—literally offered £50,000 to him for the bargain he had made. Well, was the question put by a journalist, "Were the company losers? No. Was the price above the market price? No. Was it bought in the name, or on account, or at the will of the company? No. If iron fell, who would be the loser? Mr. Hudson!"

A further charge was, that having received £31,000 on 30th December, 1845, for the payment of land, he had kept the money to himself. It appears perfectly true that Mr. Hudson received this sum, and that he paid the cheques to his own account. It was placed in his hands because, having made the purchase of the land himself, he was personally responsible to the landed proprietor. A small portion of this was immediately paid to some, but with other of the proprietors certain difficulties arose; the fact, however, is indisputable, that in 1849 Mr. Hudson repaid to the company a large amount which had been paid to him four years prior for the benefit of the landowners.

The facts of this case appear to bear the hardest on Mr. Hudson in the public mind; and the simple truth that he kept some thousands in his own hands for three years is a grave charge, and must be gravely met. But certainly a brighter aspect is assumed when it is said that the landed proprietors were repeatedly informed that the money was ready for them; that there was a large debtor and creditor account between the company and Mr. Hudson; that the former was frequently indebted to the latter, who often paid the claims for land out of his own pocket; that during a portion of the above period Mr. Hudson was in advance £100,000; that the £31,000 was probably paid to lessen the balance against the company under cover of paying the landowner; and that, paying interest on the money he received, and charging it on that he paid, the £31,000 was simply one item in a running account. And it may be added, that on the final settlement his charge for interest against the company, exceeded the company's charge against him.

It is right to treat this gravely, but it should also be treated generously; and is it to be supposed that the use of £31,000 was of importance to a man at whose name every banker bowed? Is it reasonable to conclude that there was anything nefarious in a transaction which formed only one item in a great account? And is it just to deduce unfavourable conclusions when a charitable interpretation is most in keeping with the entire charge?

It was also said that Mr. Hudson had treated £31,000 paid to him for the contractors in a similar way. In examining this, it appears that Mr. Hudson was security for the contractors to the extent of

£50,000, to which amount the latter had overdrawn their account. When, therefore, a cheque for £30,000 was paid for them, Mr. Hudson stated the case to the board, received the sanction of that board for retaining it, and remained security for the contractors. Had he not done this, a great work would have been stopped; a large number of men would have been thrown out of employ, and the contractors must have been ruined. On the other hand there was no risk of loss to the company, and there was no chance of gain to Mr. Hudson. In the words of the latter, " Nobody lost a penny, and I made nothing!"

Mr. Hudson has also been charged with the unauthorised appropriation to himself of 2,000 shares. The facts of this case are briefly these : Mr. Hudson had bought the Brandling Junction line in his own name, on his own account, for £550,000. That line was re-purchased of him by the Newcastle and Darlington company ; 22,000 new shares—appropriated to the proprietors of the last named company in exact proportion to their shares—being created to pay for it. When this was effected, 2,000 remained unappropriated ; and at an open meeting of the proprietors, it was as openly and unanimously carried, that the shares which remained should be given through the directors to Mr. Hudson. The directors consequently met, allotted 1,600 to the man they delighted to honour, and divided the remainder as they thought proper. Thus, among others, Mr. Robert Stephenson was allotted twenty-five shares. The extreme purity of this gentleman no one disputes; but if Mr. Hudson were guilty in receiving 1,600 shares, Mr. Stephenson was surely equally so in receiving twenty-five. The principle involved is the same. They were voted by the same propriatary; they were presented by the same directors; and the only difference is between Mr. Hudson's sixteen hundred and Mr. Stephenson's twenty-five : between a profit of £500 to the engineer and £37,000 to the chairman.

Of a similar character was a transaction in connexion with the York and North Midland, which created upwards of 50,000 new shares to form branches into the East and West Ridings of Yorkshire, in the proportion of one new to each old share ; it being at the same time determined to reserve a certain number to smooth the acerbity of the landowners along the line.

Of these surplus shares Mr. Hudson was allotted 1,700, of which, by virtue of a similar number of original shares, 1,000 were his due ; the remaining 700 being given him partly in consideration of his being a large landed proprietor ; partly on account of his great services, and partly on account of his position.   Nor does it seem surprising that he should have accepted them.   Would it not have been more surprising had he refused them ?   Was the moral feeling so high with railway men or measures that, with " mock modesty and bated breath," Mr. Hudson should have rejected that which had certainly been earned by him more than by any one else : which would almost as certainly have been taken by his colleagues had he refused it : and which had a value in the market solely from being connected with his name ?

It is not to be denied that in all these transactions there is something startling ; but this arises from their magnitude.   The moral principle, however, remains unchanged, whether a hundred pounds or a hundred thousand be involved.   Right and wrong are not to be measured by results ; and the question really is, whether Mr. Hudson evinced a lack of principle or a lack of discretion. In considering this subject, it must be accepted as an absolute rule, that amounts are only comparative; that all people are careless in trifling sums; and that what is much to the poor is little to the rich. It must be borne in mind that Mr. Hudson dealt constantly with accounts so gigantic that ordinary sums shrunk into insignificance by their side. That he was careless about accounts, is certain. Relying on his memory, he kept no books; he retained no copies of his letters; he paid enormous sums, and took no note of them; he gave verbal directions for the appropriation of thousands, and trusted to fate for their safety. His nerve was so strong, his energy so great, his success so astonishing, that his colleagues yielded everything. To him was assigned the task of beating down opposition, of overcoming all obstacles, of conducting negociations with landowners, of soothing the guardians of ecclesiastical property, of making terms with municipalities. Officially equal to their great coadjutor, morally they were as children before him. They registered edicts, which, if so wrong as they afterwards asserted, they should have combated. They concurred in acts which, if so criminal as

they afterwards declared, they should have opposed.
The power which was entrusted into their hands
they gave without a struggle into those of Mr.
Hudson; and it is monstrous to place upon one
the blame which attaches to many. If he was
wrong in acting as they say he did, they were
equally wrong in supporting him. They invested
him with unparalleled power; they placed him in
an unparalleled position; the management of millions
was given him. They yielded to him the interests
which had been vested in them; they assisted him in
acts which they afterwards repudiated, and their own
defence is their bitterest condemnation.

Passion and prejudice should retire when a verdict
is given; and it is right in a question which involves
the character of a public man, to think deeply
and to judge calmly. The facts, stripped of embel-
lishment, are before the reader. The period, with
all its excitement, has been exhibited to him. The
man, with the undue homage he received, has been
presented; and in considering the charges brought
against one who, whatever his faults, has done
great things for England, the writer wishes to be
impartial.

Does the iron contract—resolved into its true form —appear other than an ordinary trade bargain? Was the money received for the landowners other than a simple question of debtor and creditor? Was not the transaction with the money of the contractors an absolute benefit to all?

The shares appropriated to Mr. Hudson by two railways should be treated most seriously. But even with these there is nothing beyond acquisitiveness on the grand scale which marked the entire world of railways. The right was with him. The company voted them, and Mr. Hudson accepted them, is the simple reading of this vast transaction. It must be considered, too, that these shares were not kept to himself; his personal friends received a portion. The men who, in assisting him had assisted railways, were not forgotten; and when the purist pronounces sentence, let him bear in mind that the scrip found many recipients besides George Hudson.

These things must be left to the reader's unbiassed judgment: but let him ask himself whether it is likely that Mr. Hudson would have placed his reputation in the hands of his iron merchant? Whether he would have perilled his power by dealings which, sure to be discovered, were equally sure to ruin him ? Whether he would have endangered a position, doubly dear from its novelty ? or whether, with his keen, acute mind, he would have done acts which were certain to destroy the value of that property in which he and his were so deeply interested ?

Where the morals of a *millionaire* fade before the love of money, it is right to judge severely. England has had her share of such, and the writer deliberately asserts that, compared with some whose names are yet honoured in the land, Mr. Hudson's actions are venial. Considered on high abstract grounds, they assume a darker aspect; but judged of by the principles and practices of the Stock Exchange—and in this light they should be viewed— they are almost pure. Compared with deeds which have yet to be publicly unveiled—with the doings and dealings of provisional committee men—with the men and measures of other railways—with the uses and abuses of other directors, Mr. Hudson's transactions assume all the difference between great cupidity on his part and great crime on theirs.

It must be repeated that it is good to be generous as

well as just. If Mr. Hudson has acted unwisely, he has paid the penalty; if he has erred, he has suffered; and remembering all that he has done, bearing in mind the triumphs he has achieved and the trials through which he has passed, let him be thought of as one who, "more sinned against than sinning," has been a scape-goat for the sins of the many; and let it, too, be considered that he has done the state some service, and may yet do it much more.

CHAPTER IX.

THE episodical career of Mr. Hudson disposed of,
it is necessary to return to the progress of that
power in which he had been so prominent. Although
the mania for new lines had passed away, it is not
to be supposed that those who had received the
money of the depositors meant to return it. The
directors and provisional committee men, therefore,
proceeded gravely in their work, employed surveyors,
attended meetings, talked of their prospects, and
acted their parts with so much spirit, that their
unfortunate dupes took " heart of grace," and began
to lift up their heads. By the arrangement of the
board of trade it had been decreed that all lines

which desired to be proceeded with in the ensuing session should lodge the necessary documents by the 30th November; and a most extraordinary demand for surveyors was the consequence. As the 30th of that month approached, when the documents were to be lodged at the above office, it produced a scarcity of scientific workmen utterly unparalleled. In vain did advertisements promise high pay and make no great requirements. The demand exceeded the supply, and artists and artisans reaped a golden harvest. Professional men were tempted from abroad, trusting that they possessed the necessary information. Youths not out of their servitude were employed on works which demanded a matured judgment. Absurd impracticabilities were attempted. So long as the survey was made and the sections lodged in time, the directors were satisfied, and whether they were correct was of small importance in a majority of cases. The pay was in proportion to the urgency, and many men received for a weeks' work more than they could have honestly earned by a years' labour. Sixty persons in the employ of the ordnance department left their situations, and as their appointments enabled them to enter land

without permission from the owner, they were warmly
welcomed and largely paid. But the duties of the
surveyor were not free from danger. The landed
proprietor often refused admission to the trespasser
and to his theodolite. At Addington the surveyors
were met and defied in such force, that after a
brief fight they were secured, carried before a magistrate, and fined. At Saxby, when they were
ordered off, they produced pistols in defence, but
after a general scuffle were lodged in the county-
gaol. Near Osberton they were treated as poachers,
and only escaped the penalty from their imposing
numbers. Dukes perilled the honour of their escut-
cheons in open fights with the general enemy. Fines
were frequent, and constables were at a premium.
At Lincoln, fraud was found better than force;
and while a crafty surveyor endeavoured to persuade a
refractory landowner, his coadjutors were calmly
performing their work. In Oxfordshire a fierce
warfare arose, nor could the survey be continued
until after a severe conflict, and under the care of a
body of armed men.

The engineers were in truth driven to adopt whatever method might occur to them. While the people

were at church; while the villager took his rustic meal;
with dark lanthorns during the dark hours; by force,
by fraud, by any and every mode they could devise,
they carried the object which they felt to be necessary
but knew to be wrong.   Such was another phase of
the morality of the rail.

In extenuation of the rough and rugged opposition of the landowner, it must be said that the
surveyor and his assistants were generally indifferent
to the rights they violated: that, determined to carry
their point, they were careless as to the means:
that they would trample down the autumn harvest
as freely as they would cross the fallow land.   It
must be said, too, that no place was sacred from
their presence; that the park of the gentleman and
the flower-garden of the lady were equally disregarded
by the intruder; that he damaged fences, broke
through hedges, trod down the rising plant, destroyed
the grain, crushed the esculent, and that, too often
with an insolence only to be surpassed by his ignorance.   It was a warfare of the monied with the
landed interest, and the former rarely failed in carrying its point even if paid for with fine and imprisonment.

The 30th of November, 1845, the day by which the documents were to be lodged, fell on a Sunday, but there was no Sabbath for the restless railway promoter. "The stir of agents," said the *Railway Chronicle*, "made Sunday anything but a day of rest or devout observance throughout the country. The offices of clerks of the peace and the doors of the board of trade were stormed by breathless depositors till the stroke of midnight. Frantic 'standing-order missionaries' from Harwich—driving up a few minutes afterwards, miscarried, alas, by blundering post-boys, '*who drive for an hour and a half about Pimlico*' seeking the office in vain—have to besiege its inexorable doors, and 'fling their plans into the lobby'—breaking the passage lamp—with no effect but that of having them flung back again in their doleful faces! In Worcester so many coaches and four have never been seen in one day before, not even in race and festival weeks. Dire was the tossing on every road, and in some instances it may be feared deep groans were not wanting, nor cases of despair— of forlorn agents arriving too late, after all. On the Great Western line the haste to overtake 'spare minutes' had nearly led to a tragedy dark enough

to fill the courts of Gray's Inn and the purlieus of
Chancery-lane with inconsolable mourning. A squa-
dron of solicitors to some of the projected lines had
borrowed the wings of an express, which unhappily
broke down at Maidenhead. In this disabled condition the engine was charged by another which
had started with several legal gentlemen connected
with the Great Western and Exeter companies, and
the carriage with the learned freight was dashed to
pieces, as might have been expected—the fortune
which keeps watch over the men of law having let
the passengers off with no worse harm than the
fright and a few bruises, a better fate, indeed, than
might have been feared. The scared pursuivants
shook themselves, packed up their ruffled plans,
charitably picked up the stranded attorneys, whose
wreck had nearly caused a dismal *hiatus* in the
profession, and heroically steamed onwards, arriving,
we are glad to hear, in good time. Who shall say
that our prosaic days, even in their most prosaic
offspring, are behind the ages of adventure in ' hair-
breadth 'scapes,' or in trials of resolution? A collision between engines on the broad gauge we take
to be as smart a shock as any tilting encounter;

and the spirit of these undaunted though bruised solicitors quite as genuine, in its way, as that of your knights-errant, who bearded lions and jousted with windmills, at the cost of broken heads and aching ribs. On the Great Western on Sunday, there were *ten express trains* similarly employed; and, reading this, we deem it a great mercy that we have no worse casualty than the above to record."

It may thus be seen that the excitement was not confined to town. It spread far and wide throughout the country. The office of the clerk of the peace at Preston was invaded by an infuriated crowd of depositors. The doors were unopened, as the officials considered the orders to keep open on the Sunday applied only to the board of trade. The railway people, holding a different opinion, broke the windows and attacked the doors, that their plans might be flung in, if even they were not received with due form. One railway company was unable to deposit its papers owing to a theft of twenty sheets from the lithographer's offices, which, said the enraged promoters, found their way into the hands of a rival company at a high price. The town of Mansfield in which it occurred was violently agitated, horses were killed by violent exertion, and the police employed to trace the missing documents. The Eastern Counties ran eighteen or twenty special trains for the various projected lines. Engines with the steam up, and ready at a minute's warning, were kept for the expected wants of the projectors. Horses were scarce at the post towns, and two guineas a mile were paid for posting. One hundred and eighteen miles were steamed in an hour and a-half. " The majority of plans from the provinces," said the *Morning Chronicle*, " have been sent up by express trains, and it is whispered that those companies with the locomotives at their command, and to whom the lines belonged, availed themselves of this advantage to such an extent for the exclusive transmission of their own plans and sections, as actually to refuse special trains to their competitors." In one case they were adroitly outwitted. When an established company, with express trains at their command, refused one to the promoters of a competing line, the latter procured a hearse with all the paraphernalia of mourning, placed plans, sections, and clerk inside, and despatched it by special train to town.

The scene at the board of trade was thus related by a contemporary, " As the evening advanced, the arrivals became more frequent, and at nine o'clock they poured down Whitehall—

> Thick as autumn leaves that strew
> The vale of Vallambrosa.

The method adopted for the reception of the documents was as follows:—The parties charged with their delivery were admitted to the lobby of the office of the board of trade, where they entered the name of the agents for whom they were concerned in a book provided for that purpose. The name was then passed to an official, who conveyed the same to the inner office, where it was entered by the clerks. The several parties were then successively called in to describe the name and titles of their respective plans. This arrangement went on very well until eleven o'clock, when the delivery became so rapid that the clerks were quite unable to keep pace with the arrivals. The entrance hall soon become inconveniently crowded, considerable anxiety being expressed lest twelve o'clock should arrive ere the requisite formalities should have been gone through. This anxiety was allayed by the assurance that admission into the hall before that hour would be sufficient to warrant the reception of the documents.   Some amusement was caused by the similarity of names amongst the agents, particularly when any gentleman of the name of Smith was wanted.   At every such call there was at least half-a-dozen respondents, and it very seldom happened that the right agent was pitched upon by the subordinates below, who, being ignorant of the projects with which the agents were connected, always ushered up the Mr. Smith who happened to be most clamorous.   As the clock struck twelve the doors of the office were about being closed, when a gentleman, charged with the delivery of the plans of one of the Surrey railways, arrived, and with the greatest difficulty succeeded in obtaining admission.   These were the last notices deposited.   A lull of a few minutes here occurred, but just before the expiration of the first quarter of an hour a post-chaise with reeking horses drove up to the entrance.   In a moment its occupants—three gentlemen—alighted and rushed down the passage towards the office door, each bearing a plan of Brobdignagian dimensions.   On reaching the door and finding it closed, the countenance of each drooped; but one of them, more valorous than the rest, and prompted by the bystanders, gave a loud pull at the bell, which was answered by Inspector Otway, who informed him that it was now too late, and that his plans could not be received. The agents did not wait for the conclusion of the unpleasant communication, but took advantage of the door being opened, and threw in their tremendous papers, which fell upon and broke the passage lamp. They were thrown back into the street with as little decency as they were pitched into the hall. When the door was again opened, again went in the plans, only to meet a similar fate from the officers. The three agents were now maddened to desperation, and the principal amongst them commenced to tell his tale of woe to the bystanders, from which it appeared that they had that morning left Harwich, charged with the deposition of the plans of a certain railway proposed to benefit that district; that they had arrived in London as early as half-past ten, but, through the ignorance of the post-boy, had been driving about Pimlico and its neighbourhood in search of the office of the board of trade, for more than an hour and a half previous to their fruitless arrival thereat. The crowd, who had patiently listened to the recital of the unhappy individual, greeted its conclusion with a burst of laughter, which seemed to pierce his already broken heart."

Such were the effects of the last great money mania and its attendant panic. Many a futile effort to re-instate confidence was made by some, and many a bold attempt to regain the money they had lost was made by others. An undue depression was the natural result of the extreme excitement, and shares in lines which were not worse than they ever were, fell in price. The following table will show the variation in the value of three great companies during the year 1845 :—

	1st January.	1st August.	1st November.
London and Birmingham	228	246	214
Great Western	155	225	145
Eastern Counties	15	$21\frac{1}{4}$	$19\frac{3}{4}$

One thousand four hundred and twenty-eight companies, with a total capital of £701,243,208, demanding £49,592,816 for deposits, were actually registered by 31st October, 1845. The capital of completed railways amounted to £70,680,877. There were one hundred and eighteen lines and branches

in course of execution which required £67,359,325,
and there were 1,263 companies projected, asking
from the capitalists of England £563,203,000. The
promoters of five hundred and fourteen schemes
intimated their intention to apply to parliament in
1846—a singular evidence of their inability to comprehend the position of the monetary world.

An entirely new character marks the course of
railways from this period. No mania the world
had ever seen before was more extraordinary. It
has been compared with the tulip frenzy of Holland, with the Mississippi scheme of the polished
Law, with the South Sea bubble of the puritan
Blunt, with the distress created by Fordyce, with the
failures of 1794, and with the epoch of 1825. But
it is only so far like the tulip mania that it stirred
an unimaginative people to acts of madness; like
the Mississippi scheme, that it had a leading mind
associated with it; like the South Sea bubble,
that shares reached an unjustifiable premium; or
like the mania of 1825, that it was equal to it in
extent.

Its salient points are singularly different. The
tulip was a great fancy—the railway was "a great

fact," and no one could demonstrate that the most unlikely schemes would not pay. The Mississippi mania was caused by the issue of paper money; but the Bank Charter Act, if worth more than the parchment on which it was endorsed, prevented this in 1845. The South Sea scheme, however mischievous in itself, was the cause of still more mischief in the coarse and contemptible bubbles it evoked, and, like the fever of 1825, which sent the tangible wealth of England after the imaginary gold of America, was widely different from that great railway fever, the result of which has changed the face of the world; has developed the resources of the country; has increased the social comfort of the entire community; and with the increased commerce, capital, and population of the empire, must eventually realise a fair commercial dividend, more in keeping with the subdued expectation of the proprietor than with the extravagant promises of the promoter.

The following list of railway Acts granted during the session of 1845 will indicate in some degree the extent of the business done both by the House of Commons and by the money market.

Aberdare railway. Length eight and a-half miles. Capital £50,000. Loans £16,600.

Aberdeen railway. Length fifty-eight miles. Capital £830,000. Loans £276,666.

Ashton, Stalybridge, and Liverpool Junction railway; branch line to the Manchester and Birmingham. Length one and three-quarter miles. Capital £60,000. Loans £20,000.

Bedford and London and Birmingham railway. Length sixteen miles. Capital £125,000. Loans £41,650.

Belfast and Ballymena railway. Length thirty-eight miles. Capital £385,000. Loans £128,333.

Berks and Hants railway. Length thirty-nine miles. Capital £400,000. Loans £133,333.

Birmingham and Gloucester railway. Length one and three-quarter miles. Cost £27,422.

Blackburn, Burnley, Accrington, and Colne railway. Length twenty-four miles. Capital £530,000. Loans 176,666.

Blackburn, Darwen, and Bolton railway. Length fourteen miles. Capital £300,000. Loans £100,000.

Blackburn and Preston railway. Length three and a-half miles. Capital £30,000. Loans £10,000.

Bridgewater Navigation and railway. Length three quarters of a mile. Cost £12,000.

Brighton and Chichester railway. Portsmouth extension. Length twenty-two miles. Capital £320,000. Loans £106,666.

Brighton, Lewes, and Hastings railway; Keymer branch. Capital £140,000. Loans £46,666.

Brighton, Lewes, and Hastings railway. Rye and Ashford extension. Length twenty-nine miles. Capital £500,000. Loans £166,000.

Bristol and Exeter railway. Length twenty-nine miles. Capital £500,000. Loans £166,000.

Caledonian railway. Length one hundred and thirty-seven and a quarter miles. Capital £2,100,000. Loans £700,000.

Chester and Birkenhead railway. Length seven furlongs. Capital £300,000. Loans £100,000.

Chester and Holyhead railway. Length four and a-half miles. Cost £500,000.

Clydesdale Junction railway. Length fifteen and a-quarter miles. Capital £330,000. Loans £110,000.

Cockermouth and Workington railway. Length eight and three-quarter miles. Capital £80,000. Loans £26,666.

Cork and Bandon railway. Length twenty miles. Capital £240,000. Loans £80,000.

Dublin and Belfast Junction railway. Length seventy-three and a-half miles. Capital £950,000. Loans £316,666.

Dublin and Drogheda railway. Howth branch. Length three and three-quarter miles. Capital £150,000. Loans £50,000.

Dundalk and Enniskillen railway. Length forty and three-quarter miles. Capital £750,000. Loans £250,000.

Dundee and Perth railway. Length twenty and three-quarter miles. Capital £200,000. Loans £66,600.

Dunstable and London and Birmingham railway. Length seven miles. Capital £50,000. Loans £16,600.

Eastern Counties railway. Cambridge and Huntingdon. Length seventeen and a-half miles. Capital £150,000. Loans £50,000.

Eastern Counties railway. Ely and Whittlesea deviation. Twenty-three and three quarter miles. Cost £320,000.

Eastern Union railway Amendment Act. Capital £50,000. Loans £16,600.

Edinburgh and Glasgow railway. Length six miles. Capital £100,000. Loans £33,000.

Edinburgh and Hawick railway. Length forty-five and a-quarter miles. Capital £400.000. Loans £133,333.

Edinburgh and Northern railway. Length forty-one and three-quarter miles. Capital £650,000. Loans £216,666.

Ely and Huntingdon railway. Length twenty-two miles. Capital £194,400. Loans £64,800.

Epping railway. Length one and three-quarter miles. Capital £200,000. Loans £66,600.

Erewash Valley railway. Length thirteen and three-quarter miles. Capital £190,000. Loans £63,000.

Exeter and Crediton. Length five and three-quarter miles. Capital £70,000. Loans £23,333.

Glasgow, Barrhead, and Neilston direct. Length nine miles. Capital £150,000. Loans £50,000.

Glasgow Junction. Length two and a-quarter miles. Capital £150,000. Loans £50,000.

Glasgow, Paisley, Kilmarnock, and Ayr; Cumnock branch. Length eighteen and a-half miles. Capital £204,000. Loans £68,000.

Gravesend and Rochester. Length six and seven-eighth miles. Capital £170,000. Loans £56,666.

Great Grimsby and Sheffield Junction railway: Length fifty-nine and a-half miles. Capital £600,000. Loans £200,000.

Great North of England Clarence and Hartlepool Junction railway. Length a quarter of a mile. Capital £21,005. Loans £7,000.

Great North of England and Richmond. Length nine and three-quarter miles. Capital £150,000. Loans £50,000.

Great Southern and Western railway. Length ninety-eight and a-quarter miles. Capital £1,200,000. Loans £400,000.

Huddersfield and Manchester. Length twenty-two and three-quarter miles. Capital £630,000. Loans £210,000.

Huddersfield and Sheffield Junction railway. Length fifteen and a-half miles. Capital £532,000. Loans £177,333.

Hull and Selby; Bridlington branch railway. Length thirty-one miles. Capital £216,000. Loans £72,000.

Ipswich and Bury St. Edmunds. Length twenty-six and three-quarter miles. Capital £400,000. Loans £133,333.

Kendal and Windermere railway. Length ten and a-quarter miles. Capital £125,000. Loans £40,000.

Lancaster and Carlisle railway. Length four and a-quarter miles. Estimated cost £90,000.

Leeds and Bradford Extension railway. Length thirty and a-half miles. Capital £500,000. Loans £166,666.

Leeds, Dewsberry, and Manchester Junction railway. Length twenty and a-half miles. Capital £650,000. Loans £166,000.

Leeds and Thirsk railway. Length forty-six miles. Capital £890,000. Loans £296,000.

Liverpool and Bury. Length thirty-four miles. Capital £912,000. Loans £304,000.

Liverpool and Manchester Extension railway. Length seven and three-quarter miles. Capital £805,000. Loans £268,333.

London and Brighton railway; Horsham branch. Length eight and a-quarter miles. Capital £100,000. Loans £33,333.

London and South-Western railway; metropolitan extension. Length two miles. Capital £800,000. £233,000.

Londonderry and Coleraine railway. Length thirty-nine miles. Capital £500,000. Loans £166,666.

Londonderry and Enniskillen railway. Length fifty-six miles. Capital £500,000. Loans £166,666.

Lowestoft railway. Length eleven and a-quarter miles. Capital £120,000. Loans £40,000.

Lynn and Dereham railway. Length twenty-six and a-half miles. Capital £270,000. Loans £90,000.

Lynn and Ely railway. Length thirty-seven and a-half miles. Capital £300,000. Loans £100,000.

Manchester and Birmingham railway; Ashton branch. Length five miles. Estimated cost £93,000.

Manchester and Leeds railway; branches. Length fourteen miles. Capital £360,000. Loans £120,000.

Manchester South Junction and Altringham railway. Length nine and a-quarter miles. Capital £400,000. Loans £133,333.

Middlesboro and Redcar railway. Length seven and a-half miles. Capital £36,000. Loans £12,000.

Midland railway; Nottingham to Lincoln. Length thirty-three and a-half miles. Capital £408,000. Loans £136,000.

Midland railway; Syston to Peterborough. Length

forty-seven and three-quarter miles. Capital £750,000. Loans £250,000.

Midland Great Western railway. Length seventy-seven and a-quarter miles. Capital £1,000,000. Loans £333,000.

Monmouth and Hereford railway. Length thirty-six and a-quarter miles. Capital £550,000. Loans £183,333.

Newcastle and Berwick railway. Length ninety-five and a-quarter miles. Capital £1,400,000. Loans £466,666.

Newcastle and Darlington railway; Brandling Junction. Length six miles. Capital £650,000. Loans £216,000.

Newcastle and North Shields railway. Length one mile. Capital £50,000. Loans £16,665.

Newport and Pontypool railway. Length thirteen miles. Capital £119,100. Loans £78,163.

North British railway. Length one and three-quarter miles. Capital £160,000. Loans £53,333.

North Union railway. Length three-quarters of a mile. Capital £20,000. Loans £6,666.

North Wales railway—mineral. Length twelve miles. Capital £150,000. Loans £50,000.

North Wales railway. Length twenty-eight and a-half miles. Capital £300,000. Loans £100,000.

North Woolwich railway. Length two and three-quarter miles. Capital £30,000. Loans £10,000.

Norwich and Brandon railway. Length seventeen miles. Capital £220,000. Loans £73,300.

Oxford and Rugby railway. Length fifty and a-half miles. Capital £600,000. Loans £200,000.

Oxford, Worcester, and Wolverhampton railway. Length one hundred and one and a-half miles. Capital £1,500,000. Loans £500,000.

Preston and Wyre railway. Length eight and a-quarter miles. Capital £100,000. Loans £33,000.

Richmond railway. Length six miles. Capital £260,000. Loans £86,000.

Scottish Central railway. Length forty-seven and a-half miles. Capital £850,000. Loans £283,333.

Scottish Midland Junction railway. Length thirty-three and a-quarter miles. Capital £300,000. Loans £100,000.

Sheffield and Rotherham railway. Length half a mile. Estimated cost £45,000.

Shrewsbury, Oswestry, and Chester Junction railway. Length twenty-three and a-half miles. Capital £410,000. Loans £136,000.

Southampton and Dorcester railway. Length sixty-two miles. Capital £500,000. Loans £166,666.

South Eastern railway—Canterbury, Ramsgate, and Margate. Length nine and a-quarter miles. Capital £187,000. Loans £62,300.

South Eastern railway—Tunbridge Wells branch. Length five and a-quarter miles. Capital £180,000. Loans £60,000.

South Wales railway. Length one hundred and eighty-three and a-quarter miles. Capital £2,800,000. Loans £933,333.

Trent Valley railway. Length forty-nine and a-half miles. Capital £1,250,000. Loans £416,666.

Ulster railway—extension. Length eleven miles. Estimated cost £133,035.

Wakefield, Pontefract, and Goole railway. Length twenty-eight and three-quarter miles. Capital £365,000. Loans £121,666.

Waterford and Limerick railway. Length seventy-eight miles. Capital £750,000. Loans £250,000.

Wear Valley railway. Length eleven and three-quarter miles. Capital £82,000. Loans £27,300.

Whitehaven and Furness railway. Length thirty-two and a-half miles. Capital £350,000. Loans £116,600.

Wilts, Somerset, and Weymouth railway. Length one hundred and twenty-nine and a-quarter miles. Capital £1,500,000. Loans £500,000.

Yarmouth and Norwich railway. Length a quarter of a mile. Capital £40,000. Loans £13,000.

York and North Midland railway—Bridlington branch. Length nineteen and three-quarter miles. Capital £87,000. Loans £29,000.

York and North Midland railway—Harrogate branch. Length eighteen and a-quarter miles. Capital £230,000. Loans £76,666.

York and Scarborough railway—deviation. Length three miles. Estimated cost £38,250.

CHAPTER X.

THE TELEGRAPH.—ITS ORIGIN.—FIRST THOUGHT OF THE USE OF ELECTRI-
CITY.—THE FIRST TELEGRAPH IN FRANCE.—THE SIX SHUTTER TELEGRAPH
—DISCOVERIES OF MR. COOKE.—ELECTRIC TELEGRAPH IN ENGLAND.—ITS
USES AND EFFECTS.—ITS DESCRIPTION.

A SKETCH of the electric telegraph, one of those
agencies without which all records of the rise and
progress of the railway must be imperfect, is a fitting
conclusion to the present volume.

The polished Greek and the rude Indian alike
recognised the importance of rapid communication.
All ages, indeed, have felt, and all time has proved,
that an expeditious mode of transmitting information
is the necessary result of a people's progress. The
Roman used the flag and the banner to regulate
his armies, and for a long period it was believed
that the Greek possessed a system surpassing the
ordinary telegraph. A collation of dates has re-

pudiated this theory; and it is now only known that
from hill, from mountain, and from watch-tower,
might be witnessed the fire by night or the smoke
by day, and that the coloured standard and the rich
banner added a gorgeousness and a grace to the
scene. The untutored Indian, to produce the same
results, ascends the hill of his native land, where,
spreading his cloak or lifting his arms towards the
sky, he resembles some bronze statue of surpassing
workmanship. The Hottentot, too, almost the lowest
in the scale of humanity, lights his fire on some
tall mountain, and communicates the intelligence he
desires by this natural telegraph.

When Mexico was discovered by the haughty
Spaniard, a system of intercourse existed far superior
to anything in the country from which he came.
Couriers were trained from childhood; post-houses
were established; the colour of the messenger's dress
was indicative of his news, which with amazing
rapidity passed from station to station, filling the
towns through which it went with joy or with sorrow.

In Peru, by a somewhat similar plan, the most
distant part of the empire was brought into intimate
relation with the capital. Intelligence was trans-

mitted on the wings of the wind, and ere an insurrectionary movement was known in its neighbourhood, the tidings had reached the capital, and the imperial army had marched to suppress it.

The Hungarian, in his late unhappy struggle with Austria, adopted a system previously tried in the Netherlands, which transmitted news with an almost marvellous rapidity. Our own land in its earlier history witnessed the same rude attempts; and perhaps the most striking was the period when Elizabeth called on her subjects to rise against the Spaniard, when a fiery warning passed through the land, and Englishmen prepared to fight on English ground for their religion and their independence.*

---

* The ballad of Mr. Macaulay is a picturesque description of this telegraphic mode of communicating information. When,

> Swift to east and swift to west, the warning radiance spread.
> High on St. Michael's mount it shone, it shone on Beachy-head:
> Far in the deep the Spaniards saw along each southern shire,
> Cape beyond cape in endless range, those twinkling points of fire.
>   *   *   *   *   *   *
> Till twelve fair counties saw the blaze on Malvern's lovely height,
> Till streamed in crimson in the wind the wrekin's crest of light,
> Till broad and fierce the star came forth on Ely's stately fane,
> And tower and hamlet rose in arms o'er all the boundless plain;
> Till Belvoir's lordly terraces the sign to Lincoln sent,
> And Lincoln sped the message on o'er the wild vales of Trent;
> Till Skiddaw saw the fire that burnt on Gaunt's embattled pile,
> And the red glare of Skiddaw roused the burgher of Carlisle.

At a prior period the bended bow which passed
from city to city, and from hamlet to hamlet, was
an additional form of rapid intelligence. Every town
had then a station : the mind of the reader will at
once recur to the illustrations which enrich our
ballad literature ; and yet, in many parts of England
the beacon hill retains its ancient name, testifying
to the judgment exhibited in the place from whence
the fire and the smoke were to give the sign. Our
own time even has witnessed the same attempts in
spots where no more intelligible mode existed ; and,
in the last war, when Napoleon was expected to
invade England, and the country was one great preparation, the mountains and the hills of Great Britain
bore witness to the establishment of a similar plan
as primitively as though no other mode were known ;
and arrangements were then made to send the warning flame from hill to hill, and from mountain to
mountain, had he risked his army in the attempt.

The first idea of the modern telegraph appears
to have been indicated in the seventeenth century
by the historian Strada, who, in his essays, gives
an account of a correspondence carried on by the
help of a loadstone, which, if touched by two several

needles, the other, whatever distance it might be, moved at the same time and in the same manner. He says that two friends possessed of these needles made a dial plate, and fixed one in each of them, so that it could move without impediment to any of the twenty-four letters. Upon their separating they agreed to withdraw to their closets at a certain hour, and there to converse. To accomplish this, when some hundreds of miles asunder, each one shut himself up at the time appointed, directed the needle of his dial to every letter of the words he wished to use, making a pause at each to avoid confusion ; and his friend saw his own sympathetic needle moving to every letter which that of his correspondent indicated.

This has well been called the foreshadowing of the electric telegraph. To what extent the priest, in the early ages the depositary of European science, knew the power of electricity, remains doubtful. If, however, the Jesuit foreshadowed the great discovery, it is equally certain that in 1684—more than a century prior to the use of the ordinary telegraph —a mode of communication was mentioned to the Royal Society by which intelligence sent from any high place, could be indicated to another as quickly as it could be written. The mode in which this was to be done was minutely related; the stations, their height, and intermediate ground were described, together with the characters to represent the alphabet, which might be varied ten thousand ways.

The Marquis of Worcester, through his "Century of Inventions," appears the next claimant to the honour of originating a mechanical telegraph; and "how at a window, as far as one can discover black from white, a man may hold discourse with his correspondents" without noise or notice, by night as well as by day, is one of his rarest devices.

Its first practical use, however, was in 1794, when the French directory established this system. The report of the Convention said, "The new invented telegraphic language of signals is an artful con-trivance to transmit thoughts in a peculiar language from one distance to another. . . . A correspondence may now be conducted with Lisle upon every subject and everything; even proper names can be expressed, an answer may be received, and the correspondence thus renewed every day."*

* "At the first station, which was on the roof of the Louvre, M. Chappe received

Great Britain was not long in following the example. By 1795, this country discovered of how much avail it was to the enemy, and the admiralty adopted a plan, proposed by Lord George Murray, of a six shutter telegraph, employing it during the whole of the war.

It has been said that in the very year in which the French established their system, the electric spark was made use of by Reizen with a similar purpose, and that in 1798 a telegraph was constructed like that suggested by Reizen, by Dr. Salva, of Madrid. This, however, is but apocryphal, although the Prince of Peace is stated to have witnessed an experiment of the power which was to commucate instantaneously between the greatest distances by land or sea. About the same period, or rather

in writing from the committee of public safety, the words to be sent to Lisle, near which the French army at that time was. An upright post was erected on the Louvre, at the top of this were two transverse arms, moveable in all directions. with much rapidity. The different position of these arms stood as signs for the letters of the alphabet, and these he reduced as much as possible. Having received the sentence to be conveyed, he gave a signal to the second station to prepare. At each station there was a watch tower, on which telescopes were fixed, and the person on the watch gave the signal of preparation which he had received, and this communicated successively through all the line, which brought them into a state of readiness. The person at the second station received, letter by letter, the sentence from the Louvre, which he repeated with his own machine ; and this was again repeated from the next with almost an inconceivable rapidity to the final station at Lisle."

earlier, Arthur Young, speaking of Monsieur Lomond, "a very ingenious and inventive mechanic," says, "In electricity he has made a remarkable discovery. You write two or three words on a paper; he takes it with him into a room, and turns a machine inclosed in a cylindrical case, at the top of which is an electrometer, a small fine pith ball; a wire connects with a similar cylinder and electrometer in a distant apartment, and his wife, by remarking the corresponding motions of the ball, writes down the words they indicate; from which it appears that he has formed an alphabet of motions. As the length of the wire makes no difference in the effect, a correspondence might be carried on at any distance."

In 1816, a Mr. Ronald, of Hammersmith, also experimentalised, and in reporting the result, said, "Why has no serious trial yet been made of the qualifications of so diligent a courier? and if he should be proved competent to the task, why should not our kings hold council at Brighton with their ministers in London? Why should not our government govern at Portsmouth almost as promptly as at Downing-street? Why should our defaulters escape by default of our foggy climate? Let us have electric *conversazione* offices communicating with each other all over the kingdom if we can."

A further candidate arose in 1825, in Mr. Porter, of Harrow, who in that year memoralised the House of Commons on the subject, proposing a method of "instantaneous communication with outposts, which neither foggy weather nor the darkness of night need prevent."

If, however, these gentlemen were the forerunners of that power which, as Dr. Lardner most truly says, annihilates both time and space, the man who deserves the greatest share of his country's praise, who—the George Stephenson of the magnetic wire—by his patient search and research, was convinced that electricity could be applied to the transmission of intelligence, is to be found in Mr. Cooke. Engaged at Heidelberg in anatomical researches, he became acquainted with professor Moencke, with whom he witnessed some experiments intended to illustrate the possibility of signalising by this power, a speculation which it has been seen had occupied the scientific world for some years. The idea became fixed in the mind of Mr. Cooke; the conviction that it could be adapted to railways possessed him, and he devoted all his energy, which was great; all his intellect, which was large, to realise his fine idea. Within three weeks from this period, he invented the detector, by which injuries to the wires were easily discovered; and constructed two galvanic telegraphs capable of giving twenty-six signals. He soon returned to London, to pursue and apply his discovery, obtained a patent in conjunction with Professor Wheatstone, and it is to be trusted has secured the pecuniary reward which too rarely follows the track of scientific merit.

These were a few of the early indications of that system which has produced such wonderful results; which passes far and wide throughout the civilised earth; which promises to overspread the country with a network; and which in its infancy delivers a message at the distance of a thousand miles as promptly and as properly as for a hundredth part of it. Well was it remarked, "the philosopher is a philanthropist and a patriot, even though he may not always, like the sage of Syracuse, be able to overthrow the enemies of his country by the engines of his science. Even while he seemingly trifles, he may be achieving the highest purpose of life. The primitive electrician, when rubbing on his sleeve the bit of amber or wax, with which to hunt a feather through the air, was preparing the first steps to a valued discovery. The thunder-rod of Franklin and the thunder-belt of Harris originated in the chamber amusements of philosophical speculation. When Galvani was making dead frogs dance on the table, he was preparing for one of the most important inventions of recent times.*"

It is a great mark of modern discoveries that they benefit the people. Science, which is of no grade, is for all, and later times have proved that the patronage which the inventor once received from the monarch, he now receives from the many. It is an essential result of the high position of the people; and the day which witnessed the first public erection of the electric telegraph, was an important era in the annals of mankind. If it be not so practical in its purposes as steam; if it do not provide thousands with work like the locomotive, it yet ministers to the comfort and aids the designs of a world. The interval which elapses between the

* Athenæum.

transmission of a message from London to Edinburgh is scarcely appreciable, and the benefits which
have resulted to all classes are remarkable.   The
steam power which preceded it had prepared the
way for its acceptance, and the general spread of
the iron road rendered that easy which might otherwise have been difficult.   Probably, no new discovery of similar importance ever met with so small
an amount of opposition.   It had become the fashion
to believe that the powers of science were unfa-
thomable.   They had been treated of in prospectuses ;
they had been urged by papers ; the journalist dwelt
on that advance which was to benefit the rich and
the poor ; the inventions of mechanicians were asserted
to be illimitable ; the resources of science were said
to baffle calculation.   The public mind was, therefore,
prepared for it.   It is true that when the powers
of the electric telegraph were mentioned, there arose
scoffers, and, "what will this babbler say?" was
the unexpressed question of thousands.   It may
be true, too, that the old heard with unrepressed
astonishment, and that the young accepted this
development of the labour and the thought of years
with scarcely a consideration.   It may be true that

it met with the conscientious opposition of some
who preferred rather to quit their places than to
have dealings with one, who, like his residence,

Is never named to ears polite.

And it may also be true that men went to the
railway expecting to see the letter-bags run along
the wire, and that the power so little known was
still less understood. But this was simply ignorance,
and not opposition. The novelty was received in
accordance with the age in which it was introduced;
and it is a rare fact that one discovery was allowed
to benefit the land, without the projector being
reviled or the promoter ruined.

The first electric telegraph was tried between London and Portsmouth, and great was the excitement.
The signal was given, the needle was watched; but,
to the horror of the projector, there was no response.
The trial was again made, but still no answer came
to allay his anxiety. Once more, with trembling
hands, the signal was made, and the answer "fast
asleep by the fire," was a sufficient excuse for the
delay, and a sufficient satisfaction to the gentlemen
whose interest was so great in the experiment.

For the highest and the lowest this simple power is alike beneficial. It purchases; it sells; it equalises prices; it destroys monopoly; it places the poorest tradesman on a level with the wealthiest speculator; it renders commerce healthier; and it possesses that which it has been said distinguishes most modern discoveries, it is as free to the peasant as to the prince; as open to the mean as to the mighty; it is controlled and controllable by all. It communicates between London and Scotland in the three hundred and fiftieth part of a second; it stops runaway trains; it prevents accidents; it surprises gentlemen who pay second-class fares and ride in first-class carriages with demand for the extra money; it is a worker of social miracles as difficult properly to appreciate as it is easy to operate with.

The following is the description of Mr. Wheatstone of this wonderful application of science to practical purposes:

"Here is what may be called a dial with five vertical magnetic needles. On this dial twenty letters of the alphabet are marked, and the various letters are indicated by the mutual convergence of two needles, when they are caused to move. If

the first needle turns to the right and the second
to the left, 'h' is indicated; if the first needle
deviates to the right and the fourth to the left,
then 'b' is indicated; if the same needles converge
downwards, then 'v' is pointed to. These magnetic
needles are acted upon by electrical currents passing
through coils of wire placed immediately behind them.
Each coil forms a portion of a communicating wire,
which may extend to any distance whatever. These
wires, at their termination, are connected with an
apparatus consisting of five longitudinal and two
transverse metal bars in a wooden frame, the latter
being united to the two poles of a voltaic battery,
which ordinarily have no metallic communication
with the longitudinal bars, on each of which two
stops, forming two parallel rows, are placed. When
a stop of the upper row is pressed down, the bar on
which it is placed forms a metallic communication
with the transverse bar below, which is connected
with one of the poles of the battery; and when
a stop of the lower row is touched, another longitudinal bar forms a metallic communication with
the other pole of the voltaic battery, and the current
flows through the two wires connected with the

longitudinal bars, to whatever distance they may extend."

Such was one of the relations of the railway; and it is impossible to imagine its ultimate result. The iron road promises to place India within eight days' journey of England. The telegraph is already making efforts to fulfil its mission, and send its messages through the sea. Both are the precursors of an advanced civilisation; both are the heralds of peace and good-will among the nations of the earth.

THE END.